The Circus and Victorian Society

Victorian Literature and Culture Series

Jerome J. McGann and Herbert Tucker, Editors

The Circus and Victorian Society

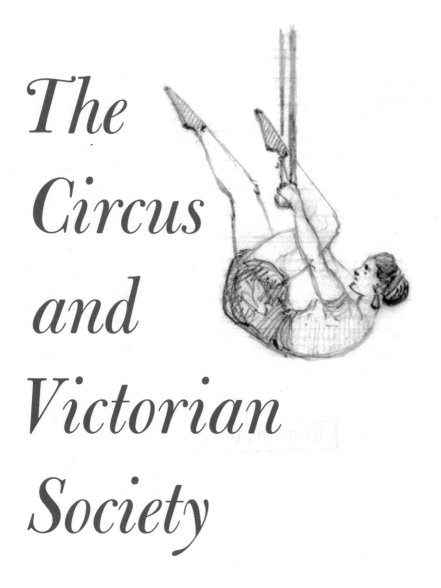

Brenda Assael

UNIVERSITY OF VIRGINIA PRESS · *Charlottesville & London*

University of Virginia Press
© 2005 by the Rector and Visitors of the University of Virginia
All rights reserved
Printed in the United States of America on acid-free paper
First published 2005

9 8 7 6 5 4 3 2 1

Library of Congress Cataloging-in-Publication Data

Assael, Brenda, 1967–
    The circus and Victorian society / Brenda Assael.
        p.   cm. — (Victorian literature and culture series)
    Includes bibliographical references and index.
    ISBN 0-8139-2340-9 (cloth : alk. paper)
    1. Circus—Great Britain—History—19th century. I. Title II. Series.
GV1805.G7A77 2005
791.3'0941'09034—dc22

                                                                2004024950

For my parents

Contents

Illustrations

Acknowledgments

When I first began researching this book I discovered an anecdote by Thomas Frost, the Chartist journalist, who complained in *Reminiscences of a Country Journalist* (1886) about the scarcity of source materials he encountered as he set out to write about the circus in England: "I wrote to the proprietors of the principal circuses for information concerning the history of their respective establishments [but] I found them disposed to be reticent on the subject" (218). Turning to the catalogues of the British Museum, "I was scarcely more successful," he added, finding only "the autobiography of Wallett, the clown, a few passages in Elliston's memoirs, and a collection of bills of Astley's from 1819 to 1845" (219). Fortunately for me, his conclusions about scarcity were wrong; in fact, much material on the circus—in the form of playbills, newspapers, and business correspondence—survives. For discovering these sources I am grateful to the archivists and librarians at the Mander and Mitchenson Collection, the British Library, the Bodleian Library's John Johnson Collection, Trinity College Cambridge, the Minet Library in Lambeth, the Public Record Office, the Royal Society for the Prevention of Cruelty to Animals, the Lancashire Record Office, the Birmingham Central Library, the University of Glasgow Special Collections Library, the Tyne and Wear Archives in Newcastle, the London Metropolitan Archives Library, the Dickens House Museum, the London Library, the Cheltenham Library, the Liverpool Public Library, the Family Records Centre, London, the Brighton Reference Library, and the Southwark Local Studies Library, as well as various other local studies libraries in London. The Colindale Newspaper Library, in the British Library, provided the most extensive support throughout my research. Further afield, Columbia University's Butler Library Special Collections and the Billy Rose Theatre Collection in the New York Public Library at Lincoln Center provided me with key materials that I was unable to get in Britain.

Librarians to whom I am particularly grateful for providing me with expert help with their collections include Nicholas Malton, of the National Society for the Prevention of Cruelty to Children; Victor Bryant, of the Earl's Court Exhibition Centre; John Fisher and Jeremy Smith, of the London Guildhall Library; John Turner and Malcolm Clay, of the Circus Friends Association, Liverpool; Steve Gossard, of the Milner Library, Illinois State University; Ian Glen, the arts librarian at the University of Wales Swansea; and Clare Hudson and Cathy Haill, of the Theatre Museum, London.

I owe heartfelt thanks to the Leverhulme Trust for a six-month fellowship and to the Arts and Humanities Research Board for research leave in 2002 and 2003, which enabled me to complete the manuscript. I also wish to thank the British Academy, the Society for Theatre Research, the Midwest Victorian Studies Association for the Walter L. Arnstein Prize for Dissertation Research in Victorian Studies, the Theodora Bosanquet Trust, and the University of Toronto for helping to fund this project with research grants earlier on. The trustees of the Marc Fitch Fund, in Oxford, deserve special thanks for giving me a prepublication grant.

Richard Helmstadter, Trevor Lloyd, and Paul Bouissac, at the University of Toronto, also deserve many thanks for their comments on this work when it was in its earliest stages as a doctoral thesis. My editor, Cathie Brettschneider, her editorial team, including Mark Mones and Joanne Allen, and the anonymous peer reviewers at the University of Virginia Press also deserve thanks for their help on this manuscript as it was being revised from a doctoral thesis into a book. In the revision process I restructured my ideas and materials. For their very useful insights on the manuscript I would especially like to thank Kelly Boyd and Rohan McWilliam. In addition, Marc Baer, Peter Bailey, David Cannadine, Anna Davin, David Eastwood, David Feldman, Deborah Gorham, Martin Hewitt, Anne Humpherys, Marius Kwint, Peter Mandler, Lynda Nead, Roland Quinault, F. M. L. Thompson, and Noel Thompson provided helpful suggestions at important junctures. Henry Tillotson and his colleagues at University College London offered invaluable computer support at another critical stage. I also thank Ashgate Press for permitting me to reproduce chapter 6 from my chapter in *An Age of Equipoise? Reassessing Mid-Victorian Britain,* ed. Martin Hewitt (2000).

The following audiences gave me useful feedback on various papers connected with this work while it was in progress: the inaugural conference of the British Association of Victorian Studies; "Streets of London, 1660–1870," a conference at the University of Hertfordshire; the Social History

Society; the Charles Booth Centre for the Study of Social Investigation in the Open University; the "Beggars Description" conference, University of Gröningen; the Mid-Atlantic Conference on British Studies; the Midwest Conference on British Studies; the Leeds Centre for Victorian Studies; the History Workshop seminar; the history department staff seminars at the University of Wales Swansea and the University of Manchester; the Modern British History seminar at the Institute of Historical Research, and the Victorian Studies seminar in the Graduate Center in the City University of New York. For any errors that remain, however, I accept full responsibility.

Academic support aside, my happiness during the process of transforming this work from a Ph.D. dissertation into a book was vital. Swansea colleagues Dan Healey, Julian Jackson, and Jill Lewis have enriched my daily academic life, making fun at work possible. Outside the office I am grateful to the following friends in particular: Rhiannon Ash, Diana Burton, Matthew Cragoe, Natalie Fingerhut, Ross Forman, Vishal Gulati, Grace Koh, Beth Linklater, Chad Martin, Saho Matsumoto, Elizabeth Ransom, David Sarphie, Janelle Scialla, Heather Shore, Adam Sutcliffe, Elizabeth Tarr, and Elizabeth Zimels. Martin Francis, whom I met at the end of writing this book, makes me look forward to married life beyond it. My family and especially my parents, Henry Assael and Alyce Friedman Assael, to whom this book is dedicated, deserve the most thanks for their unconditional love and support and, moreover, for encouraging my creative interests at an early age.

The Circus and Victorian Society

Introduction

Fascinated by spectacle, the Victorians flocked to the ring to see acts that spoke to the eye.[1] It was in the Victorian period that the circus emerged as a commercialized entertainment that we would recognize today. The equestrian who somersaulted on the backs of his bridled steeds, the female acrobat who nimbly tiptoed across a high wire forty feet above the ground unsupported by a net, the gymnastic clown who fell over his own feet, the animal tamer who pacified his wild beasts with a steely look and the tap of his whip, and the sword swallower whose knife edge threatened to puncture his vital organs—all defied the limits of man and nature. All were physical embodiments of that quintessentially Dickensian love of "fancy," an inalienable human desire generated by spontaneity, freedom, release, enjoyment, curiosity, and the wonder of life.[2] The circus at once both fed off and fed its audience's desire to see the artist's spectacular body in motion and thereby served as a laboratory of sorts for investigating human potential.[3] In this consummate age of industry and empire the strong body became a metonym for progress and power. Because it featured the body in terms of skill (rather than abnormalities such as birth defects), the circus was no freak show.[4] But like such displays, circus performance was an embodied experience. This was so for the artist who realized his unique potential and for the spectator who gaped at his display, heard the roar of the drums, smelled the sawdust, and felt the velvet on the seat or the hard wood of the bench. In Charles Dickens's *Hard Times* (1854) the children of the Benthamite schoolmaster Mr. Gradgrind clandestinely steal glimpses of the "hidden glories" in Mr. Sleary's circus by peeping (a different kind of embodied experience) through a hole in the amphitheater's deal boards, which only adds to their fascination and excitement.[5] By appealing to the senses, the circus attracted a wide variety of spectators of both sexes and different classes, regions, and ages. As the acts struck the eye and stimulated the imagination, they triggered a system of meaning to be activated and released. This book is concerned with that process and what it tells us about Victorian culture.

The circus's display of the extraordinary body had its roots in a variety of cultural sites: the ancient amphitheater, the medieval fair on the ancestral village green, the Lord Mayor's Day procession, the aristocratic court, and the eighteenth-century virtuoso's cabinet of curiosities. Though greedy eyes had feasted on similar acts throughout the ages, it was in the late eighteenth and early nineteenth centuries that the organization of these acts into one program performed in a tent or amphitheater was turned into a commercial enterprise. But like many other cultural forms, it exemplified the survival of traditional recreation from the preindustrial to the industrial period.[6] The circus emerged at the moment when the performer and the entrepreneurial manager combined their creative efforts and organized a variety program. Together they engaged in the serious business of making money by presenting to the public their spectacular and gaudy dream. In the second half of the nineteenth century, when the trade really developed, small-scale proprietors dominated the field and were distinct from that small number of large-scale managers who had access to vast amounts of capital.[7] Midcentury developments in the workaday world, such as the reduction of the working week from six days to five and a half days and a new range of leisure forms, sites, and services, engendered "a new leisure world" in which the circus's growth took place. And new technologies like railways gave proprietors and artists greater mobility, increasing the public's exposure to their entertainment. In addition, railways afforded many spectators the opportunity to visit circuses in nearby places. In the last quarter of the century a rise in real wages encouraged consumer spending, which in turn fueled the leisure market.[8] Both small and large managers' steady efforts at profit making and their shrewd, highly adaptable management skills contributed to their success in this climate. Theirs was an enterprise that, like many others, reflected Britain's industrial culture, as well as its growing culture industries. By the end of the century, a period marked by consolidation as well as growth and innovation in the leisure market, the circus had many of the hallmarks of an organized and respectable trade, with friendly societies and trade unions, trade newspapers, employment agencies, and extraparliamentary pressure groups, for instance.

The emergence of the circus, which was rooted in the industrial landscape, pointed to an important change in the traditional festive calendar.

Simply put, those strolling players who traditionally toured villages and towns on feast days adapted to a commercialized leisure market that provided employment opportunities year-round. Theirs was a trade open to talent, and sometimes this talent was also displayed in the theater and later the music hall, depending upon public demand. Over the century the acts and therefore the circus program changed so as to satisfy the public's demand for variety, although the chief feature of the program—trick riding—remained. Trick riding was important because equestrianism distinguished the circus from other types of entertainment.

Chronologically, the circus's development may be divided into four key (although overlapping) periods: 1768–1820, 1820–60, 1860–80, and 1880–1900.[9] The first phase begins with the creation of Astley's Amphitheater in Lambeth in 1768, when circus enthusiasts argue the modern circus was born (a point to which I will return).[10] As in any market ripe with possibilities, there was competition. In 1799 Charles Dibdin the younger wrote of amphitheaters erected in various parts of England, Wales, Scotland, and Ireland.[11] In these early establishments spectators viewed discrete scenes in the ring that combined low comedy with skilled horsemanship. Astley's went on to develop a theatrical genre of circus involving burlettas (brief plays relying on song) and later *gloires militaires* (military pieces on horseback portraying recent news, especially of the Napoleonic Wars). During the winter of 1778–79 Astley's built a stage on which these took place, although it also had a ring in which variety acts were performed.[12] Impressed with the popularity of equestrian plays, patent theater managers adapted them to their stages, giving rise to criticism that the national drama was in decline. At the lower end of the scale were those smaller, more numerous circuses run by families, who performed two or three acts of horsemanship on the three or four horses they owned. These acts were often followed by tumbling and tightrope performances in a short program repeated from noon till midnight "as often as the seats could be filled," as Thomas Frost put it. Frost noted that in the north and midland counties Holloway's, Milton's, Wild's, and Bannister's could be found, whereas Saunders's, Cooke's, Samwell's, and Clarke's traveled the eastern, southern, and western regions. In contrast to Astley's, these troupes appeared mainly at fairs, often in tents and booths but sometimes in a primitive open-air ring.[13] Other companies soon sprang up, often run by artists who had learned about the business from their former managers.

In the second phase (1820–60) the material differences between Astley's and the rest of the circus establishment became greater. James Grant remarked in the thirties on seeing the company's entire stud, numbering twenty to thirty horses, in the ampitheater. They dominated the first and main part of the program, an equestrian play, which was then followed by "scenes in the circle" featuring all the other variety artists.[14] A short burletta or tableau usually ended the program. Typical of the grand equestrian drama in this period was *The Battle of Waterloo,* which during its first season at Astley's, in 1824, enjoyed a run of 144 performances, an impressive figure in comparison with the much shorter runs typically on the boards in that period.[15] A platform connecting the stage to the ring allowed the military spectacle to take place on two fronts, thereby giving a "greater effect to the war-scenes" as one reporter noted in the 1850s.[16] The pit, the area closest to the action, held the largest section of the audience, typically artisans, governesses, and tradespeople, who paid 2 shillings.[17] The gallery, at the top of the theater, was often frequented by servants, private soldiers, manual labors, and apprentices, who paid 1 shilling, while those in the upper gallery paid 6d.[18] Boxes, by contrast, cost 4 shillings and were usually occupied by local elites, foreign visitors, and the bourgeoisie (fig. 1). This class of patron traditionally had places in the theater reserved for them by "place keepers." All others were required to queue outside the theater for as much as an hour before the program began, which was usually at six, although half-price seats were available in some areas of the theater midway through the program. Traders in Bond Street and libraries in Piccadilly also sold tickets to the public.[19] For those coming from the north side of the Thames, therefore, or from Greenwich, further afield, steamboats and omnibuses were available to shuttle them across or down the river, although Astley's also relied on local audiences from Lambeth.[20] Social stratification also characterized audiences in smaller circuses, but because they generally had no stage, their patrons looked into the ring, where discrete acts like clowning, trick riding, acrobatics, and juggling were performed.

Variety acts overshadowed elaborate equestrian dramas in the third phase, 1860–80. Commenting on the metropolitan scene in particular, the dramatic critic Edward Dutton Cook was moved to write in 1876 that "of late years a change has come over the equestrian drama. The circus flourishes, and quadrupeds figure now and then . . . but the 'horse spectacle' has almost vanished."[21] The closure of some important metropolitan fairs, such as Bow, Bartholomew Fair, and Greenwich, by this period contributed to the change,

Fig. 1. "Astley's Amphitheatre," aquatint from *The Microcosm of London; or, London in Miniature,* 1808–11. (By permission of The British Library)

as many variety artists pursued employment opportunities with a new crop of circuses, thereby rendering the equestrian drama a less important part of the program. Even where the fairs survived, such as in Oxford during Whitsuntide, in Birmingham, and elsewhere, there were still efforts by local authorities to clean up the events, reduce their length, and make them more orderly.[22] That said, restriction was by no means universal, and some fairs were created anew. In Northamptonshire, for example, there were more fairs in the 1850s than a century before, and those most likely to succeed mixed business with pleasure.[23] While some circus artists certainly continued to perform at them and in other open-air spaces, they were also encouraged by the growth of amphitheaters, stages, assembly rooms, and halls in this important period of growth in the leisure industry.

In the fourth phase, 1880–1900, the increases in capital and size continued, and wild animals became a star feature of some circuses that had the money necessary to make large investments in lions, tigers, and elephants from the far corners of the globe. Legal influences like the introduction of protective legislation for child performers in 1879 and the lack of such protection for wild animals contributed to this shift. Moreover, the arrival of the Barnum and Bailey three-ring circus (with two stages and a menagerie) to London's Olympia during the 1889–90 season offered a new benchmark for circus managers. (George Sanger disputed this novelty, insisting, in a tit for tat that characterized the circus and its members' preoccupation with artistic authorship, that his 1856 show was presented in three rings and on two platforms.)[24] Like menageries and some circus troupes earlier in the century, such shows afforded spectators, particularly children in the provinces, their first glimpse of the strange and the wonderful.[25] Writing of his turn-of-the-century Lincolnshire childhood, the son of a farm laborer recalled that for weeks before the circus arrived, "the walls and shops [of Digby] were plastered with highly coloured pictures of the delights in store." And when it finally rolled into town, "the whole village turned out . . . [to see] the star turn . . . , the elephant, because of his size."[26] Companies with smaller budgets might settle for performing dogs, so that their programs resembled those of the variety stage rather than those of large-scale circuses in this later period. While rooted in the culture of the fair, variety acts were developed commercially in the circus ring (and elsewhere). Moreover, they were later appropriated by artists in the early-twentieth-century variety theater (and vaudeville in America), as well as the silent-film industry.

Like the music hall and other performance trades, the circus depended on artists who observed industrial time-work discipline.[27] As skilled workers, these performers required constant training and practice to perfect and maintain their unique talents. Posters, drawings, and, from the second half of the century, photographs serve as important historical reminders of what those skills were. The mid- to late-century *carte de visite* (a small photograph sent to managers by artists to secure engagements) reveals a great deal in this regard and, moreover, tells us about "presentation of self."[28] Adorning their bodies with spangles or stripping them of all clothing except tights and body stockings, artists struck poses before special studio sets and constructed public personae through the camera's eye. These images were encoded with meanings about fame, celebrity, and, most of all, individuality. In this sense, the performer's work was emblematic of nineteenth-century individualism, liberated from the industrial world of the machine, particular, and irreplaceable.[29] Yet in another sense, and like many other artisans dependent on new technologies, they were integrated into the new industrial order and compelled to adhere to a strict time-work discipline in rehearsal, in performance, and in getting and maintaining engagements. Thus, they contributed to a perfect assembly line of production: on the one hand, unique and autonomous; on the other, disciplined and part of an organic whole. And like workers in other trades, artists at the top end, such as "star" equestrians and their managers, enjoyed comparatively good benefits in the form of lucre, status, and membership in respectable institutions. Those at the very bottom, by contrast, were no more than poor players, isolated and despairing.[30]

Unsurprisingly, historians have been concerned with detailing the "romance of the ring" rather than its structure and tedium. Thomas Frost's *Circus Life and Circus Celebrities* (1875), a wonderful, detailed study, marked the start of this tradition and has influenced several generations of writers.[31] For Frost and more recent circus enthusiasts, the circus originated with Philip Astley and the foundation of his riding school in Lambeth in 1768. They have seen Astley as the father of the modern circus. Their picture of the circus is generally London-centered and spotlights Astley's role. Only recently has the story been set in the wider context of the eighteenth-century theatrical world, characterized by petty jealousies, plagiarism, and litigation, as well as sawdust and tinsel.[32] The circus has been discussed in a national framework only in larger studies concerning the impact of industrialization on leisure during the nineteenth century.[33] While I am certainly interested in addressing these problems and absences, this book is not simply intended to fill a gap in the historical writing on the circus.

The main concern of this book is to link the cultural history of the Victorian circus with contemporary politics, religion, economics, and society in the widest possible sense. It does this at a national level and thus, in contrast to many studies on nineteenth-century leisure, does not focus on a specific region.[34] Because some circuses traveled, they linked industrialized areas with rural ones. Meanwhile, others remained fixed and flourished in major urban centers throughout the kingdom. Set against this complicated spatial backdrop, the circus occupied a contested role in Victorian Britain. Some believed it was safe, while others considered it transgressive. Whether supportive or critical, most were fascinated by it and were involved in a dynamic process of thinking about it, ordering and reordering its place.[35] This book attempts to map those processes. As a consequence of its ambivalent place, the circus allows unique access into a Victorian universe fraught with contradiction and anxiety. The main goal of this book is to locate the circus within this cosmos and thus untangle problems and contradictions that preoccupied the Victorian mind and informed a way of seeing—or rather, multiple ways of seeing. It thus investigates how the circus spoke to the eye and triggered a system of meaning that had relevance far beyond the ring itself. Methodologically, it has been necessary for me to isolate specific acts—equestrianism, clowning, acrobatics, and so on—in order pursue this line of inquiry, a point to which I will return. In doing so, I offer not a narrative of the acts but a series of historically contextualized "snapshots" that reveal a picture of the Victorian world at key cultural, social, and political moments.

The intellectual model for this book has been the rich study of Rabelais by the Soviet structuralist Mikhail Bakhtin. Like Bakhtin, I assume that carnival exists throughout all periods and places, informing us about liberation and repression, the sacred and the profane—dialectics that lie at the heart of all human society.[36] Carnival serves to reinforce the "official" order by inverting it temporarily, but as Natalie Zemon Davis has written with respect to early modern France, it also creates something new and "unofficial," dynamic and culturally specific, that invites and requires historical contextualizing. In slave and feudal societies it becomes a "second life" that is separated from power and the state but is nonetheless public and perennial. In bourgeois society, including in the nineteenth century, it has often been "reduced," to use Davis's word, to the home and holiday.[37] That said, the circus was the Victorians' carnival and defied the limits of "a mere holiday mood."[38] It offered a "second life" to the people, but rather than inverting power relationships for a day or a week, it had a more permanent role to play in this society. As part of the commercial leisure market, it was quite literally just around the corner, in the local amphitheater or tent, functioning to overturn the sacred in favor of the profane any day of the week and throughout the year. The carnival of the marketplace in Rabelais's day was thus succeeded by the carnival that took place in the commercial amphitheater in Dickens's. With good reason, therefore, Dickens contrasted Mr. Sleary's academy of feats with Mr. Gradgrind's Benthamite academy of facts in *Hard Times*.[39] The circus's emphasis on the materiality of the body meant that it traded in excess. The body (belonging to the clown, equestrian, or acrobat, for instance) became grandiose, exaggerated, immeasurable, and heroic and was a manifestation of what Bakhtin termed "grotesque realism."[40] The spirit of the circus was not to be found in the body's physiology or in the nineteenth-century bourgeois ego but in the people—in the widest possible sense—who were "continually growing and renewed."[41]

It is notable, especially in light of what has been said about carnival's public, democratic, all-embracing tendencies, that the historiography on nineteenth-century carnival culture in Britain has placed so much emphasis on class conflict.[42] Inspired by Antonio Gramsci's hegemony thesis, early work in the field stressed the struggle between the classes and located this battle on the shifting sands of ideological, cultural, and social ascendancy. Also stimulated by E. P. Thompson's *Making of the English Working Class* (1963) and the attendant shift toward "history from below," it aimed to discover an authentic class consciousness in the popular culture under early industrial capitalism. This was a culturalist response to the (then) growth area of labor history.[43] Gareth Stedman Jones provided a sober warning of the "real danger of overpoliticising leisure as an arena of struggle" in the 1970s,[44] but this was often ignored. While the social-control thesis to which he referred has fallen into disuse, class interpretations (Marxist or variations thereof) have nonetheless cast a long shadow over historical writing to the present day, with its emphasis on class or trade-specific pursuits. Because the circus catered to a wide public, it (along with other forms of carnival) does not fit easily into this long-established framework. Rather, much of what was seen and appreciated by the public was experienced in terms of a universal human spirit.

My analysis reveals cultural threads connecting "low brow" and "high brow," and at the circus the visual language of the fine arts and that of the fairground booth was appropriated.[45] The classical body of the male equestrian and the vulgar, grotesque body of the clown exemplify this aesthetic mixing. Not only were "high" and "low" culture reassembled and rendered a hybrid in the ring but this cultural form was then displayed outside it.[46] Circus acts were also performed in democratic spaces such as the street or park and in elite spaces like the private party. The performer's origins at the fairground and at court were thus perceivable. With this in mind, we need to revisit the dichotomy between public, democratic spaces and private, elite ones and how their cultural bases were constituted. As both sublime and ridiculous, artists inspired and encouraged a desire for excess and excitement and, moreover, crossed important class and spatial boundaries. While the circus is of primary interest here, examples of other spaces are provided where relevant and beg consideration in relation to the larger project.

Since this analysis focuses on the performing body as text, it is influenced by linguistic and cultural turns that have shifted the direction of social history over the past generation, especially with reference to studies on the gaze and spectacle, two concepts that are necessarily linked. Framed by the ring—beyond the audience's grasp, sometimes above eye level—the artist became a spectacle or an object of the gaze.[47] Standing at a crossroads between self and society (i.e., the audience), the male performer's body was inscribed with meaning—as grotesque, heroic, bold, athletic, and astounding. So too was the female performer's body, which became glamorous, beautiful, erotic, fearless, and transgressive. As Rabelaisian lords and ladies of misrule, they embodied carnival spirit. Constructing or enhancing the foreignness of their bodies, they paradoxically domesticated them. Trading their shillings for the privilege of "epistemological authority" that the display bestowed, spectators came away with a revised or reinforced understanding of the order of things.[48] Feasting their eyes (quite literally) meant more than just engaging with a specific display; it also involved a process of defining, ordering, and classifying the exotic, the strange, and the wonderful in relation to "other" specimens, as well as to oneself. The early modern cabinet of curiosities, Enlightenment taxonomies, and, later, Darwinian theories about natural selection and evolution served as cultural and intellectual frameworks structuring this knowledge. Above all, this mental process was an exercise in cultural power that the Victorians enjoyed in an expanding commercial marketplace for leisure.

Pinpointing what exactly was being consumed by the audience, and why, involved serious moral searching.[49] To be sure, it was widely believed that the spectator's "gaze" involved more than just looking: complex feelings of fear, sympathy, lust, awe, bewilderment, and shock arose in the process.[50] This presents methodological questions about how the displays were understood and how audiences and the gazes of individuals in them are "read." I would argue that audiences are more "readable" through the eyes of individual spectators, whose pluralized selves appear in a variety of ways and attitudes, confusing and complicating notions of class identity.[51] Focusing on subjectivity in this way permits an interrogation of those social values that have been used to define the age, such as respectability, progress, and improvement, to name just a few, and those categories that have been used to delineate social groups within it, such as class. Letters, memoirs, travelogues, newspaper articles, and evidence before parliamentary bodies and police court magistrates shed enormous light in this regard. Privileging the individual in this way makes the spectator appear atomized and alone in the crowd, guided by shifting stimuli that shape his or her responses, which, in turn, were shaped by his or her own cosmos or way of understanding the world.[52] Such an approach might be seen to run the risk of ahistorically normalizing the viewer "by abnormalising—indeed spectacularising—the body on view, fixing it in a position of difference."[53] Yet, while this gaze was fixed on points of difference, it was nevertheless unstable and shifting, perpetually engaged in a process of envisaging and reenvisaging the spectacular subject.[54]

At the same time, and perhaps in contrast, the stimuli created by the act served as a glue, linking individuals—in pursuit of ocular adventure—around a ring. In doing so, they provoked responses that sometimes were contagious; fear, shock, and other such reactions were thereby shared.[55] The individual's subjective response could be reinforced or overwritten by the audience's collective one manifested by screams, laughter, or open-mouthed awe, for instance. This is not to deny the importance of class and other dominant analytic categories for understanding the complex historical self. Rather, it is to argue that class must be seen in relation to a whole host of other factors, such as the symbolic structuring language of the display and its impact on spectators.[56] In general, a study of the acts in the ring leads us to question just how improving this culture was and therefore to expose the limits of "rational recreation," a contemporary movement built on Enlightenment rationality and evangelical zeal that historians previously used to exemplify Gramsci's hegemony thesis. An examination of the circus at times reveals an anti-improvement narrative of the nineteenth century.

As the circus evolved and assimilated into the world of commercialized entertainment, its program was adapted to satisfy the public. And as the number of companies grew, demand rose, and the market became increasingly competitive, these displays became ever more daring, dazzling, and awesome. Striving to go ever further, higher, deeper, and faster in their performances, circus artists sometimes drove a wedge between respectable entertainment and transgressive thrill, thereby disrupting Victorian notions of improvement. In the process, they destabilized midcentury equipoise and provoked late-century moral panics.[57] The claim that leisure was by the end of the century "now safely neutered," as Hugh Cunningham has written, does not stand up.[58] Unabashed display in the ring, when viewed from a moralistic perspective, rendered the human body grotesque, dangerous, or lewd. Far from being sweetness and light, as Matthew Arnold would have it, such display was anything but. Its proliferation gained the attention of re-formers concerned about how the working classes, benefiting from a shorter work week and relatively higher wages, spent their leisure time. Rather than take walks in the park to renew their minds and bodies, for instance, the working classes, so the argument went, corrupted themselves by participat-ing in irrational amusement like the circus; but so too did the middle classes and elites, who also flocked to the ring.

In the 1860s, when a relatively small but vocal minority (often of nervous bourgeoisie) made their critical voices heard, MPs, magistrates, and police throughout the kingdom responded with deep ambivalence, an ambivalence that persisted until the end of the century. Despite the pressure initiated by certain extraparliamentary groups and morally-minded individuals, politi-cians with laissez-faire leanings (including a mix of Radicals, Liberals, and Conservatives) prevented the passage of regulatory legislation affecting the circus, at least until the tide of change, in keeping with Shaftesbury's Factory Acts earlier in the century, could no longer be stemmed. When a law pro-tecting children performing in dangerous exhibitions was passed in 1879, the door to reform could no longer be shut, and subsequent protective statutes were passed in the next two decades. Even then, change was not as radical as some reformers had hoped. However moderate, such measures presented real ideological problems, particularly for Liberals.[59] While some favored noninterference, others sought to protect "victims" who could not help themselves. Pro- and anti-interventionist positions divided the Conser-vatives as well. If the circus became political, politics resembled the topsy-turvydom of the circus, at least where state intervention in the ring was concerned. The circus thus stood at a main political and social intersection, pitting reformers against libertarians, while exciting fascination for a broad range of social classes.

This dispute became the subject of investigation and fantasy for some whose ideas found expression in protoanthropological and literary studies propelled by Darwinian questions about racial distinctiveness. From the

1850s onwards, and in the tradition of Henry Mayhew, explorations of "low life ways" and "adventures" filled the pages of popular periodicals and books for "wanderers' libraries," allowing the reader to travel into an unknown land inhabited by apparently foreign people.[60] Perceived as a race apart, these rootless "foreigners" were also seen as undefinable socially because of their unstable employment patterns; many were British, however.[61] The dual perception of the circus—that it was foreign yet ubiquitous and therefore familiar—made it not only an intellectual contradiction but also a real problem, particularly for those concerned with the transmission of disease.[62] Critics considered the spread of "low-life" ways from the circus to the communities it visited, whether for days or months, to be not only possible but likely. Revisiting attitudes about early-nineteenth-century fairs, which underwent restriction and in some cases closure, censorial onlookers generalized about the "disreputable" circus in association with the "illegitimate" fair in order to prey on the public's sense of collective vulnerability.[63] By "othering" the circus in this way, critics constructed an anxious view of their world.[64] The circus thus stimulated opinion on itinerancy and on the need to control public space, the latter of which was so critical in a society whose public life was built on the foundations of civic virtue. Like the blind man in the crowded street, it stood in the way and disrupted the order of things—at least in the eyes of some critics concerned with "marking difference."[65]

The circus was, to be sure, fraught with contradictions—order versus disorder, transgression versus respectability, foreign versus familiar—that invite historical untangling and lead us into an exploration of the values that contemporaries held dear or eschewed. Such tensions, and the "tug of war" underpinning their mediation, provided the basis upon which I have problematized and explained the circus's contested role in Victorian society. And this points to something larger than the circus itself: amusement was no laughing matter. Its provision was profoundly influenced by the contradictory and corresponding impulses underpinning the interplay between morality, censorship, individualism, the free market, and the continuity of tradition. Thus, how the circus developed from an ad hoc fairground entertainment at the start of the century into a regulated and organized trade by the end; how it negotiated with baroque enthusiasms for the bizarre, daring, or curious, on the one hand, and spoke the language of improvement, on the other; how it withstood reform movements that called for increased intervention into the affairs of individual troupes—all constitute key concerns leading this investigation. If we are interested in Victorian values that the circus at once challenged and embodied, these problems and others arising from them need to be explained.

In doing so, it is first necessary to locate the circus within a vibrant and dynamic leisure market and the society that shaped it. This task, which until now has never been undertaken with any historical rigor, is the focus of the first chapter. Each chapter thereafter takes one element of performance and examines the complex desires that it fulfilled and the cultural problems it raised. These analyses of visual texts help focus attention on what stimulated the Victorian imagination and peaked interest in the world outside the ring. While thematic, the chapters follow a chronological order, although the periods often overlap according to changes in the circus program over time, as detailed above. Chapter 2, on early-nineteenth-century patriotism, deals with equestrian battle scenes, in which popular attitudes about nation, heroism, and divine rule were given visual force. Influenced by the Romantic tradition and a vision of the past as subjective, panoramic, and radiating moral righteousness, these spectacles presented viewers with readable, recognizable narratives that not only told about recent events but also, in much the same way as the narrative historical painting of the period, visually filled them in with color, detail, and human empathy. At the center of these stories was the military leader, spectacularly celebrated in the role of the hero. As such, he engaged a desire for both authenticity and highly emotive pictures, thus helping to construct national memory and anticipating Britain's future at a crucial moment of consciousness-raising in the decades after the Napoleonic Wars.[66]

Chapter 3, on curiosity, takes a closer look at national identity and the imperial display as it considers the "wonderful" and "strange" items in the circus program, such as the educated pig and the Chinese juggler, brought from abroad. Such acts astounded viewers in a manner akin to the early modern cabinet of curiosities. This chapter reveals how a baroque enthusiasm for the bizarre vied with ambitions for intellectual refinement. The history of material acquisition is located in the cultural history of public curiosity. Chapter 3 develops an anti-improvement thesis of the nineteenth century by arguing that enlightened ideas of progress and rationality driven by a desire to learn were contradicted by a desire to gape at, objectify, and possess the "other."

Chapter 4, on laughter, explores the relationship between the clown and his audience, between spontaneous expression and social values. By examining the delicate boundary between innocent fun and subversive humor, the circus's place on the margins of respectability, especially after the passage of the Theatre Regulation Act of 1843, when performance was increasingly policed, is considered. However central the clown's role in "letting off steam," his low social status spoke volumes about how out of step he was in the march of progress and material improvement that characterized the trade to which he belonged. Tears, for him, were the natural corollary to laughter.

Chapter 5 considers the lady-acrobat "frenzy" of the 1860s, which attracted the critical attention of moral reformers, MPs, and even the Queen. In so doing, it sheds light on contemporary attitudes about public representations of the female body, sexuality, danger, and athleticism. It also brings into focus the materially precarious lives that acrobats led. Given the public's insatiable and irrational appetite for transgression, her performance invoked ideas about progress while disrupting and destabilizing notions of sexual propriety and civility. Sometimes ironic gesture was one way of coping with these tensions, as when, for instance, the acrobat covered up her naked legs with dark stockings, which only provoked further bourgeois anxiety. This then became liminal play of an entirely different order.

The sixth and final chapter revisits the theme of danger in relation to child performers and their would-be rescuers, whose efforts culminated in the passage of protective legislation in 1879 that was revised in 1897. The complementary relationship between popular taste and some regulatory pressures at times made the act a safe and innocent amusement. However, the antagonistic tensions arising from popular taste and moral reform rendered it socially transgressive. This found anxious expression in evangelical children's literature of the period. Here (and elsewhere in the book) we see that the Victorians lived a strange double life.[67] On the one hand, they created a world for themselves marked by public-spiritedness, humanitarianism, and Enlightenment ideas of improvement and refinement. On the other, unruly appetites for danger (and in this chapter, child acrobatics) contradicted that spirit of progress. It is a cliché to talk about the Victorians as hypocrites, as unofficially indulging in forbidden pleasures and yet officially eschewing them. However the contradictions showcased in the ring pointed to larger contradictions regarding the place of the carnivalesque in this society.

In many cases, an act's wondrous quality and its transgressiveness blurred the boundary between respectability and unrespectability, making the circus, in turn, a highly contested institution. As we will see, the topsy-turvydom of the ring extended beyond it, rendering the circus's role in this society far-reaching. My purpose is to explore what lay behind the Victorians' fascination with the circus—or how the acts spoke to the eye—triggering a complex system of meaning and mediation. In doing so, I do not imagine that I will have the last word on this, though I am in the rare and fortunate position of having the first.

One

The Rise of the Victorian Circus

7 May 1857, Brentwood, Essex. William Henry Cooke wrote to his fiancée, Caroline Heginbotham, the daughter of a London hotelkeeper (figs. 2 and 3). Although it was only a few hours since she had visited him, he wrote, "I cannot describe to you how lonely I felt when I looked round . . . my little room where we sat and talked so happily [and] how deserted it looked now. . . . I could have cried."[1] Over the next weeks his letters to her became more emphatic. Only two things kept them apart: his work and his prospective in-laws, especially Caroline's brother Charles, who, Caroline admitted to Henry, "did not at all like the life I shall lead [and] thinks it too much like a wandering Arab's."[2] Henry, an equestrian rider in the circus, was in the middle of his provincial tour with part of his father's troupe from Astley's Amphitheatre. The couple had only recently revealed their plan to marry the following month, which suited Henry's busy itinerary, and the news had both "astonished" and "rather annoyed" her family, particularly Charles, who had expressed reservations about Henry's "precarious" financial status on the grounds that he received his salary from his father. But, as Caroline wrote, Charles "does not know how large a concern it is."[3] Henry hoped that she would continue to resist her family's interventions, but it was hard not to be persuaded by some of the arguments they put to her.

Because of the demands of his tenting schedule, he had asked to meet with her family on a Sunday at the end of the month in order to allay their doubts. Charles was less than happy with this proposal, thinking that the Lord's day—incidentally, the only day in the week when the circus did not perform—was inappropriate for such a meeting. "I represented the distance you were from London and your difficulty in leaving business [in the week, but Charles] said sixty miles . . . is an hour's journey and a thing that happened once in a man's lifetime was of more importance to him than business. . . . he was quite sure you could come if you chose, and really Henry I think so too if I were you I *would* come tomorrow [Monday]," Caroline wrote, suggesting that she thought he should be able to drop everything and go to London.[4] Instead, Henry wrote the following day, saying that he would have paid the visit, but "the notice was too short. I could not leave without making some extra arrangements which I had not time to do."[5] Her family's rigid middle-class aspirations for respectability conflicted with the equally respectable demands of Henry's work, pointing to a basic incompatibility between them.[6]

Because she was on the outside of the trade, it was hard for Caroline to imagine the pressures that Henry faced. His longing for her was complicated by very real problems during that season, which included his having to discharge some servants, or "hands," in the company because they had "behaved . . . very bad."[7] In addition, he dealt with the normal but heavy demands of running his father's troupe; he often woke at three in the morning, and he and his troupe toured daily from town to town, covering distances of up to twenty-one miles along narrow, muddy country roads. When they arrived, Henry supervised the circus's construction; organized the morning procession through the town, which included "Fifty Mounted Knights in Real Armour" with "arms, standards, banners and their esquires, pages, [and] attendants[,]escorted by a body of yeomen"; directed and performed in the afternoon and evening shows, which comprised "a grand historical and magnificent tournament," gymnastic and equestrian scenes, and "Richard III; or, The Battle of Bosworth Field and the Death of White Surrey" on horseback; and finally, supervised the tearing down and loading of everything into carriages.[8] His father's sudden request to see him in a spectacular display driving forty horses meant that he had to make time to rehearse, thereby shortening what little time he had to write. "I am interrupted again," he protested in a letter from Worksop. "I shall never get this written and the post leaves so soon here."[9]

Thus, Henry's life on the road was mentally and physically exhausting.

Fig. 2. W. H. Cooke.
(The London
Borough of Lambeth
Archives Department
& Minet Library)

Fig. 3. Caroline
Heginbotham. (The
London Borough of
Lambeth Archives
Department & Minet
Library)

Still, he was desperate to allay the concerns of Caroline's family about their proposed marriage and to meet with her brother. He pleaded in another letter from Bedford, "Please God . . . if your brother has an objection to an interview on that day [Sunday] I will contrive to stay and see him early on Monday."[10] In the interim, he attempted to get a "likeness" taken of him so that Caroline could preserve the memory of his face in a locket. Unfortunately, however, "the towns where I have been this week were so small and I did not see a place where they could take them well at all."[11] Picture or no picture, Caroline thought of Henry, and he of her, as their continued correspondence makes clear, and they married on 13 June, but not without the infamous meeting between Henry and Charles. Lurking behind the scenes was a benign uncle who may have swayed opinion in the couple's favor. Unlike most women who married into circus families, Caroline obviously did not belong to this world. The reality of her settled life and Henry's itinerant one led them both to participate in a courtship that involved almost daily letter writing and constant negotiations with her family. Their correspondence not only informs us about the uniqueness of their union but also provides insight into two worlds—the circus and the world outside—and how their lives intersected, if only temporarily and by post. Probably because of Henry's frenetic schedule, most of Caroline's letters to him have not survived, whereas his to her do. We do not know how Caroline and Henry met—it is possible that members of his troupe stayed in her family's hotel—but the mere fact of their meeting and indeed their engagement and marriage speak volumes about the circus's integration into Victorian society.

The circus developed from a fairground entertainment into an organized trade that took place in tents and amphitheaters. Popular demand kept these shows on the road and inspired change to the program over time. These changes affected labor arrangements, particularly among artists. A knowledge of what artists earned and how this affected new hierarchies in the trade is central to understanding how the circus functioned. As the circus rooted itself deeper and deeper into Victorian society, it became more contested; the nervousness displayed by Caroline's family about her proposed marriage to Henry is testament to this. Throughout, companies like Henry's pressed hard for respectability and carved out a niche for themselves in a competitive entertainment market. In doing so, they established a resilient trade that was integrated into modern, industrial life. In the move from her respectable Islington home to Henry Cooke's gaudy carriages that traveled along muddy provincial roads, Caroline stepped inside a world with a colorful and dynamic past, present, and future—and it is to this we must now turn.

Like most circus troupes in this period, Henry's tented during the summer season, which for him extended from 14 April until 5 November in 1857. As stated above, he spent approximately one day in each town. Early in the day, the caravans containing the properties had to be set up, as did the tent where the artists performed in the afternoon and evening. Before the performance, townspeople were given a preview of things to come in the form of a circus procession, which thus complemented advertisements in the local newspapers and the posters that would have been placed on town walls and in shop windows. Figure 4, a rare late-century photograph of Sanger's procession, shows shopkeepers and their customers standing on the pavement to observe the visiting circus parading through the streets. The Italian ice cream seller points directly at the procession while engaged in conversation

Fig. 4. Sanger's circus procession. (A. H. Coxe Collection, Theatre Museum, London; © V&A Images)

with a passerby. They stand alongside other tradesmen and school or work-ing boys, as well as women out with their children and husbands. Above their heads are curious residents, some standing on the balcony of a town-house in the background, while others peer from the windows of modest dwellings in the foreground. T. J. Hunt, the son of a paper mill foreman, re-called how in Dartford in the 1860s the visiting circus, with its procession of animals, "caused a flutter of excitement."[12] Cooke's procession was similar in kind, although the artists in the parade wore different costumes, and as the grand finale Henry drove forty horses through the town.

During the winter season, from November to April, circuses generally performed in amphitheaters built for the purpose, some of which, unlike Astley's, were no more than a "tin roof and wooden boarding round [and in] severe weather could not be kept warm," as Ginnett's 1860 circus was de-scribed.[13] Recalling one that was put up in his native town of Merthyr at the end of the century, the union leader Jack Jones wrote, "It had everything a boy could ask for: trapeze, tight and high wire, tumblers and acrobats, funny clowns and a few of the world's greatest bare-back riders," on which the cir-cus depended.[14] Whether paying a fleeting visit during the summer season or staying in town during the winter, the Victorian circus created a carnival-like atmosphere throughout the calendar year.

The antecedents of the circus can be traced back to the village green. John Timbs noted in 1855 that Londoners had been flocking to see equestrianism for more than a century, although evidence suggests an even longer trajec-tory. One of the first performers, he wrote, "was Thomas Johnson, who exhibited in a field behind the Three Hats, at Islington, in 1758; he was succeeded by one Sampson, in 1767, [and rivaled] Price . . . opposite the Belvedere Tavern, Pentonville, . . . where Wildman exhibited his docile bees in 1772" (fig. 5).[15] Another attraction for Londoners was ropedancing, which had been around since the days of Samuel Pepys. On 29 August 1668 Pepys took his wife to Bartholomew Fair, where they saw "Jacob Hall's dancing of the ropes, a thing worth seeing and mightily fallowed."[16] Nearly half a century later, Hogarth depicted such players in his 1733 engraving *South-wark Fair,* which shows a rope flyer leaping from a church tower while ac-tors perform on a collapsing stage in a traveling theater booth (fig. 6).[17]

Posters, municipal reports, newspaper reviews, memoirs, and woodcuts indicate how artists banded together and traveled in troupes from town to town. For example, in a report on the doings at "Bartlemy's," or Barthol-

Fig. 5. Engraving, Mr. Price on horseback, ca. 1768. (Guildhall Library, Corporation of London)

omew's Fair, in 1833, Clarke's equestrian troupe was listed as one of the many entertainments to be found there. Clarke, who was billed as formerly an equestrian at Astley's, ran a company that presented "the old performance of going round the ring tied up in a sack. . . . During the going round, a transformation took place, and he [who] went into the sack a man came out a woman on throwing off the sack."[18] Astley's, the training ground of many famous circus equestrians, was founded in 1768 in order to present trick riding to the public. Following Clarke's performance at the fair, a Miss Clarke was said to balance with and without a pole on the tightrope. After her, an eight-year-old boy called Benjamin Saffery did slack-rope vaulting. Contortionism and feats of strength by two "exotics"—"a Chinese" and "a Black Man"—followed. The program closed with a "countryman" masquerading as an unskilled rider who mounted a horse and "after a short time, beginning

Fig. 6. Engraving, William Hogarth, *Southwark Fair*, 1733. (Guildhall Library, Corporation of London)

to grow warm, he pulls off his coat, then his waistcoat, then another and another . . . and at last with apparent modesty and reluctance his shirt . . . then he appears a splendid rider . . . and does a few evolutions."[19] A program such as Clarke's, combining skillful feats with exotic displays, was the hallmark of any good company. Mr. Samwell's troupe performed at the same fairground in the same year with a program that included "tumbling, dancing and a real Indian Warrior who showed the manner of performing a true war dance."[20] The scene at Bartholomew's was generally one of confusion in which "there thundered the clanging of gongs, the firing of pistols, the springing of rattles . . . and the hoarse voices of showmen, all uniting in one loud, discordant and ceaseless roar."[21]

Open-air sites continued to attract a burgeoning group of circus troupes outside of fair times. Mr. Saunders's company, for instance, appeared at Ranelagh Gardens, in Norwich, in 1809.[22] Some companies occupied country meadows or metropolitan streets. Lloyd's company staked out a piece of

The Rise of the Victorian Circus

ground opposite Fischer's Hotel, near the Nutshell Orchard, in Cheltenham in 1822.[23] Similarly, in 1831 Messrs. Brown and Chaff erected a temporary ring at Bell Street in Marylebone, where they displayed some artists who had previously been employed at Astley's, suggesting the fluidity of artistic engagements in the metropolis.[24] Some years later, in 1838, Messrs. Bridges' company played before an audience at the Cattle Market in Canterbury, where they presented a program that included the "young Master Bridges on the tightrope, the Mandarin Jugglers, the Automaton Tumblers, a Comic Antipodean, and an interesting panoramic view of the 'doings' of the fair."[25]

Among those who saw working-class leisure as a problem, there was agreement that the fairs needed to be put down or restricted. In London in the 1820s, for instance, there was a concentrated attack against the fairs, but some important fairs survived and even experienced a rejuvenation. Furthermore, such fairs as those at Deptford, Chalk Farm, and King's Cross sprang up for the first time. Commentators nonetheless were convinced of their decline. The closing of a few key ones like Bartholomew Fair in 1855, Camberwell in 1856, and Greenwich Fair in 1857 added strength to the argument.[26] One aggrieved conjurer went so far as to say that "the Honorable MPs might have thought that we had wives and children to support before they decided to close Bartholomew Fair and Greenwich Fair." The effect of restriction on those existing fairs, he added, was that they "lose their importance every year," making it difficult for the artist to earn a living.[27] Yet, nineteenth-century circuses did not rely exclusively or even mainly on fairs for survival. By traveling from one town to the next as Henry Cooke's did, they created their own holiday atmosphere outside of traditional fair days. With the restriction of Greenwich and Bartholomew in the middle of the century, managers and their artists simply went elsewhere.[28] Coincidentally, in this period a new wave of construction occurred, evidenced by new assembly rooms, theaters, music halls, and amphitheaters, opening up a new world of possibilities for the hungry manager and artist. The emergence of these enclosed commercial spaces suggested that they had new and different opportunities in which to ply their trade, rendering the fairground and other open-air spaces like the street less crucial, although still useful, for earning their daily bread.[29]

Not only a period of construction, this was also a period when the number of circuses rose. According to my sample compiled from the *Era*, an entertainment and sporting weekly founded in 1837, there was an impressive increase in the number of individual companies over the period (although there is reason to think that these numbers underestimate the increase since they do not account for the less commercial and smaller troupes that the paper neglected). While in 1847–48 there were ten companies, the figure had risen to fifteen by 1857–58, twenty-one by 1867–68, thirty-two by 1877–78, forty-seven by 1887–88, and seventy-four by 1897–98.[30] Whereas in the 1840s most of the troupes were descended from old fairground families, the pattern changed in the next decades, with new names from both home and abroad (including the United States) cluttering the trade paper. The Cookes, for instance, belonged to the former, more established group. Henry's father, William Cooke (1808–86), inherited the business from his father, Thomas Taplin Cooke (1782–1866), who in turn had inherited it from his father, Thomas Cooke (born ca. 1752).[31] However, by the 1860s approximately half of the companies belonged to the new breed.

By the end of the century, most managers were first generation and had companies in industrial towns, where demand was high, making the Cookes a minority in the trade. Of all the counties, Lancashire had the greatest number of circuses. According to the sample, 31 percent of all troupes in Britain performed there between 1847–48 and 1897–98, concentrating in major industrial cities and towns such as Manchester, Liverpool, Southport, Preston, Wigan, Bolton, and Blackburn. Yorkshire followed close behind, attracting an overall average of 29 percent, while regions like Middlesex, Essex, Surrey, Warwickshire, Cheshire, Gloucestershire, Nottinghamshire, and Northumberland trailed by a wider margin.[32]

The increase in the number of amphitheaters in these places encouraged a sizable minority of troupes to abandon tenting altogether. Beginning in the 1860s a growing number (about one-third) undertook residency throughout the year. At the start of the twentieth century one acrobat lamented that "there are so few circuses on the road . . . the days of the [traveling] circus in England are almost over."[33] While a good number of the remaining two-thirds (about 40%), like Henry Cooke's troupe, spent some time on the road, this pattern declined steadily over the period.[34] The one thing preventing greater decline was the growth of seaside towns, which circus managers, particularly those with large concerns, found to be ideal spots for drawing holiday makers. Sanger's tenting show in the Cinque Ports in the 1890s suggests as much (fig. 7).[35] Railways transported patrons to these populous places that

Fig. 7. Sanger's tenting circus, Cinque Ports, ca. 1890s. (Theatre Museum, London; © V&A Images)

circuses also visited. A few others, such as Howes and Cushing's in 1860, tented in the winter months, although this was generally unpopular with audiences, who complained of the wet and cold they experienced under the "soaked" canvas.[36]

However important the traditional practice of tenting remained for some troupes, the construction of these new amphitheaters was remarkable and implied a new way of conducting business. At least twenty-three had been built across the country by the late 1850s, coinciding with the boom in building of music halls and theaters. The pattern continued, and a decade later the number of amphitheaters had increased dramatically, to fifty-nine, although there may have been many more for which the *Era* did not account. Reflecting on the general trend, one contemporary was moved to write that in South Shields, North Shields, Sunderland, and Middlesborough, "the increase of these places of amusement has been something astonishing in the last few years."[37] Considering that there were at least twenty-one circuses in 1867, the rise in the number of amphitheaters to fifty-nine implied that some circus companies had more than one.[38] Charlie Keith, for instance, built six in the north of the country, from Douglas on the Isle of Man to Southport to Halifax. He received a patent for them, a variation on the old theme of portable theaters, in 1882. Like Ginnett's, Keith's ampitheaters were made of wood, but Keith's design was slightly more elaborate, consisting of "convertible vehicles placed in a circle with a roof formed by erecting a pole in the center, which supports a cover secured by ropes to rings fitted to the roofs of the vehicles." It also contained "moveable seats, shutters . . . [while] spaces are left in the circus for the entrance and exit of the horses, etc., and a portico [where a] pay office and other moveable buildings may be fitted."[39] Such buildings, like Keith's in Southport, could hold 250 persons in the boxes and stalls, 800 in the pit, and another 1,000 in the gallery.[40] A late-century photograph indicates that rough and respectable members of the audience were separated by different levels of seating (fig. 8). Tradesmen sat with their children at the top, while those in finer apparel occupied ringside seats and, paradoxically, were closer to the smells of the animals. It is notable that audience

Fig. 8. Unknown circus interior, probably British, n.d. (A. H. Coxe Collection, Theatre Museum, London; © V&A Images)

capacity at circuses like these was greater than at many music halls, which could only accommodate a fraction of the number of patrons.[41]

In theory, architects and builders to construct these ampitheaters could not be hired until the circus manager had obtained permission to build from the town authorities. In order to get this permission, managers like Keith had to ensure the safety of the structures, which were otherwise shabbily constructed and dangerous. Fire was not an uncommon occurrence. In the period 1833–67 the *Era Almanac* listed fifty-five serious fires in London playhouses; circuses performed in nearly a quarter of them.[42] In the provinces the story was no different, and Henry Cooke's Portsmouth circus burnt down in 1861, foreshadowing the end of his circus career.[43] Building collapse was another serious problem, as Charles Hengler discovered in 1872, when one of the side galleries in his Sheffield circus fell down. Offering a rare insight into at least part of a circus audience, and one that was notably working class, the accident victims are recorded in table 1.[44] While most victims suffered injuries ranging from "dislocations of the ankle" to broken legs, Robert Knewwshaw died in the hospital after sustaining a fracture to the spine.[45] At the coroners' inquest, where Hengler's culpability was disputed, it was decided that circus buildings must be "inspected by the Borough Surveyor or some other competent official before being opened to the public in order to prevent such accidents for the future."[46] This corresponded with a general pattern of building inspection whereby municipal committees reported to the town council on a building's safety and hygiene before the building was opened.[47] London had its own system—emboldened by the 1878 Metropolitan Management and Building Acts Amendment, which, among other things, gave greater powers to the Metropolitan Board of Works (MBW) for theater inspection, especially concerning fire safety, until it was replaced by the London County Council a decade later. (The latter body was responsible for ending Astley's 125-year existence in 1893 due to breaches in its building codes.)[48] That most members of the gallery audience at Hengler's were artisans or from artisan families—this class of customers usually sat in the gallery—was important to the story.[49]

The fixed nature of these amphitheaters meant that locals were exposed to the circus more than ever before. In Manchester the public had the opportunity to see 120 circus performances in 1847–48 and 134 in 1857–58. The number had escalated to 348 a decade later, remaining relatively constant for the rest of the century.[50] As audiences had more exposure to the circus,

Table 1 Casualties from the Hengler Circus Accident, Sheffield, October 1872

Name	Occupation	Age
George Booth	Furnace man	43
Thomas Hanson	White metal smith	26
Jane Hanson (wife)	Warehouse woman	24
Angela Gambels	—	21
Ellen Barker	—	13
Mary Ann Parkins	Scholar	11
Thomas Woodhouse	—	—
William Gould	Razor grinder	43
George Hunt	Fish salesman	45
Thomas Grey	—	24
Mary Grey (daughter)	—	1
Thomas Needham	Pen blade grinder	47
John Breckenbridge	—	26
Russell	Propertyman for circus	—
Allan Scott	Scholar	11
George Hurst	Fishmonger	42
Harry Gillot	Laborer/moulder	36
Robert Knewwshaw	Ironmonger	37

Source: Census Return for England and Wales, 1871, Sheffield, RG 10/4681, 53; RG 10/4684, 59, 62; RG 10/4689, 53; RG 10/4676, 98; RG 10/4678, 56, FRC.

they became more discerning. Like music hall managers, circus managers who wanted patrons to return in the same season were compelled to change the acts.[51] After visiting Madame Newsome's circus twice in the winter of 1866, one reporter for the *Carlisle Examiner* complained, "We have seen their 'different' performances so often that some of them are necessarily tiresome to witness."[52] Madame Newsome's agent withdrew the company's advertisements from the newspaper, only to change his position a week later, when he ordered new ones to be printed announcing "an entire change of programme." In a gesture of "tit for tat" the reporter returned to the amphitheater a third time to witness the "new programme," which, he wrote, "amounted only to a reshuffling . . . the season is flat."[53] The criticism supported Charlie Keith's comment that with the resident circus, "the visitor frequents [the ampitheater] more times in a week, consequently he becomes a better judge of our business."[54]

Knowing the importance of fresh novelties and wishing to ensure continued support among his patrons, Mr. Transfield promised the opening-night audience at his amphitheater in Hyde in 1898 that "there will be an entire change of programme weekly [loud applause]." According to the reviews, Transfield's audience that night saw the Three Zaros on the horizontal bar; the Scorey Trio, a musical specialty; the Two Cosmos, a musical mélange; Tom Hall and his dogs, monkeys, and a high-leaping greyhound; Paganni Rediviuus, a clever violinist; the Brothers Lloyd on the tightrope; Rosco with his performing pigs; and a troupe of equestrians.[55] Reportedly, the next week, true to his promise, he varied the program and presented Six Welsh Glee singers; Mlle Selma and the Leopards in a gymnastic performance; Captain Zodiac, who showed his innovative "shadows on a screen"; and a troupe of jugglers called the De Wynne Trio, among others.[56] If the *Era*'s reviews are accurate, the cast changed weekly for the rest of the season, with highlights including Japanese performers, the Mitsutas; the stiltwalker Rosini; "natives" from the Burmese village of "Tebeton"; and Bosco and his Bi-Fantoscope.[57] This variety program thus resembled a collection of those individual acts once seen at Bartholomew and still seen at other fairs where skillful artists and curious subjects were displayed.

These circuses thus relied on a revolving door of talent, which had important implications for the movement of labor in the trade. While some members of the company were permanent and generally remained because of their family connections, other artists regularly moved between tenting troupes and resident circuses that needed fresh talent for blasé customers like the ones in Carlisle and Hyde. Popular artists often commanded a series of short-term engagements and thus moved from company to company with even greater frequency. The experience of the clown Edwin Croueste was typical. Between 2 June and 20 October 1878 he worked for six companies: Atrato and Allen's at Sunderland, the Pavilion circus at Lincoln, Stoodley and Harmston's at Nottingham, Keith's at Southport, Tournaire and Reed's at Guernsey, and Charles Adams's at Scarborough. His engagements with each one lasted from one to five weeks.[58] As proof of Croueste's popularity, Keith employed him for a two-week engagement in August, a key holiday period, in the resort town of Southport.[59] The clown was in such demand that season that the manager of the Colosseum circus at Cheltenham attempted to secure an engagement with him for the following winter by advertising in the *Era* in September that Croueste was needed, along with the musical clown Abe Daniels, to complete the company.[60]

The Colosseum manager's advertisement pointed to an important development in finding employment: both artists and managers relied increasingly on the *Era* for information about work. With its "Help Wanted" and "Wanted" columns the paper created a space for connecting people and troupes in disparate parts of the country. In their advertisements, managers sometimes requested that performers send them their *cartes de visite,* revealing one way that technology was adapted to suit the new labor market. Alternatively, artists made their timetables known to managers by advertising their schedules in the paper. Those less known and particularly hungry maximized their marketability by drawing attention to the diversity of their talents. M. and Mme Ozmond told prospective employers in an advertisement of 1858 that the two of them could perform on the elastic wire and that M. Ozmond could double as a clown if needed.[61] Although more will be said about this in chapter 4, it is worth remarking here that artistic specialization, on which the circus relied, was often undermined by the reality of the job market in cases where the performer claimed to be a jack-of-all-trades.

The agent system helped other artists to fill employment gaps. By negotiating salaries and representing the interests of his clients, the agent loosened traditional bonds between the circus manager and the artist. For many agents, having control of a performer's career provided them with a degree of power, as well as money. Instances of artists being accused of breach of contract by their agents suggest just how uneven the power struggle was. For instance, in a dispute between the blind Sardinian minstrel Picco and the agent John Gay, of Fitzroy Square, the latter warned the public in an *Era* advertisement that he was "the only authorised director and [artistic] manager of Picco" and that "any engagement, contract or agreement" must be entered into with him, indicating the degree to which some artists were both protected by and beholden to their middlemen.[62]

Agencies were not all the same, however. In organizations like the General Dramatic, Equestrian, and Musical Agency and Sick Fund Association, in Covent Garden, established in 1855, the agent system and the friendly society were combined. In keeping with its founding principle, the organization promised all members that profits derived from all agency business would go into a fund to support members during times of sickness and misfortune.[63]

It required an initial membership fee of 5s., and thereafter contributions depended upon the age and health of the member. For men who were forty years old or younger and in good health (women were not mentioned in the further particulars), all that was required was "three pence . . . to make provisions for a 'rainy day.'" The sum was notably smaller than the weekly fee, which ranged from 5¼d. to 7½d. for skilled craftsmen belonging to friendly societies in Kentish London in the 1860s, for instance.[64] As part of its function as friendly society, it founded a burial ground at Woking for its members, a project that was said to have cost £11,000.[65] By design, the association was meant to fill the gap created when established theaters such as Drury Lane and Covent Garden set up small-scale friendly-society schemes for their theatrical employees, while the Actors' Benevolent Fund catered only to the acting elite, excluding auxiliaries and choristers. Given the association's aspirations to be a national body, its leaders also hoped to supersede provincial agencies like Harry Wilson Barnes's General Theatrical Agency on Market Street and H. Franklin's Dramatic Agency on Windmill Street, both in Manchester, which attended to actors' needs only.[66]

Despite the association's populist intentions, equestrians and other such artists were not its principal members. Charlie Keith noted in his memoirs that in the four years that he belonged to it, actors had had "the greatest and most legitimate claim" as a consequence of their large membership.[67] The donation lists tell a similar story. Of the seventy-three subscribers in 1858 sixty-six belonged to the theatrical trade. Among them were some of the most important London managers, including Benjamin Webster, of the Royal Adelphi Theatre; E. T. Smith, of the Alhambra; and J. J. Towers, of the Royal Victoria. Among its dramatists were J. S. Coyne and Mark Lemon, as well as Nelson Lee, who wrote equestrian plays for Astley's. Others more directly connected with the circus included Henry Cooke's father and Astley's manager, William Cooke Sr., and his wife, as well as the equestrian J. W. Anson and the manager and clown W. F. Wallett. Receipts from Henry Cooke's papers show that he also paid into the organization in March 1859, although Caroline was not a member.[68] (Her role as manageress and occasional equestrienne meant that she played a part in her husband's business and therefore had cause to join.)[69] The representation of circus folk in fact declined over the period for which we have records. Whereas in 1858 they constituted 12.1 percent of the association's membership, in 1859 the figure dropped to 11.8 percent. By 1862 it had fallen to 7.1 percent, and it fluctuated little over the next five years.[70] Meant to serve the interests of both artist and manager, the association discriminated against the rank and file who could not afford to join.

The absence of performers' subscriptions is explainable by their low wages, but Anson's presence may have been something of an anomaly. In the 1860s, "top" equestrians like him generally earned more than other specialty artists. According to a weekly salary list from Cooke's Portsmouth circus in 1861, the leading horseman, Edward Moffatt, earned £3. Meanwhile, a performer named Oxford, who did a turn on the perpendicular ladder, and the clowns earned on average £2.[71] By contrast, the salaries commanded by male actors at the Royal Surrey Theatre in the same year varied between 12s. and £6.[72] Considering that the average skilled engineering laborer earned 35s. weekly in London and 23s. weekly in Scotland in 1861, circus artists were comparatively better off, and elite actors better off still.[73] Yet unlike many skilled laborers, circus performers usually did not have a constant wage throughout the year owing to the casual nature of engagements. The artist was thereby compelled to save his pennies for those rainy days in between, which sometimes extended to several months at a time.

The state of affairs had improved significantly by the end of the period, particularly for star male riders at big commercial establishments, who could earn between £15 and £20 weekly. In 1899, for instance, the Clarke brothers were hired by the Tower of Varieties and Circus in Birmingham to perform their bareback riding act for £40 per week over a four-week period. In real wages, the difference between riders who earned £3 weekly in 1861 and those who earned roughly £18 weekly in 1899 was enormous, amounting to more than a 700 percent increase.[74] Compared with what female riders had earned in the sixties, those in the nineties experienced an even greater rise in real wages. Mlle Pauline Sivado, for instance, was hired to perform a bareback trick act for £9 weekly over nine weeks with Mr. Edward Wulff's circus in 1893, although her engagement was cut short because the owner, on reflection, said "there was not enough dash" about her act.[75] Sivado's promised salary was nonetheless a considerable improvement over that of her female counterparts at Cooke's in 1861, who earned between 10s. and £1 10s.[76] Taking into account the price of deflation over the period, this represented an increase of approximately 1,100 percent in real terms by 1893.[77] Although she did not earn as much as her male counterparts in the 1890s, her proportionate wage rise from the 1860s suggests something about the increased value attributed to skilled women riders. Rises were, of course, relative depending on specialism, and Madame Sivado's earnings were almost three times those of the husband-and-wife variety team Charles and Enone Mack, who were engaged in the same year as general "variety performers" (probably comics) for £3 10s. weekly at the Circus of Varieties in Salford.[78] The Macks' real wages increased by a comparatively small margin—40 percent—when compared with the £2 weekly average earned by Cooke's clowns in 1861. Overall, money earned by horsemen, equestriennes, and clowns in these two decades—the 1860s and the 1890s—reflected large salary improvements that conformed to price deflation and a general rise in wages among workers in the last quarter of the century. For the individual, these rises depended on the wealth of the hiring company, as in the Clarke case, as well as gender and specialism. But big salaries created a false picture of the trade, said one acrobat turned dancer: "The public hear that a performer is earning £10 a week, and they think it is a noble salary for two hours' work each evening." "Thousands of girls employed in shops and factories think that the life of the gymnast or dancer is a very easy one," she said, without realizing how important it is to "strike originality" in order to succeed.[79] The dismissal of Madame Sivado from Wulff's company affirms this.

In this climate managers had a lot to gain—and to lose. Henry Cooke, for instance, spent an average of £70 weekly on salaries in 1861, to say nothing of the general expenses of running a show.[80] In her account book/diary of 1858 Caroline Cooke (née Heginbotham) noted that the troupe earned £13 9s. on a single day in January.[81] The year before, the company had taken £20 at their afternoon show which performed at Hull, a sum donated to the Infirmary and Sailors' Orphan Home as a mark of the company's public-spiritedness.[82] (If most patrons paid 6d. per ticket, then the performance was seen by approximately eight hundred people, which, considering the charitable act, secured Cooke's good name in the town, a point to which I will return.) Assuming that the average earned for each show was £16 and that the company gave two shows daily over a six-day period, Cooke netted £192 on average per week in this period. After salaries were paid (assuming the Portsmouth salary list to be typical), the troupe grossed £122, which was meant to cover the normal costs of running the company, including advertising, repairs, stabling, ground rent for the amphitheater or tent, and so on. The clown Peter Paterson estimated these costs to be £50–60 daily, meaning that the Cookes probably suffered loss, although it is hard to know precisely how great.[83] When

Fig. 9. Photograph, Cooke's Victoria Riding Establishment, Wimbledon, ca. 1921/22. (The London Borough of Lambeth Archives Department & Minet Library)

William Cooke Sr. gave up his lease at Astley's in 1860, the family focused on their provincial circuses, a change that may have drawn attention to their financial stresses. The fire at the Portsmouth circus the following year may have provided the blow that eventually forced the senior Cooke, Henry, and his brother to decamp to Wimbledon, where they set up a riding school (fig. 9).[84] At Wimbledon, Henry gave lessons just as he had at Astley's in the 1850s.[85] Their failure may have been more keenly felt than most because of the family's century-long connection to the fairground world; that said, the name carried on as other members of the family continued to run circus companies. But Henry Cooke's experience was not uncommon; other troupes were also forced to dissolve over the period. Whereas in 1867–68 three companies (or 14%) went bust, in 1887–88 nine (or 19%) failed, and in 1897–98, twelve (or 16%), according to my sample.[86] While the percentages were not overwhelming, they did suggest a basic instability in the trade.

In the latter half of the century, when the circus both expanded numerically and consolidated commercially, big firms like the Tower of Varieties

The Rise of the Victorian Circus

and Circus at Birmingham wielded much power, which was reflected in their treatment of employees. In particular, the ubiquitous contract defining terms and conditions changed the dynamics between employer and artist, making their dealings more formal and legally binding. The signature replaced the traditional handshake. At the Tower of Varieties and Circus the Clarkes agreed to obey forty-four regulations outlined in their contract, including rules about timekeeping, noise backstage, drunkenness, and absenteeism.[87] The Alhambra at Blackpool, where they performed later that year, demanded £100 from them, recoverable in a court of law, if they failed to fulfill their engagement for any reason other than sickness.[88] To prevent impropriety, management also threatened to retain a week's salary for offences such as obscenity or vulgarity in the display. And finally, to preempt their performance being seen elsewhere, the Alhambra's management demanded that the Clarkes absent themselves from venues within a ten-mile radius of Blackpool from the time they signed their contract in January, although the engagement was not to start until July. For all this, the Clarkes received a combined weekly salary of £30 for the season. This was less than the two of them had earned in Birmingham. It was also less than the £20 weekly that Alfred Clarke Jr. had earned when he performed alone in a somersault and bareback jockey act with the Barnum and Bailey Circus when it toured Britain the previous year. This engagement had been especially lucrative since his contract with the American company had lasted for eleven months, during which period the troupe had visited seventy-one cities, traveling 2,976 miles.[89] He had been one of three hundred employees.[90] But like the Alhambra, the Tower, and many other circuses, Barnum and Bailey insisted on Clarke's "faithful fulfillment" of the contract and retained a portion of his weekly wage as insurance until he had completed the engagement.[91]

Much like Henry Cooke's tenting circus in 1857, only bigger, Barnum's compelled its employees to obey a tight, logistically complex schedule that included breakfast, a morning procession through the town (on a much grander scale than Cooke's or Sanger's), lunch, a noontime rehearsal, an afternoon performance, a dinner break, and an evening performance.[92] Penalties for individual infractions such as being late for rehearsals or performances ranged from 4s. to £1.[93] After the evening performance, artists packed their things while the properties were dismantled and loaded onto train wagons and taken to the next town, where the "operation" was again

Fig. 10. Animals getting off the wagons, the Barnum and Bailey Circus, European tour, ca. 1899. (Museum of the City of New York)

performed. One contemporary writing for the Anglican *Record* marveled how like "a small army" Barnum's was, with "every man [having] an allotted duty and [knowing] exactly what he is expected to do" (fig. 10).[94]

Long before the use of the contract, managers strove hard to ensure the admirable conduct of their employees. Though inconvenient, Henry Cooke's decision to dismiss some men in the middle of his troupe's 1857 tenting tour suggests as much. Besides hiring respectable workers and firing bad ones, managers like him tried to secure local patronage from mayors or other dignitaries, who sometimes presided at their opening nights. The circus was seen by some, therefore, as a needful alternative to other forms of social intercourse, such as drinking. And in keeping with midcentury Smilesean discourse, the idea that the interests of capital and labor were the same meant that harmless release from toil would only strengthen the work ethic. Or as the fictional Mr. Sleary famously says in Dickens's *Hard Times,* "People mutht be amuthed" since "they can't be alwayth a working, nor yet they can't be alwayth a learning," an idea that town elites articulated as well.[95]

Giving evidence before the Select Committee on Public Houses in 1853, the Reverend John Clay observed that in his own community of Preston there were not enough rational recreations that could produce desirable effects on the inhabitants. Recalling the existence of some curiosity rooms nearly a generation earlier, he said that such displays would be welcome again since they drew together "the poor, the working man, and working boy . . . [and] the higher classes also."[96] Cheap entertainment encouraged popular participation in a sober pleasure, which Clay believed discouraged drink. A decade later, in Middlesborough, where it was said "drunkenness is a besetting sin," the visit of a circus was likewise seen to improve the character of the town. "It seems from the records of misdemeanors that convictions for that offence decreased by 152 cases. It was officially stated that [the decrease] was clearly traced to the counteracting influence of a well conducted place of amusement . . . Newsome's circus."[97] Some years later, Aberdeen's elites went so far as to honor another branch of the Cooke family at a dinner for the same reason. The city councilman presiding over the event believed that "all would be agreed that it was desirous to wean the people from the public house . . . and that this could best be done by providing for them legitimate and proper entertainments such as have been given by the brothers Cooke [John Henry and Alfred Eugene, first cousins of Henry] in their circus."[98] Its reputation as an innocent amusement was, moreover, borne out by the attendance of children accompanied by their artisan parents. Favorable status thus hinged on official perceptions articulated in the press, at town council dinners, and before select committees, as well as visits by local dignitaries and children. In this way, the circus vied with, and in some ways surpassed, the concert hall, the assembly room, and the well-run theater.

All that glittered was not gold, however. The longer troupes stayed in a town, the more prone some were to stir petty jealousies among rival theater managers irritated by their success. These jealousies provided the fuel that launched legal campaigns by theater managers to stop some circuses from performing. And after 1843 their crusades gained further legitimacy as a consequence of the Theatre Regulation Act, which gave justices of the peace (in the provinces) or the Lord Chamberlain (in parts of the metropolis) authority over the licensing of stage plays, which extended to any "tragedy, comedy, farce, opera, burletta, interlude, melodrama, pantomime or any entertainment of the stage."[99] In more cases than not, circuses did not need to hold the license, one of the few exceptions being during the Christmas season, when many performed pantomimes protected under the new statute.[100] Even when circus managers applied for the license, the magistrate's court often refused on the basis that they had no stage on which to perform stage plays, nor did circus acts, narrowly defined, require one.[101] Under these circumstances, circus managers were extremely vulnerable. The Christmas season was a time when children and their parents frequented pantomimes and managers competed fiercely for custom. In cases where a circus insisted on presenting pantomimes and was found guilty of breaking the law, its manager was forced to pay a fine (not exceeding £10) for each day his company offended. To add insult to injury, he was also compelled to change the program or close down altogether.[102]

In other cases, local interest groups attempted to halt the circus even before it entered the town. In a complaint registered with the Newcastle Town Council in 1868, for instance, Mr. Craggs, of the marble works on Percy Street, objected to the opening of a proposed wooden circus building in the Haymarket, immediately opposite his site, on the grounds that it would be an obstruction. His petition was eventually dropped because the land had been leased by the time of his complaint.[103] Several years later, in 1876, when a permanent circus was proposed nearby, ninety-seven local residents signed a memorial opposing it. In general, they (like Mr. Craggs) believed that there was no room for the building, which would be an obstruction and generate noise in what was otherwise a quite neighborhood. In addition, with a boys' school nearby, there was concern about the possibility of the boys' temptation. This potential problem was injected into a wider debate that focused on the likelihood of the neighborhood's steady decline if the circus was set up. A local resident and supporter of the petition, the Reverend A. Griffiths, stated that he did not want to see the area "degenerate" into something like the one in New Bridge Street, where there were several public houses and shops owned by beer retailers.[104] While the matter was referred to the Finance Committee for further discussion, the structure was eventually approved, thereby exposing the limitations of local protest and confirming a paternalistic and widespread perception among town authorities (the clergyman excepted) that a well-conducted entertainment was valuable to the town.[105] The amphitheater was rented by Messrs. Cooke in February 1879 for the winter season before being advertised in the *Era* as available for leasing from mid-April.[106]

Of course, there were circuses and then there were *circuses,* as letters of complaint from householders to the Metropolitan Police and the Home Office in this period reveal.[107] In most cases, property holders objected to the "low order" of adults and feral children who frequented the lots on which these shows "rolled up." As in the Newcastle case, it was feared that they would encourage crime and cause an obstruction, as well as noise, and, moreover, corrupt the moral welfare of local children.[108] How long they intended to stay was a key concern. Residents objected to open-ended visits by troupes. As one Metropolitan Police report noted in 1884, "The shows stop in such positions for a week or more at a time and they differ in that respect from the ordinary traveling circus or menagerie which only stops for a day or two and then moves to another town or place."[109] The view expressed in this report, which encapsulated the distinction between troupes like Henry Cooke's, with definable touring schedules, and less commercially organized ones, was important to later debates on the subject. In an attempt to regulate the movement of those "gypsy-run" shows, the author of the report called for the police to be given greater powers to intervene, a view that was in agreement with those of other police inspectors, like the one who suggested that "a fee should be extracted for a license; and the local authority should have power to stop such shows or exhibitions after they opened if they proved to be a nuisance."[110] Something had to be done because at present, "the police have no power to interfere in the matter."[111] But this argument fell on unsympathetic ears at Whitehall, where Home Secretary William Harcourt admitted to being "very much surprised at these police reports" calling for interference in those "cheap pleasures" enjoyed by "children in their humble amusement." After receiving a deputation from various vestries that wanted to close down these entertainments in 1889, he ordered letters to be sent to the chief commissioners telling them to refuse involvement.[112]

The householders' complaints and police reports were reminiscent of those lodged against the fairs before pressure had led to the closure of many, for example, at Greenwich in 1857.[113] As stated earlier, Charles Heginbotham expressed fears about his sister, Caroline, joining a company of "Arabs." Such fears revealed a constellation of anxieties about rootless people that found expression later in the century in the Canal Boats Act of 1877 and the Moveable Dwellings Bill put before Parliament between 1885 and 1894, both the work of the evangelist George Smith of Coalville. The latter proposal was designed to regulate itinerants and make them subject to the laws and controls falling on settled populations. Acting on behalf of the circus and fairground community, the Van Dwellers' Association, created in 1889, opposed Smith's bill. After a few years of anti-Smith agitation, the association drew up twenty petitions with thousands of signatures, which were forwarded to the Royal Household and sympathetic MPs. It also sent them twenty thousand letters from friends of the organization. James Ellis, a Liberal MP from Leicestershire, was moved to write to the association that "I have given such good reason [for your case in the Commons] that I have increased your friends [at least among] the Radicals."[114]

Representing their interests in the fight against Smith was Henry Stephens, of the Liberty and Property Defence League, a Conservative MP from Hornsey. Together, they successfully opposed Smith's bill, whose main clause was to give local authorities the right of entry into van dwellers' caravans at any hour of the day between six in the morning and nine at night in order to inspect them for overcrowding, disease, and other related public nuisances.[115] This was of extreme concern to the circus community. A census return from 1861, for example, recorded George and John Sanger as inhabiting traveling carriages with their families near their Manchester amphitheater.[116] In the same census, William Bouse, an American equestrian, was registered as living at the Queen Arms in Liverpool in 1861, probably while performing with Hengler's circus, which was resident in the city at the time.[117] This mixture of hotel lodging and caravan dwelling was practiced by tenting companies as well. An 1871 census return from Crewkerne, Somerset, shows that while the managers Anthony Powell, George Foottit, Alfred Clarke, and their families stayed in caravans, their equestrians and other artists lodged nearby with local artisans or in hotels.[118] A photograph from 1878 shows the big top and caravans of Powell and Clarke's Paragon Circus in Ireland; those at the top of this hill were probably the ones in which they lived (fig. 11). Thus, the resident and tenting circus embodied a strange mixture, being both rooted and itinerant. It is not hard to imagine a growing sympathy among reputable circus managers for "low" van dwellers, who belonged to that invisible class of companies traceable only in police reports like the one from 1884. For managers who, like Sanger, possessed authority in the trade and wealth, there was both a practical and a moral principle that needed to be challenged. Assuming van dwellers to be unclean and prone to incestuous relationships, Smith believed that tight regulation over the van-dwelling community was necessary because it posed both a moral and a health risk to settled society—a re-

Fig. 11. Powell and Clarke's Paragon Circus, Ireland, 1878. (A. H. Coxe Collection, Theatre Museum, London; © V&A Images)

flection of his evangelical missionary zeal, his so-called investigations of these people, and traditional prejudice against fairs. Ultimately, Smith's bill was not voted upon, largely because his plans for registration were seen by MPs as impracticable.[119]

In addition to small and large circus proprietors, the Van Dwellers' Association was made up of steam engine drivers and managers of roundabouts, who shared a similar political agenda with their circus brethren. Through its rhetoric of collectivity and its motto, "Unity is strength," the association fashioned itself as a populist organization that aimed to attract a diverse body of converts by fostering "firstly, friendship; secondly, friendship; and thirdly, friendship."[120] The association's subcommittees throughout the country—in Salford, Liverpool, Glasgow, Newcastle-upon-Tyne, Birmingham, Hanley, Buolem, Manchester, Nottingham, Rotherham, Aston, Neath, Swansea, Cardiff, Oxford, Rochdale, Peterborough, and Wigan—supported this effort. The membership fee was 5s. per year, although contributions of larger amounts were welcome from those who could afford them. Among the association's ranks were the acrobat Chevalier Blondin, the lion tamer Madame Salva, the menagerie proprietors E. H. and Frank Bostock, and the circus manager George Sanger. Membership grew from 533 in 1891 to 680 in 1892, 700 in 1893, and 780 in 1894.[121] Through efforts like the fight against Smith, circus managers and artists mobilized and sharpened their political bite. Faced with threats to their business and family life, those in the trade had little choice.

In his remarks to Caroline in a letter of Thursday, 28 May 1857, Henry Cooke wrote that he was "counting the hours till . . . early on Sunday," when he would meet with her brother, who had finally consented to the "interview." Given his anxious mind and aching heart, as well as the uncomfortable May heat, it is small wonder that he complained to her that "for these last two days I have been rather unwell . . . my head ached so I must now conclude as my time is short."[122] Time was short indeed: in the three days before he was to leave for London, his show had to move from Peterborough to Stamford and to South Oakham in Rutland, a total of forty-two miles. As at all the other stopping points, he had to help set up the show, perform in it, and then move it on. His stress apparently was not evident, however: one reviewer in Peterborough noted that "everybody appeared to be pleased," especially with the procession featuring chivalric knights in armor, "the finest sights of the kind seen here since King, Bishop, or Mitred Abbot with their trams and attendants visited the monastery centuries ago."[123] This was the life led by Henry and many others.

The expansion of the leisure market and all that this entailed contributed to a new kind of organization that enabled the circus to develop into a trade. The rise of new companies with organized programs performing in tents and amphitheaters was a key feature of this development. Residents in towns in which circuses played came to expect new and different acts, or "variety." The *Era* and the agent system facilitated the process of seeking and filling jobs by refashioning an "imagined community" that previously existed between managers in one part of the country and performers in another.

Assimilation in the commercial marketplace, as we have seen, was not without its problems, particularly when internal squabbling took place between theater and circus managers, who competed for the public's favor. Nor was it unproblematic in the eyes of nervous bourgeoisie and religious zealots who eschewed the circus's noise and immoral ways. But such protest, when it was expressed through official channels, was often stifled by paternalistic authority. The pressure on managers to cultivate and maintain community goodwill was intense, and they were compelled to respond to social, cultural, and legal pressures accordingly. "Hands" and artists likewise were forced to respond to a work discipline that relied above all on respectability or else face dismissal. As it expanded commercially, the circus became engaged in a delicate balancing act between an appreciative public and a critical minority. The irony was, of course, that the more assimilated and respectable its role in the leisure market, the more contested it became. But this was not at all amusing to Henry Cooke. Instead, as he said, his head ached.

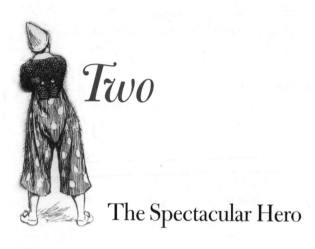

Two

The Spectacular Hero

While the London literati toured the rooms of the Royal Academy observing the heroic in narrative painting, another kind of hero was on display even more spectacularly across the river at Astley's Amphitheatre. The male equestrian's performance, set within a story about nation, revealed his courage and fearlessness. The Royal Academy and the circus inhabited parallel universes where similar themes and overlapping messages concerning war, leadership, and patriotic duty were given visual force. The hero unified these high and low cultures, which in the metropolis were separated by neighborhood and, often but not always, socially disparate audiences. At the circus, feats traditionally portrayed on canvas were transformed into live representations of national heroes and the battles they fought, offering important readings on the forging of British national identity.[1] Given that Philip Astley served in the king's army during the Seven Years' War (1756–63) and the wars against France (1793–1815), it was no accident that the genre developed at his amphitheater, where his patriotic sympathies literally took center stage. Astley was not alone. Hundreds of these dramas appeared at every theatrical level, from the Theatre Royal Drury Lane to penny gaffs in the East End. They were featured outside London at small circuses, as well as at more established Theatres Royal in provincial towns.[2] In the first half of the nineteenth century no fewer than one hundred different spectacles dealing specifically with the Napoleonic Wars appeared in these places.[3] Considering that the state was generally reluctant to get involved in matters of national consciousness-raising because of fears about the impact this would have on the lower, disenfranchised orders, these plays took on an important life of their own in the political and popular culture.[4]

The popularity of the equestrian military drama arose from a culture of memory, or to use Lord Acton's phrase in 1895, "historical-mindedness," forged by such practices as battle-site tourism and souvenir collecting.[5] Moreover, it was connected to the impact of histories, newspapers, journals, cheap book printing, ballad sheets, and prints that manufactured heroic images that came to dominate the popular imagination.[6] Local voluntary subscriptions to raise monuments for the commemoration of war leaders further testified to a popular enthusiasm for valorizing heroism.[7] It was consistent, therefore, that in contrast to the funerals of George III, George IV, and Albert, those of Nelson and Wellington riveted the nation and surpassed the former in splendor and popularity.[8] The role of these military leaders was vital in a war fought on an unprecedented scale, involving mass armies for the first time. France and Prussia employed universal conscription, and Britain mobilized its male population in a way hitherto unknown. It has been estimated that in 1805 one in ten British men capable of serving in the military fought in the army and the navy and that an equal number served in auxiliary forces.[9] Within this context, the cult of the hero so evident in high art and literature also found expression in the popular culture, especially in the early-nineteenth-century circus.

When visually articulated in the ring, these military spectacles contributed to a culture of remembrance and hero worship in the same way as processions, parades, thanksgivings, and anniversaries. These displays in the circus broadened the notion of the "political" beyond the boundaries of Parliament.[10] Furthermore, by glorifying the nation's military achievements—as opposed to radical or antiestablishment activities in an unfinished revolution—the circus participated in a "flag-saluting, foreigner-hating, peer-respecting" plebeian culture that social historians (in search of proto-Labour movements) were once inclined to overlook.[11] In its evocation of individual and national memory, spectacle was more than just entertainment: it addressed a need to find explanations for the present that history was assumed to provide. Not just recounting "facts," it contributed to a culture of myth-making and, like most myths, obliterated "the boundaries separating legend, historical reminiscence and actual history."[12]

Perhaps no part of the Napoleonic Wars caught the public imagination more than the Battle of Waterloo, a conflict that effectively ended Napoleon's struggle against the Allies after his surprise return from exile during his Hundred Days of power. For any contemporary, the truth of this historical episode was stranger than fiction. The battle was the stuff of spectacular melodrama, with the underdog/villain returning from the brink of destruction only to meet his final cataclysmic defeat in the field of Waterloo at the hands of Wellington and his men. It was thus dramatized and memorialized repeatedly in the circus ring and elsewhere. Spectacles like this one added, in visual terms, to developing discourses about recent history and British national identity.

A sergeant major in the Fifteenth Light Dragoons during the Seven Years' War, Philip Astley went on to establish amphitheaters in Paris, London, and Dublin in the 1760s and 1770s.[13] The spectacles he produced emerged from a tradition of parade ground evolutions and marching, as well as his own experience.[14] Their most salient feature, recalled the actor-writer Henry Barton Baker, was "noise, blood, thunder and gunpowder. . . . Every great battle from Waterloo to Kassassin, probably, was depicted."[15] One of Astley's earliest military displays was in October 1781, when he invited the public to witness Chinese shadows "of the [recent] engagement between the English and Dutch fleets."[16] The genre evolved from shadow to spectacular theater. Within weeks of the event, he represented the fall of the Bastille to an overflowing house: "150 disciplined troops . . . charging with bayonets, firing, storming" on a stage able to support eight horses.[17] When Britain joined the fight against France in 1793, Astley rejoined his old regiment as horse master and meanwhile sent messages from the front back to his amphitheater in London, which in turn represented the battles on horseback. He also penned two accounts a year later based on his earlier wartime experiences.[18] Until his death in 1814 he continued to construct war narratives, creating a theatrical convention that mingled news events and spectacle; the tradition was carried on by his son, John, who died seven years later, and several successors (as late as the 1850s) eager to build on it. In popularizing the genre, Astley's competed with neighborhood theaters such as the Royal Circus and Vauxhall Gardens' Rotunda and, slightly further afield, with Cooke's in the Haymarket, Sadler's Wells in Islington, and the Theatre Royal Drury Lane, which presented similar dramas.[19] Smaller companies presented discrete scenes or *tableaux vivants* rather than entire plays.[20]

At Astley's the equestrian drama was featured at the start of the program and ran from 6:30 until 9:00 in the evening. The writer James Grant observed in 1836, "You will sometimes see twenty or thirty horses, some of them single with riders, and others yoked in twos and fours in carriages, chariots, &., . . . Battles are often fought on horseback as well as on foot."[21] If audiences wished to see this part of the program they had to pay full price for a ticket otherwise they paid half price and saw what followed: "Scenes in the circle" featured independent acts of trick riding, acrobatics, juggling, and clowning and usually lasted forty-five minutes. The program concluded with "a non-descript sort of afterpiece," usually a farce or melodrama.[22]

The development of the military spectacle coincided with an important period when attitudes about the nation's soldiers were undergoing change. Although the encyclopedist Chevalier de Jaucourt condemned the "warrior hero," Adam Ferguson's writings on man's natural instinct for war in the creation of civil society vindicated him.[23] Drawing on Platonic notions of civilization, Ferguson argued that such a man became a "guardian" of his society and said that his was the most "illustrious career of human virtue," a view shared by Adam Smith.[24] Romantic writers and painters later insisted that great men were responsible for great actions that affected the course of history, leading to what they saw as a heroic, civilized age. The numerous contemporary biographical histories of famous men, notably Sir Walter Scott's nine-volume *Life of Napoleon* (1827), reinforced ideas about military glory.[25] This is not to say that Romantic ideas about leaders were monolithic; Wordsworth differed from Scott in his views on Wellington, for instance.[26] Yet, the pervasive fascination was with leaders who stood at the center of a historical struggle that changed the course of European history.

In perceiving the glorious careers of these leaders, which ended cataclysmically (as in the case of Napoleon) or victoriously (Wellington), the Romantics made a crucial distinction between the leader and the common soldier. At the same time, and in opposition to this view, a gradual acceptance of the military led to a relaxation of age-old prejudices about the common soldier's lower-class associations and quieted more recent concerns immediately after the French Revolution about his radical sympathies.[27] By the 1830s, and with the expansion of the empire, there were further signs that "imperial soldiery was coming to be re-envisioned at home and abroad," according to Linda Colley.[28] If Britain wished to sustain its imperial enterprise, it needed its armed services. The rise of schools for soldiers' children, garrison hospitals, regimental libraries, and army chapels was evidence of an active concern for their spiritual and physical welfare.[29] The expansion and acceptance of the militia and the construction of welfare programs for soldiers and their families had important democratic implications.[30]

For good reason, therefore, many felt that the ranks needed strong leadership lest their brutal passions reign and they turn against the state. Thomas Carlyle argued in *Past and Present* (1843) that "man is created to fight; he is perhaps best of all definable as a born soldier; his life 'a battle and a march' under the right General."[31] The final qualification—the focus of lecture 6 in Carlyle's *On Heroes, Hero Worship, and the Heroic in History* (1841)—was key: Carlyle argued that in contrast to great heroes like Cromwell, Napoleon, because of his self-delusion and self-aggrandizement, lost that noble purpose and sense of order that Carlyle believed true heroes possess.[32] In other words, unlike Cromwell, he violated established practices of just rule in order to pursue selfish ends, becoming an antihero in ways that recalled Thomas Hobbes's *Leviathan.* In an age of limited franchise reform, the relationship between the leader and the led was highly ambiguous and contested. Developing notions of citizenship came together in minds and on maps in the post-Napoleonic era; for Carlyle and others, the leader who commanded great armies served as a cultural reminder of how far he had changed both. This perception of military heroes hardened during the war scare and invasion panic of the early 1850s.[33] Colonial campaigns, as in 1857, added to the fascination with individual actions believed to have changed the course of history, leading to Britain's imperial greatness. The heroic leader therefore came to embody, in multiple ways, British justification for war against European rivals like the French and, later, the Russians and colonial "inferiors" like the Burmese, Chinese, and Indians, as well as stability at home.[34]

The development of narrative battle painting anticipated some of these changes in attitude. Anglo-American artists like Benjamin West, John Singleton Copley, and John Trumball provided a grand-style formula of the hero who sacrificed his life for a patriotic cause.[35] According to West, the hero must "excite awe & veneration & that which may be required to give superior interest to the representation must be introduced, all that can shew the importance of the Hero. . . . To move the mind there should be a spectacle presented to raise and warm [it]."[36] Referring specifically to his 1806 painting *The Death of Nelson,* West added that Nelson should not be depicted as dying like an ordinary man. At the war's conclusion, the Royal Academy and British Institution made concerted attempts to elevate this genre to the status of historical art. Artists such as Abraham Cooper (whose uncle, not coincidentally, managed Astley's Amphitheatre) won premiums in British Institution competitions. It was at the circus that Cooper is said to have received his early training in equestrian drawing.[37]

There was a historical precedent for a close connection between pictorialism in the theater and in painting.[38] In the 1760s, theater managers began hiring skilled artists to paint more sophisticated set designs. A decade later the marriage between the fine arts and theater was strengthened by David Garrick's appointment of the artists Phillipe de Loutherbourg and Robert Carver as scene painters at Drury Lane.[39] These bonds tightened with Cooper's generation of Royal Academy artists, who began their training as theatrical scene painters.[40] Cooper's painting *The Battle of Ligny,* depicting a battle fought two days before Waterloo between the French and the Prussians under General Blücher's leadership, said to be the first documented essay in battle painting, was entered into the British Institution competition of 1816. It won, and Cooper pocketed 150 guineas.[41] The battle was seen as evocative because Ligny was fought with particular fury, resulting in 11,500 French and 25,000 Prussian casualties.[42] One reviewer noted that Cooper's painting depicted the complex reality of war: "Advance, retreat, attack, defense and death are in unison with the particular nature of the event."[43]

When such scenes were presented in J. H. Amherst's *The Battle of Waterloo* at Astley's in 1824 and later at Vauxhall, admirers said the extensive panoramas and action provided a "truthful" account of soldiers' life-and-death struggles. In addition to representations of anonymous soldiers, audiences saw "living pictures of heroes," including Wellington, Bonaparte, and the Marquess of Anglesey, in contrast to the motionless wax ones popularized at Madame Tussaud's in the same period.[44] "The work of destruction then proceeds," involving loud noise caused by horses charging, soldiers firing, and gunpowder exploding, which heightened the effect.[45] The play ran for 144 performances during its first season, a bona fide success considering that shorter runs were typical early in the century (fig. 12).[46]

Given the number of times that circuses like Astley's burned down and were rebuilt, it is difficult to estimate their audience capacity, to say nothing of the average attendance, without complete box office receipts. That said, it has been estimated that in the period 1804–30, when Astley's suffered no such catastrophe, its auditorium could hold approximately two thousand persons, although James Grant noted in the 1830s that upwards of twenty-five

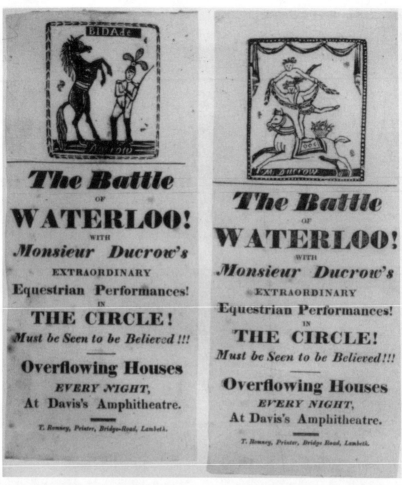

Fig. 12. Poster, *The Battle of Waterloo*, 1824. (John Johnson Collection, Bodleian Library, University of Oxford)

hundred had been known to be crammed into it.[47] By contrast, the Theatres Royal Covent Garden and Drury Lane could hold more than three thousand each in this period.[48] These theaters were accused of importing equestrian spectacles from Astley's, a move that some critics saw as contributing to the decline of the national drama.[49] If Astley's auditorium was full every night during the 1824 run and performed to a new audience each time, then *The Battle of Waterloo* was witnessed by more than a quarter of a million people in just a few months. The popularity of the play extended into the provinces and even as far as New York's Bowery Theater (formerly the Zoological Institute) in 1840, suggesting close links between New York and London theatrical trends.[50] It was presented in three acts, each of which culminated in a battle on horseback, but was interspersed with love entanglements, comic relief, spectacular parades, and patriotic declarations set against a "scenery of views taken on the spot by Mr. Wilkins and assistants."[51]

Having attended the 1824 production with his friend, Colonel Dickson of Limerick, the author and ex-artillery officer Benson Earle Hill recalled that he had expected "much food for mirth" but instead had been "amazed at the accuracy with which the military evolutions were executed."[52] They provided living proof of newspaper descriptions and "episodes picked up from military conversation," said one reviewer.[53] A contemporary who had seen a version of the play at Vauxhall as a boy recalled that "it seemed a wonderful spectacle with real horses, real Highlanders, real Dragoons, real Horse Guards and Coldstream [Guards], real Old Guards which 'died but never surrendered,' real guns, real cannon, real gunpowder and smoke and real red fire."[54]

The exhibition's authenticity was central to its attractiveness, fueling contemporary imaginings of warfare and of Britain's military prowess.[55] Perceived as an extension of "the parade ground, the camp, the ship, or the barrack," these displays were, as stated above, akin to many military performances, contributing to what Gillian Russell has called the "masculinisation" of the theater in the late Georgian period.[56] This may explain why circuses like Astley's received patronage from Dickson and Hill, along with other men of rank, including the Duke of Wellington. It was reported that at one performance some sailors in the pit recognized the duke in one of the boxes and "got some wine, drank his health, and gave him three cheers, in which they were joined by many in the gallery and pit."[57] Noise from the gallery (above) and the pit (below) surrounded dignitaries, who sat in the boxes in between. At the performance Wellington attended, it was reported that the Marquess of Anglesey and the Countess Lieven sat in a box adjoining his.[58] The right to hiss, shout, or cheer during theatrical performances assumed a special importance among spectators who had no formal political rights. As Marc Baer has argued, "A place in the audience was also a voice," something that Wellington, no friend of franchise reform in this period, was reminded of at this performance. The transmission of ideas was not just a one-way street; it moved between them (from patron to actor and from actor to patron) and within the crowd (from patron to patron).[59] As a site of "clamorous exchanges," the late Georgian circus joined the theater in becoming a politicized and unified social body.[60]

And yet, the audience's apparent patriotic zeal was at odds with changes evident in the immediate postwar climate. These included an economic slump that persisted until the early 1820s, the national debt, indirect taxation, unemployment, destitution, social unrest, strikes, and an insufficiency of army pensions, which affected more than a third of a million demobilized men.[61] Linda Colley points out that we know little about these men, "but many were clearly angry about returning to poverty and neglect, and even those who were able to find jobs often seem to have found it difficult to settle back into ordinary working life."[62] Practiced fighters, they were seen to be dangerous and potentially subversive in peacetime society, where an inflammatory press flourished underground while radicals took secret oaths and hatched conspiracies against the Tory government. Moreover, public fear of soldiers in this period coincided with repressive legislation that prohibited drilling and military exercises and restricted public meetings and the press.[63] At Astley's, the spectacle played up patriotic themes that focused, not on the ordinary soldier, but on generals who commanded. Importantly, it contributed to what was becoming a civic religion, founded on patriotism, which could, in theory, mitigate popular dissent arising from the depressed material realities of the day.[64]

The tradition of military patronage at these performances continued into the next decades, albeit in a more rational and respectable form than that demonstrated in Astley's galleries, which had the reputation of attracting "wags," according to the actor and musician Arthur William A' Beckett.[65] Performing in the Cattle Market in Canterbury in 1838, Bridges's circus, for instance, was patronized by the Earl of Cardigan and officers of the Eleventh Dragoons, along with the "distinguished band of the Regiment," which played several airs at the display. Bridges's circus combined patriotism with civic-mindedness: posters advertised that children of various local charities would be admitted free.[66] In the same season, with the "kind permission" of Major Westonry, the Fifth Dragoon Guards assisted in a version of *The Battle of Waterloo* performed at Batty's circus in Newcastle.[67] At T. Cooke's, in Glasgow, in 1844 the officers of the Royal Irish Fusiliers brought with them the regiment's band, which played "concerted pieces, overtures and popular airs" during the intervals between the acts. These included "a grand chivalric spectacle" that hit another nationalist note, "St. George and the

Dragon."[68] Six years later at Manchester, Lieutenant Colonel Nicol and the Thirtieth Regiment promised to patronize William Cooke's performance of *The Battle of Waterloo*.[69]

With real soldiers in the audience, playing in the band, or both, these exhibitions assumed an authentic air that elevated not only the circus to the level of parade ground but also the viewers to the level of patriots. Locality played an important role as individual regiments interacted with their communities in a way that paid tribute to local heroes. Given that many individuals had enlisted as an act of camaraderie, to serve alongside friends and relations from their own villages and county, their participation at the circus was in keeping with other commemoration rituals. That they exhibited solidarity not just with one another but also with the needy suggested another kind of loyalty—to community—which could easily coexist with patriotic feeling.[70] The circus thus provided a site where different levels of allegiance intersected, producing a ritual that at once celebrated nation, community, and individual duty. Moreover, through these acts, the circus constructed and mobilized national memory decades after the conflict had ended and the surviving troops had returned home. They thereby provide an example of what Eric Hobsbawm meant by "the invention of tradition," that is, the process by which groups, usually nations, use the past to construct identity and give meaning to and legitimize social values and actions.[71]

In these plays offering a vision of the nation the hero provided a neat focus. In *The Battle of Waterloo* Napoleon and Wellington are portrayed as equally matched leaders—talented, ambitious, and resolute.[72] Thus depicted, Wellington's eventual victory over Napoleon becomes that much sweeter and heroic. He is seen as the protector of English political stability, the embodiment of Burkean conservatism, and a reflection of how patriots liked to see themselves.[73] Notably, the duke is rarely seen or heard and is more often spoken about, usually by Napoleon. His cameo appearances no doubt raised him to even loftier heights in the audience's collective imagination. At the same time, his absence may have been intended to add dramatic tension, building up to the desperate encounter.

In act 1, scene 3, Napoleon addresses his troops on the eve of the Battle of Ligny, declaring, "This defensive war must on our part be conducted on the same great principle which has elevated France to the highest rank among the nations." Here and elsewhere, the rhetoric of the patriot and that of the nation were intertwined, as in contemporary political oration, in the discourse of the leader in whom the soldier must place his trust.[74] Napoleon admonishes his troops, "With soldiers so resolute, and generals so talented, great results may be expected. . . . He is with you who has always pointed out their victorious flight; he will now share your toils, your marches and your daring."[75] The actor who played Napoleon in 1824 and again in 1844, Samuel Gomersal, cut an impressive figure, earning credit for his "prodigious likeness" to the emperor: he was "curiously exact—broad shouldered, well limbed, sallow, serious," one critic noted.[76] The scene that follows involves "a dreadful contest on the bridge" and "continual skirmishes below" between the Prussians and the French. Finally, Blücher is fired at, and "his horse rears and eventually falls wounded, and [he] with [it]." Tearing at his hair, he seizes his pistols and places them in his aide-de-camp's hands, pleading with the latter to put him out of his misery "rather than let him become a prisoner to France." In an act of devotion, the aide-de-camp lifts up the infirm old man and carries him off.[77] The fighting scene, conducted entirely without words, visually articulated conventions from melodrama and narrative painting, combining feeling with stoicism, spiritedness with melancholy.[78] Externalizing thought and feeling in such ways, the general, the officer, and the common soldier revealed themselves to be bound by the same obligations and emotions surrounding nation and citizenship.[79]

In these equestrian representations, being a man ultimately meant sacrifice for *patrie,* as Wellington's character also shows. In the second act, when he first appears, "a gay flourish of fifes and drums" announces his arrival. Following this, the chorus sings, "May war, that source of sorrow, ne'er cause us to morn, mayst though before tomorrow, with victory return." With spirits raised by the music, Wellington addresses his foot soldiers, telling them that "the world has fixed its eye upon us, England expects much; no one is here, I trust, who would not rather die than disappoint his native country's hope."[80] Later he makes clear the steadfastness of Napoleon's army: "None of you will fall into the vulgar error of having to deal with an inactive or untalented enemy. The man who is now opposed to us, is by nature and circumstances compelled to make a desperate stand."[81] The author of one contemporary acting handbook, the *Thespian Preceptor* (1811), recommended that when giving such speeches the hero must not "roar" but rather must "have a distinct articulation, clearness, compass and strength of voice."[82] Strong words commanded obedience from Wellington's men.

In the battle scene at Quatre Bras, Wellington's troops exchange fire with

DEATH *of the* DUKE *of* BRUNSWIK *at the* BATTLE *of* WATERLOO.

Fig. 13. Frontispiece from *The Battle of Waterloo*, by J. H. Amherst, 1874. (By permission of The British Library)

and charge at the French, who initially "obtain possession of the wood after a struggle and from the most advantageous situation defend their positions." They later lose it to the English and Allied troops, who, in turn, suffer the death of the Duke of Brunswick, who is shot from his horse (fig. 13).[83] Such action contributed to a narrative structure that, far from revealing a foretold victory over the French, lacked "fixity." As the play unfolded, the spirited efforts of both sides allowed for this instability and thus raised tensions and excited the audience, as earlier accounts suggest. "The effect throughout on the auditors resembles that produced at a race course when favorites are neck and neck," said one viewer at the Vauxhall production in 1827.[84] The cut and thrust of military battle not only portrayed two strong enemies but also glorified the "triumph of freedom and humanity over military despotism," in the words of a poster for the Surrey Theatre in May 1814, when Wellington's entry at Bordeaux was re-created.[85] The dramatic tension was connected to a "terrible uncertainty" that resulted in the triumph of goodness over chaos, darkness, and terror, which Napoleon and his army embodied. In the final scene, the English and Allied troops emerge—led by Wellington—from a burst of light amid the screams, shrieks, and the double crash of shells and fire. As hero, Wellington inspires thoughts of greatness about nation, power, and virtue, as well as eternal loss and emptiness, amid this apocalypse. He was seen to act with "God-like moderation" in the hour of victory.[86] For any viewer versed in contemporary aesthetic doctrine the scene was sublime.

So successful was *The Battle of Waterloo* in 1824 that Astley's presented another of Amherst's plays, *Napoleon Bonaparte's Invasion of Russia; or, The Conflagration of Moscow,* a year later. Like the previous production, this one featured extensive panoramas. The most impressive came at the end of act 2, in the scene "Moscow in Flames," in which there were crashes and an enormous conflagration. According to the text, "Alarm bells [ring] . . . many of the inhabitants half naked with blankets or carpets about them . . . an immense pile of building falls," creating a splendid "spectacular effect." In the foreground, Napoleon rescues a woman and child trapped in a burning house.[87] His action at the foot of the stage or center of the ring (since Astley's had both) and the landscape in the background combined in powerful ways before audiences accustomed to spectacular "metamorphosis." Such stage transformations grew from innovations like the magic lantern and the moving diorama, or Eidophusikon, as well as new painting technique.[88]

These dramatic portrayals of the emperor's character as chivalrous and virtuous appeared in more than just circuses, as demonstrated in the play *Napoleon: The Hunter of the Alps,* by W. Dimond and John Walker (author of the 1832 play *The Factory Lad*), performed at the minor theater Sadler's Wells in 1828.[89] In this play about compassionate leadership Napoleon, disguised as a prisoner held captive in his own army, is confronted by a man about to be taken prisoner who, it is revealed, served as a soldier for Louis XVI. The man hates what Napoleon has done to his country, insisting that "after laying waste other countries he has brought war on his own." Just as the soldiers were about to fire at the man, the disguised prisoner yells "Hold" and reveals his true identity as emperor, inspiring surprise and adulation. In an act of modesty, however, he implores, pointing to the prisoner: "Kneel not to me but rise and imitate that man." And he adds, "I trust the actions of this night will prove that my heart is not callous."[90] Thus presented, Napoleon is "a head of state who can both create order and intervene with humanity and justice," as Louis James has argued.[91] Moreover, in the final days of the Regency period Napoleon offered an important lesson on meritocracy that fueled current ideas about democracy and electoral reform. One of the key attractions of Napoleon, inspiring the cult of Bonaparte for generations, related to his rise from "the ranks of the people, entirely by his own talents and courage," as described in an 1843 catalogue of the Napoleon Museum, housed, appropriately, in the Egyptian Hall.[92] It was a theme pursued in other contemporary plays, notably Bulwer-Lytton's *The Lady of Lyons* (1838), in which the noble cousin of the Lady observes that "in the French army, now-a-days, promotion is not a matter of purchase. We are all heroes because we may be all generals. We have no fear of the cypress because we may all hope for the laurel."[93]

Posterity, so important in Dimond and Walker's play, is the theme explored in *Napoleon's Glory; or, Wonders in Saint Helena,* first performed at the Adelphi Theater in December 1840. Like Banquo's ghost, Napoleon's rises from the dead and confronts a soldier who guards his tomb on the island. Astounded by this apparition, the sentry draws his weapon. The ghost appeases the man by reassuring him that he has only come before him to renew a friendship: "You served under Abercrombie in Egypt," France's enemy, the ghost reminds him, "where you may remember I saved your life, when sadly wounded on the sands, and sent you prisoner to Toulon from whence by exchange you again entered the service of England." "Recovering his arms," the sentry confirms this and says, "I'll do nothing to harm you!" He adds that he "will do anything to serve you, and yours; not injuring the Country I serve," importantly implying that no conflict necessarily would arise from his being devoted both to England and to Napoleon.[94]

This favorable depiction of Emperor Napoleon persisted, and on the eve of the Crimean War, a decade later, when Britain's old enemy became its new friend in the fight against Russia, it was given even greater visual force.[95] In the military spectacle *Bonaparte in Egypt,*[96] produced at Astley's in April 1852, when it had an eight-week run, "everything . . . is done to elevate the character and achievements of the ten young generals of the French army and afterwards [of the] Emperor," one reviewer noted, adding that "no one word is said in favour of British valour, all is given over to French bravery," and this was greeted with "a spontaneous burst of applause from every part of the theatre."[97] No doubt the applause was even greater in Paris, where it appeared before its London debut.

The London production, approved by the Lord Chamberlain's office, featured scenery, *tableaux,* and incidents at "The Fortress of El Haric, near Alexandria" and the "Mystic Tombs," where the Arabs pray and where "the wild, young prophet El Mohdi" incites violence against the approaching Napoleonic army in the background.[98] "Behold this Sacred Scymitar . . . its darling blade shall strike the infidel," he yells to the crowd that surrounds him, adding, "*Allah-hu'* . . . death leads but to life; to all who battle for our holy Cause." When the French army marches to Alexandria, the peaceable Napoleon cautions his soldiers to resist fighting: "I wager victory and glorious triumphs! as friends—unless they [the Arabs] declare war against us." This policy becomes increasingly difficult to maintain when he is confronted with El Mohdi, who tells him, "My mission is to exterminate the Enemies of our holy Prophet." Mohdi's followers do so by poisoning the water in a well that some of Napoleon's men drink from in a later scene. Those who survive swear their allegiance to the dead and to France, promising to punish the enemy. Following this is an attack on the village Rochech, where Sally, a servant to the British consul, and Helena, a Greek girl, are abducted by a slave merchant called Kalfoh, anticipating white-slave narratives made popular three decades later. They are soon saved, however, by the French soldiers. Two Britons, Paddy and Ben, of the Thunder Gun Brigade, later join the French in their fight, agreeing that the common aim is to defeat the ruling Mamelukes. With this new alliance, they redundantly insist that they do not wish to fight against "Old England, no never."[99] The most spectacular scene comes at the end: the overthrow of the Mamelukes at Aboukir, near the Pyramids, by Bonaparte, who explodes the "Powder Tower" in an "imposing denouement" that received great applause, according to one reviewer.[100]

Concerns of the 1850s, rather than unsettled scores between the French and the British, informed the production. Instead of exposing differences between the two former enemies, the spectacle highlighted the compatibility between current British policy abroad (in the empire and, more pressingly, in the Crimea) and past French expansionism. Far from being mutually exclusive, they were politically and diplomatically complementary, at least where Western hegemony and colonial encounters with despotic dynasties were concerned. This double narrative therefore was an exercise in historical displacement: it featured the Napoleonic Wars as the subject of the play but was informed by the new diplomatic reality of the 1850s, thereby providing an interesting, if not also self-serving and bizarre, mix of past and present.[101]

Presented in the period preceding colonial consolidation, this narrative also revealed imaginings and fantasies about Britain's projected imperial greatness, attitudes that were projected onto the French soldiers in their celebrated invasion of Egypt. Represented thus, cultural imperialism preceded political imperialism by three decades, at least in the case of Egypt.[102] The military hero—not the politician, the bureaucrat, or the merchant trader—was responsible for its success in this spectacular display.

In conclusion, the equestrian military spectacle contributed to an important process of national mythmaking, one that did not originate with the state but arose within the unofficial, popular culture. It was, to be sure, complemented by high cultural developments at the Royal Academy and elsewhere. As in painting, the battle scene foregrounded heroic action, providing the material necessary for national storytelling and engendering patriotism. And as in contemporary biographical histories, the great man or hero in these spectacles provided a focus for understanding war and the complex relationship between the leader and his men. Thus, circus equestrians portrayed famous men battling against dangerous odds and for virtuous ends. The performers' grand speeches, statuesque poses, and real-life resemblances only heightened the artistic effect, rendering them as much like paintings or sculptures as actors in a ring. As *tableaux vivants,* they appeared lifelike, stylistically caught in a historical moment that was part of a living drama.[103] Surrounded by the carnage of war and "terrible" noise, they embodied the heroic, although Napoleon's heroism did not become truly apparent in the ring until mid-century, when Britain's current foreign entanglements were justified in terms of France's past expansionism. These scenes structured knowledge about war for a popular audience in the period before photography utterly and permanently changed how war would be remembered, as occurred in the Crimea. In presenting these dramas, circuses like Astley's told a "flag-waving" and selectively "foreigner-hating" story about recent history that corresponded to other artistic forms, local rituals, and national ceremonies and, moreover, contributed to "the invention of tradition."[104] The indefatigable, courageous, virtuous, strong, godlike hero was at the very center of this story, and on his body the heroic was inscribed. Depicted thus, he had an important story to tell his "historically minded" popular audience in this age of limited (but widening) democracy.

Three

Victorian Curiosity

The *Oxford English Dictionary* defines *curiosity* as a descriptive category ("an object of interest; any object valued as curious, rare or strange") and in terms of intellect ("a desire to know or learn about anything, especially that which is novel or strange").[1] An important change in the history of curiosity occurred in the Victorian period, when a desire to know aroused a fascination with exotics brought from the far reaches of the colonial world and beyond. This fascination spanned the class divide, and with it came a new way of seeing and thinking about curiosity. This reimagining was central to the culture because through it the Victorians made sense of themselves and of their role in the world.

But this marked a great departure from age-old assumptions about curiosity. For many ancient and early modern philosophers, little or no virtue was to be found in it.[2] Plutarch called curiosity vulgar, and Thomas Hobbes associated it with greed. If greed was its hallmark, then it also spurred "a desire for totality," particularly among early modern collectors, who traded in the luxury goods that were ubiquitous in a budding New World economy.[3] Aristocrats, gentry, natural scientists, and other elites collected rarities that filled their extensive and elaborate cabinets. Stuffed animals and birds, fossils, small artifacts, articles of costume and weaponry, religious accessories, mechanical devices (e.g., clocks), and wax models were prized and sought after.[4] Such collections, like the one belonging to Isabella d'Este in the late fifteenth and early sixteenth centuries, were said to cost far more than a painting by a leading artist such as Mantegna or Perugino.[5]

The private rooms in which they were exhibited stood in stark contrast to the public marketplaces, inns, and streets where a wider public gathered to gape at related "eccentricities." During the Enlightenment, members of the literati, such as Chevalier de Jaucourt, deemed curiosity to be "the indulgence of the folk" or the "portion of the lazy."[6] Against the backdrop of the heaving, chaotic, and commercial streets of London, for instance, James Boswell observed "a vast museum of all objects" in 1775. A decade later such sights included Mr. Loutherbourg's Eidophusikon, as well as a grand scene from Milton and a Polish dwarf at Exeter Change.[7] At the Camberwell Fair in 1829 rare stuffed birds, shells and fossils, and other items that had once been part of the Leverian collection were displayed in "several commodious caravans."[8] Likewise in the following decades, the circus became a repository of all that was strange and wonderful, offering rare specimens of natural history and human perfection and exoticism—a change that coincided with midcentury colonial market expansion.[9]

In turn, those assumptions born out of the Enlightenment (and earlier) about the perceived incompatibility between "noble curiosity" and "vulgar wonder" began to wane, and the gulf between learned and lay culture began to close. The hunger to know and the desire to gape became increasingly intertwined; the gape—an open-mouthed, stupefied condition—literally and figuratively implied openness, incompleteness, and therefore a capacity to change or confirm one's ideas. Visual demonstrations acted as a great social leveler, uniting unskilled workers, working-class tradesmen, and elites who were attracted to the circus ring and other democratic spaces. This social mixing complicates historiographical assumptions about the fracture between low and high culture resulting from the explosion of print culture since the Reformation. At the circus, the boundary separating the two was a thin and transparent one, necessitating constant negotiation where matters of knowledge and intelligence competed with a baroque enthusiasm for the grotesque, bizarre, or exotic.[10]

This was a delicate balancing act. Throughout the nineteenth century, parliamentarians, theater critics, and other social observers commented on the link between exhibition and moral education or its corruption. The assumption that audiences involuntarily imbibed lessons from display provided one rationale for the 1843 Theatre Regulation Act, which consolidated the Lord Chamberlain's authority to license and censor.[11] The circus for the most part remained outside his control because of its emphasis on visual rather than written texts.[12] Therefore, what the public saw in the form of "the strange and wonderful" had to be legitimized in other ways if the company's good name was to be upheld. Considering the mid-nineteenth-century preoccupation with respectability, and the fact that it was in this period that the circus expanded commercially, the link between rational amusement and visceral fascination had to be carefully mediated. Occupying a central place in the history of popular culture, the history of curiosity informs us about what contemporaries valued and what excited their minds. In addition, the subject sheds considerable light on the history of the body not only because performance represented the body but also because the act of seeing was, after all, an embodied experience. Thus, the history of curiosity becomes a story of the subjectivity of the visual encounter, one reflected in the interested gaze and the bewildered gape.

Curious exhibitions and the responses they provoked, moreover, illuminate broader cultural shifts that challenge historiographical assumptions about the importance of antislavery and radical opinion in the first half of the century and anticruelty in the second. The public's fascination with curiosities hampered the development of humanitarianism and sentimentality. At the same time, it was propelled by contemporary scientific findings and protoanthropological investigations. Underpinning the agenda of many was a fundamental belief in the desirability of curing physical deformities and taming emotional excesses, an idea that had obvious parallels with the civilizing project in the colonial world. Contemporary notions of progress were thus complicated by these exhibitions. Moreover, they force us to interrogate previous historiographical assumptions about the mid-Victorian's pursuit of rational recreation.

The display of natural history, so integral to the early modern collector's cabinet, was also an important part of the circus and offered visual examples of new scientific theories in an age when evolutionary biology transformed man's way of seeing himself and the world around him, particularly after the publication of Jean Baptiste Pierre Antoine de Monet de Lamarck's *Philosophie zoologique* (1809) and, decades later, Charles Darwin's *Descent of Man* (1871).[13] Monkeys, for instance, constituted links in the great chain of being. In a remark affirming those gradations, Rao Nadkarni, a Bombay lawyer visiting Regent's Park Zoo at the end of the century noted that the faces of the African monkeys in particular "approach much to that of the negro."[14] In addition to serving as specimens in what might be called an imperial showcase, animals performed "wonderful," anthropomorphic feats. Educated pigs and stallion horses demonstrated "unusual" intelligence by allegedly counting with their hoofs or walking backwards on tightropes. Extending upward, the links in the great chain of being connected beast and man.[15] The Chinese juggler, the Bedouin acrobat, the Indian sword swallower, the American conjuror, and the German Hercules, for instance, provided visual proof of the "wondrous" abilities of men from around the globe. Coming together in London and other cities and towns, these artists (many of whom were, in fact, Britons masquerading as foreigners) provided real or imaginary insight into other, more exotic worlds.

In "Oriental" spectacles displaying, among other things, perceived habits, manners, and rituals of Easterners, these imagined worlds were exposed further, thereby illuminating what some Victorians thought of as their developing empire, as well as areas they had not yet conquered, and all the curiosities in it. According to non-Western travelers to the metropole, this vision was highly ornamental, sometimes bizarre.[16] To such onlookers from the periphery, this brand of curiosity was curious indeed. By "speaking to the eye," these writers contributed to the developing genre of metropolitan travel writing and in turn represented the complexities of the city and its curiosities as only outsiders could.[17] The colonial encounter is further explored below by examining the responses of such travelers.[18] Aiming to keep this quintessentially Victorian show on the road, managers concerned themselves with finding increasingly more "wonderful" and exotic specimens culled from home and abroad. During Victoria's reign the opportunities were vast, especially in the great metropolis, where the pickings were abundant.

Many contemporaries flocked to see and shared an enthusiasm for the unexpected, the hitherto unseen, the inexplicable or, wonder. In *The Old Curiosity Shop* (1840–41) Dickens romanticized "the vague smell of horses suggestive of coming wonders" that the youthful audience at Astley's eagerly awaited.[19] In the same period, two Bombay naval architects, Jehangeer Nowrojee and Hirjeeboy Merwanjee, were duly impressed by the horses' "admirable training" at the amphitheater. Like the snake charmed in India, "they rise up and lie down at the word of a command; they lie as if dead at the bidding of the rider; and when the tune is played they dance with their feet as if they were human beings."[20] Some decades later, Jhinda Ram, of Lahore, commented that he had never seen a circus before visiting the one at the Albert Palace, where the sagacious horses were "like human beings."[21] It was in this period that Mr. Ginnett's circus, then on the auction block in Oldham, reportedly sold "a talking horse."[22] The visual pleasure roused by wonder and enchantment gave rise to an enthusiasm to see more. As acts became more skilled, trainers such as the visiting American J. S. Rarey received popular attention. Advertising his "novel" system of "subduing and training unmanageable horses" at the Royal Cirque Unique in Margate and at more esteemed venues like Tattersall's in London in 1858, he encountered a mixture of applause and criticism. Many doubted the wildness of his steeds and therefore his "magical abilities," sparking age-old concerns about the connection between fakery and wonders.[23] In cases like these, the boundary between childhood credulity and adult skepticism was therefore heightened rather than relaxed by the alleged display of the "real," the "abnormal," and the "fantastic." Here and elsewhere, the gape and the interested gaze combined. "Noble curiosity" hardly "froze inquiry," as the Encyclopedists had believed a century earlier; to the contrary, the former spurred the latter.[24]

But impresarios had more to worry about than the public's disbelief. Humanitarian sensibility occasionally asserted itself in ways that threatened the showman and his livelihood. Street performers were the most vulnerable because a broad public witnessed their shows, often without contributing to their purse and sometimes with the intention of driving them away. One penny showman told the *Morning Chronicle* in 1850 that formerly he had strapped a donkey to a ladder and balanced him. But "the papers attacked the performance and I was taken to the Union Hall . . . and fined 7s 6d and they kept the donkey in default," referring to the anticruelty law of 1849 protecting domestic animals.[25] While some members of the public gathered before the animal in awe and amazement, others worried about the impact of the performances on those witnessing these displays. The reformist impulse underpinning these discourses raises important questions, as did the female-acrobat controversy (discussed in chapter 5), about what excited interest in curiosity exhibitions and how much more it would take to gratify it.

The problem was exaggerated when exotic animals were involved. After seeing the revered lion tamer Mr. van Amburgh perform at Drury Lane, probably in January 1839, when the Queen also paid a visit, Nowrojee and Merwanjee fretted about a fatal outcome: "Although a wonderful performance, it was not pleasing; for we thought if their savage nature should return to them the man must die, and then people would reproach themselves for going to

Fig. 14. Sir Edwin Landseer, *Isaac van Amburgh and his Animals,* 1839. (The Royal Collection © 2004, Her Majesty Queen Elizabeth II)

encourage him [to put] his life in danger."[26] Apparently joyful rather than fearful, the rest of the audience in the cheap gallery seats "made much noise, whistling and yelling," they added. Many more applauded van Amburgh's heroic triumph over the savage nature of his beasts, a point borne out by his successive performances in Britain and on the Continent and emphasized in newspaper reviews and in Sir Edwin Landseer's 1839 painting *Isaac van Amburgh and his Animals* (fig. 14). One Mr. Carter, a rival, similarly enjoyed iconic status for his role as "civilizer." And "that is more than many of his fellow creatures can say who undertake hazardous expeditions to displace aboriginals and rob them of their home and birthright," said another observer, alluding to humanitarian sentiment that underpinned some of the contemporary discourse.[27]

Others, like traveler John Howison, made their observations more pointed, noting that wild animals like the lions and tigers kept in Lord Somerset's Cape Town menagerie appeared "active, well grown, and in high condition" due to "the size of their cages that affords them sufficient room for exercise." Consequently, he added, "they have a very different appearance from those animals of the same species that are exhibited in England."[28] The latter's apparently inferior condition may have given Carter the necessary edge to subdue them, although the publicity surrounding his performances with wild beasts emphasized his abilities.

One 1844 poster for Cooke's circus in Glasgow went so far as to boast that the tamer worked "miracles," drawing important parallels with missionary work abroad.[29] That year at Astley's in London, Carter performed with lions, tigers, and leopards in a variety of displays, including "Mungo Park" and "The Lion of the Desert, or the French in Morocco," in which he, not they, was king of the forest. To be a "civilizer," one had to be tough, a point given visual force in the posters featuring Carter holding back a lion with one hand while beating off an attacking tiger, whose claws ravage his chest, with the other (fig. 15). "This is a frightful exhibition and really worth the money," wrote the lawyer Henry Crabb Robinson about the display.[30] This aesthetic revealed in the posters reflected Romantic discourses on the sublime and in

Fig. 15. Poster, "Astley's," 26 August 1844. (Theatre Museum, London; © V&A Images)

Victorian Curiosity

some sense anticipated muscular Christianity in the late 1850s.[31] Moreover, it revealed, in visual terms, tensions evident in colonial discourse between the ideas of combating barbarism and teaching civility. To civilize and to trade went hand in hand, and it was encounters like these that underlined Britain's reliance on its colonies and other trading nations to provide raw materials (e.g., wild animals) so that the wheels of cultural and economic progress could turn.

Whatever the criticism articulated by Howison and later writers, companies were keen to emphasize that the more domesticated and skillfully trained these erstwhile wild animals seemed, the more respectable their display. One advertisement in 1855 even assured the fainthearted that a lion and three Bengal tigers on display at Drury Lane were not only "serene" but "also free from all disagreeable smell[s]" that "in exhibitions of this kind generally create disgust." Should they be in any doubt of the class of patrons that came to see them, the poster added that "nearly the whole of the Royal family . . . the rich [as well as] the poor, the naturalist and the learned have all concurred in announcing them to be the most interesting and novel sight ever witnessed."[32] The reference to the "naturalist and the learned" reinforced midcentury ideas about rational recreation and bestowed on the exhibition a measure of respectability, at least in advertising terms. Furthermore, as visual reminders of an expanding colonial order, with its emphasis on free trade, the animals in the display served to justify the merits of the civilizing project. Rivaled only by the zoological display, the scientific lecture, and the schoolbook, they informed the curious-minded about the natural world and the unstable boundary between wildness and submission, much as Dr. Jekyll and Mr. Hyde did decades later.[33] Here and elsewhere, colonialism, politics, education, and morality combined in a complex representative structure in which the exotic animal, once subdued, became a metonym for progress. And in the streets of London that progress was evident as "wild domestics," like those belonging to Edwin Hughes's company, were paraded before a crowd, thereby providing—in that free, democratic space—a "living picture" of the Orient that spectators would otherwise have had to pay for. The procession through the City, symbolically illustrated in figure 16 before the Royal Exchange, emphasized the connection between progress, commerce, and empire even further. For well-traveled onlookers it also visually recapitulated the Indian procession celebrating marriage, religion, or ruler, in which priests and other local elites rode in ornamental carriages on the backs of elephants.[34]

Fig. 16. Lithograph, view of Edwin Hughes passing the Royal Exchange in a gilt coach drawn by two elephants, 1847. (Guildhall Library, Corporation of London)

The representation of such themes in the display of exotic animals effectively transformed the circus arena (as well as the streets through which circus companies processed) into one enchanting, global village. And its capital was London, with its docks and trading companies, which enabled the trade in "exotics" to thrive (fig. 17).[35] Beginning in the late eighteenth century, London-based impresarios like Astley made use of their geographical advantage. In 1796 Astley advertised "a cabinet of monkeys," along with Signor Lioranardi and his famous comic cabaret, "just arrived from Hamburg in the Good Ship Elizabeth."[36] Within the metropolis the same animal might be passed from one showman to the next, as in 1829, when Mr. Wombwell borrowed a Burmese elephant performing at Astley's in order to complete his show at Bartholomew Fair.[37] From the docks these animals spilled into nearby thoroughfares.[38] At the end of the period, Nundo Lall Doss, of the London Missionary Society, remarked on seeing five elephants hired by a circus as they were being taken to their destination, "a sight I had never seen in Calcutta, where alephants [sic] are forbidden by law to appear on the streets."[39] Sometimes the trade worked in the opposite direction, with English mercantile companies supplying the Continent with animals imported from colonial lands. The existence of warehouses, stables, and cellars along the Thames made it possible to hold animals before the transfer.[40]

Victorian Curiosity

At midcentury, with the help of the railways, troupes transferred such creatures from ship to carriage in order to provide audiences in the provinces a similar thrill. In 1866, for example, Mr. Manders's "private secretary" boasted that Manders had a double-striped Bengal tiger, "the largest animal of his species," obtained at the East India Docks and then sent to Carlisle, where it was exhibited.[41] Some managers relied on importers like William Cross or Mr. Jamrach, who owned shops specializing in rare animals near the docks in both Liverpool and London, to act as their dealers. The clientele of these importers included not only showmen but also elites who collected rare species. Carl Hagenbeck, for instance, claimed to supply such "distinguished" persons as Victor Emmanuel of Italy, the emperor of Austria, and the mikado of Japan, indicating that the early modern court mascot was still alive and well.[42]

A motley of customers also bid at auctions for the stock of bankrupt companies. Mr. Batty, lessee of Astley's, purchased items from the auction of the

Fig. 17. Sketch, "Shipping Wild Animals in the London Docks," *Illustrated London News,* 21 May 1864. (By permission of The British Library, Colindale Newspaper Library)

bankrupt Hughes held at Vauxhall Gardens in 1847, some of which he then resold to country managers.[43] For buyers looking for deals, the opportunities here were great. When Wombwell's menagerie came under the hammer in 1872, the "Tasmanian Devil" reportedly sold for "the small sum" of £3 5s., while Hannibal, "the largest and handsomest lion" in Britain, went for £270.[44] This must have been a bargain since one commentator noted that £250 could buy merely "a good lion."[45] At James Newsome's circus auction in 1899, two thousand persons, including "representatives from all the best known shows on the road," were present, some of whom were able to pay these prices.[46] George Sanger, seated sixth from the right in row 2 in figure 18, featured among those at Bostock's auction in Dalston in 1896, when its stock of menagerie animals was put on the block. Yet the exceptional cost of lions (and of what they ate daily, which one contemporary in 1888 estimated to be 8s.), in comparison with the cost of monkeys, for example, meant that only showmen like John and George Sanger, with big concerns and capital, could afford to buy them.[47] This obviously drove a wedge between them and those circus troupes with smaller budgets.[48] Auctions often indicated that the company doing the selling had gone bankrupt. Massive speculation in an unstable entertainment marketplace in the 1860s, combined with economic de-

Fig. 18. Bostock's auction, 1896. (A. H. Coxe Collection, Theatre Museum, London; © V&A Images)

Victorian Curiosity

pressions in the 1870s, put financial pressure on many companies that in the next two decades could no longer be sustained.[49] Thus, there was a minority that could afford to buy up the properties, some of which included wild animals. With increasing numbers of exotic animals on the market (at auctions and elsewhere), those circuses still in business and with big budgets were more likely to feature them than ever before.

Yet, a rising humanitarian concern for animals employed at circuses in the second half of the century threatened to remove them from the display. This movement had its roots in the late eighteenth century and arose from a combination of Romantic ideals, evangelical piety, and rational humanitarianism.[50] The emergence of the Royal Society for the Prevention of Cruelty to Animals (RSPCA) in 1824 paved the way for organized protectionist activity, and its members concentrated their efforts on making bullbaiting and other cruel sports illegal. Their successful action, culminating in Martin's Act of 1835, opened the door to further animal-protection legislation. Not only did the organization campaign for legal change but its activities extended to inspection. To this end, RSPCA inspectors sometimes paid visits to circuses, especially after the passage of an 1849 law protecting domestic animals such as horses and donkeys from cruelty. Generally speaking, however, their efforts resulted in little change to circus programs.[51] The application of the law was uneven, and the definition of cruelty was unclear and open to interpretation.[52] As reform became more urgent, animal-rights discourse came to be allied with debates on antivivisection and cruelty to children in order to encourage a widening of the 1849 law.[53]

In response to this agitation, a trainer known as "Professor" Parker suggested in an editorial printed in the *Era* that the problem be kept in proportion and that "one or two brutes" not be made to represent the whole trade.[54] Manager George Ginnett added in another letter that these cases did not amount to hundreds, as the many stories of this period implied, but only twenty or so.[55] Proof was therefore at the heart of successful investigations, RSPCA officials later admitted in an act of distancing themselves from more radical opinion.[56] But in the absence of behind-the-scenes access, proof remained a real challenge that even legal reform in 1900—resulting in the protection of wild animals—could not remedy.[57] Criticism like that articulated by Howison or the Bombay architects in the early to middle part of the century was probably more common than direct interference by RSPCA inspectors or other social reformers who tried to police showmen's activities.

Generally, neither affected managers' programming decisions. The public's keen interest in the exotic, wild animal persisted, compelling managers to make choices that suited this market demand. If they were rich like Sanger, they stood a better chance of surviving.

The curiosity that motivated observers to seek out spectacles involving exotic animals also stimulated an interest in "exotic" people. Anticipating the protoanthropological studies by Henry Mayhew, James Greenwood, and, others in the 1850s, many early circuses offered "ocular" studies of foreigners. At Bartholomew Fair in 1833, for instance, Clarke's equestrian troupe featured not only horses but also "a Chinese and a Pierrot [who] walk around the ring with each a leg put up to their necks." Following this, "a Black Man . . . threw himself backwards and resting on his hands, formed an arch, and then two heavy men stood on his stomach, with ease."[58] In each case a particular body part was emphasized in a display of skill whose overall effect was heightened by the performer's racial difference. The distinction between them and monstrosities with birth defects, who sparked repugnance, horror, and fear, was vital; it distinguished the circus from exhibitions at Exeter Change (until it closed in 1829), from penny booths at fairs (until they were severely restricted in the 1840s), and from the Barnum and Bailey show, which toured the kingdom in the late 1880s and 1890s.[59]

The removal of freaks from the fair or Exeter Change by midcentury paved the way for their reemergence in the second half of the century not only at Barnum's circus but also in metropolitan assembly rooms, scientific lecture theaters, and other such venues largely attended by the middle classes.[60] A display of "Zulu Kaffirs" in 1853 at Hyde Park Corner caught the attention of Charles Dickens, who commented in *Household Words* on their physical and moral savagery.[61] Bourgeois metropolitans remained gripped by these curiosities for decades. Readers of the *St. James Gazette,* the *Times,* and *Nature,* for instance, would have found advertisements for "Krao, the missing link," half-ape and half-man, at the Aquarium's new lecture room, where reserved seating cost one shilling in 1883.[62] Here and elsewhere a baroque interest in the grotesque was dressed up by scientists and other elites as legitimate interest in Darwin's theory of evolution. An example of this cultural appropriation was the Hottentot Venus, whose sexuality was pathologized in medical discourse.[63] In another example of scientific ordering, a paper published in 1864 by Dr. John Shortt in the *Journal of the Anthropological Society* on Indian acrobats described their languages, habits, caste, ceremonies, dress, and ornaments and listed their age, country, height, and head, neck, chest, arms, and thigh measurements.[64] In cases like these the relationship between "noble curiosity" and "vulgar wonder" was fused for respectable audiences. But this was different, at least in degree if not in kind, from circus entertainment, which was characterized by the Chinese and black performers at Clarke's in 1833, who made their living by performing unique skills rendered even more spectacular by their racial distinctiveness.

In the second half of the century, when the circus shifted from the fair to the tent or amphitheater, the acts became more elaborate and ornamental, a change that coincided with Britain's transition from colonial authority to imperial power in the second half of the century.[65] Like previous Continental wars, imperial conflicts provided a theatrical occasion for narrating a version of the recent events. In these narratives about the colonizer and the colonized, clear boundaries were drawn between a savage East and a civilized West. In November 1857, for example, Astley's staged *The Storming and Capture of Delhi!*—a grand military spectacle in three acts—which appeared for twelve weeks.[66] Using the greased-cartridge scandal as its starting point, the play opens with two British officers speaking darkly about "dangerous signs" and "suspicious" actions among the sepoys. They rise up and spare no mercy for the British "infidels"—a reference to Nana Sahib, "the Demon of Cawnpore," who was said to have been responsible for the massacre of British women and children and was subsequently demonized in contemporary novels, as well as plays like this one.[67] It also corresponded to narratives about captivity written by those Britons cut off and incarcerated by "natives."[68] (As a sign of solidarity and sympathy, some circuses, such as Howes and Cushing's in Norwich, contributed to a fund for the relief of these victims of the so-called Indian Mutiny.)[69] At the display's end, however, the British prevail and enjoy "a glorious victory of civilization over Barbarians."[70] Like equestrian dramas before it, this one combined patriotic military scenes with domestic themes, melodrama, and panoramas that "authenticated" or dazzlingly represented newspaper reports, broadsheets, song, and hearsay.

As a projection of a perceived reality about the East as untrustworthy, wild, ungovernable, and barbaric, such spectacles shed light on what excited the Victorian imperial imagination.[71] This also extended to trading regions over which the British had no formal rule or administrative control, like China. In 1858, during the Second Opium War, Astley's manager, William Cooke, staged *The Bombardment and Capture of Canton*. In it he featured a mixture of historical scenes involving "night attacks," panoramas of "a street in Canton," "the interior of a Chinese fort," and "a Chinese landscape," followed by celebrations of the imperial victory in which "British and French flags wave triumphantly upon the walls of Canton."[72] These panoramas, like the postcard in later years, transformed exotic places and the "natives" who inhabited them (in this case, the Chinese "rebels") into a knowable and tangible, if also highly fantasized, form.[73] Enhancing this fiction, all the actors were British, including Mr. Vokes, who played the emperor of China; Mrs. W. Dowton, the empress; Mr. G. Claire, the "gallant Moo Sing"; and Mr. James Holloway, "the Brave Kwangchoo." By assuming "Oriental" identities in the struggle, these artists presented a "truth" about the East-West encounter that was, to metropolitan eyes, more real than the event itself; to use Clifford Geertz's words, "the real is as imagined as the imaginary."[74]

As in other demonstrations of cultural inversion, such as blackface clown acts, the East's character was represented by white Britons.[75] As Brave Kwangchoo or one of the auxiliaries engaged in attack, the British portrayed the Chinese as cunning, treacherous, and unrelenting. They waged war against "white devils in Red coats and Blue jackets," whom *they* label "audacious barbarians," a cliché in these narratives. British sailors in the play, like Cable, characterized their foes as "winkey-eyed monkeys," whose plot to overwhelm them anticipated "yellow peril" anxiety in late-nineteenth-century invasion novels.[76] By having its performers assume colonial identities, Astley's departed from the practice later adopted at the Royal Aquarium or the Colonial and Indian Exhibition of using real foreigners as symbolic trophies. Significantly, the circus became even more distinct from "low" booths and its middle-class successor, the assembly room or special colonial exhibition, and arguably more respectable because it represented the East with white actors; in short, it was no sideshow.

Offering a monolithic view of both East and West, such circus spectacles presented a clear hierarchy whereby the British (read English) or French—strange bedfellows admittedly, although that relationship was changing—established authority over their colonial subjects.[77] *The Rajah of Nagpore; or, The Sacred Elephant of the Pagoda,* a production that ran for six weeks at Astley's in 1846 and coincided with British efforts to annex the Punjab, made this point. In the opening scene the people of the city literally kneel, not before a British ruler, but before a real elephant that will appoint the next king.[78] This underscored contemporary, particularly Christian, preconceptions about Hindu indulgence in idolatry, superstition, and heathen ritual, which was said to hamper British missionary activity.[79]

When Peter, a simple shoemaker from Cripplegate, is anointed as king, his new identity fools even his wife, who approaches him in his disguise and asks about her husband's whereabouts. She emphasizes that she is "a respectable, married woman and . . . not to be kept by you or any other man."[80] The woman's assertion of racial and sexual boundaries signaled both the potential for and fear of an intimate encounter. According to Patricia Murphy, without such a clearly established boundary between East and West in the plot, "the justification for imperialism would be weakened and the ideological structure underpinning it would be vulnerable to challenge."[81] The possibility of cultural entanglement is a point of tension that the king's disguise both heightens and, when ultimately revealed, appeases. The worshipping Indians who accept Peter as their king (like the defeated Chinese in *The Bombardment and Capture of Canton*) are depicted as heathens who stand to benefit from British civilization; they are also seen as challengers to it. Productions like these foregrounded, through violence, ritual, and pageantry, a view of Western imperialism that was superior and total.

These displays assumed even grander proportions later in the century, for instance, at Astley's in 1878, when two hundred auxiliaries were used to play sepoys, British troops, and Hindu servants in *Relief of Lucknow; or, Jessie Brown*, although a version of this had been produced on a smaller scale during Cooke's provincial tour in 1858 and at Drury Lane in 1862, indicating that public interest had increased by the seventies.[82] More impressive still was Imre Kiralfy's *India* two decades later at Earl's Court. With a cast of a thousand, it covered almost a thousand years of Indian history and offered a justification for the British Raj.[83] With this show Kiralfy established himself as a great impresario. During its summer runs in 1895–96 it had an estimated audience of at least one and a half million, to say nothing of the millions more who attended the Empire of India Exhibition, which accompanied it. Presided over by Indian princes and British government officials, Kiralfy's show radiated authenticity, displaying a mirror image of the highly ornamental, hierarchical empire that these dignitaries had helped to fashion overseas.[84] Indeed, these exhibitions helped to define, classify, and order visually the deeply conservative hierarchy that by the 1880s was showing signs of strain.[85]

These spectacles, therefore, became theatrical occasions for both reflecting and distorting peculiarities about British experiences of and attitudes toward empire and hitherto unconquered territories.[86]

The Eastern spectacle not only sparked keen interest but also reflected anxieties during crucial years when Britain's economic and, later, political hegemony came under threat. Conflicts with India and China in the fifties were followed by the Maori Wars of the sixties, the rejection of British rule by Afrikaner trekkers of the Cape, and the Jamaica Rebellion of 1865.[87] Besides the nationalist threat, the British had to cope with pressures arising from European imperial expansion. Competition for imperial territories, particularly with the Russians in central Asia, the French in Southeast Asia and Africa, and the Germans in Africa, created other anxieties.[88]

The representation of British power over foreign subjects assumed greater urgency by the end of the century, when cracks in the imperial facade were apparent and ministers and colonial officials alike were doing their best to paper over them. The jubilees of 1887 and 1897 illustrated this, but the circus had done so decades earlier, when Britain's imperial destiny had been far from certain.[89] As early as midcentury, when mercantile expansion had turned into administrative control (in India) or resulted in continued war (as in China), the circus presented a version of the East to a public that clustered around the ring in order to gratify its visual appetite for imperial color, ornamentalism, and pageantry. This consumerism grew directly from a commercial market for exotic things unloaded at the dockside. The greater the empire became over the next fifty years, the greater this appetite and the more elaborate the spectacle, as exemplified by Kiralfy's *India*. As nationalist uprisings threatened to usurp Britain's authority, Eastern spectacles cloaked the reality in an imperial fantasy. This was an important fiction to get across to an audience that included working-class men at a time of electoral expansion, especially after 1867. By projecting patriotic themes and rousing audience sympathy, managers at Astley's and elsewhere acted opportunistically in an effort to secure respectability for their shows, much as they had in the post-Napoleonic era, when military dramas were staged. Seen in this light, the circus, along with similar entertainments like Kiralfy's, presented to the public conservative messages about the "Orient." But lurking beneath the surface of this Eastern fantasy were deep anxieties about the future of imperial domination—and its limits.

The presence of Indian princes as spectators at Kiralfy's *India* suggests another kind of imperial encounter. Fraught with similar tensions, this story was narrated by foreign visitors whose gaze challenged and disrupted the representation of British authority. Narratives of their visits to Astley's and other metropolitan "spaces" from the 1830s onwards provide an interesting reading of curiosity, therefore. In these narratives the gape is not admitted to by the observer (e.g., I do not gape) but by the one at whom it is directed (e.g., He gapes at me). Thus, it is not surprising that the narrative of the gape in combination with the interested gaze is here told by colonials and other non-Britons who are the subjects of others' focus. As such, they shed light on the culture as only outsiders could. These accounts not only provide unique insight into the complex question of what motivated Victorian curiosity but also illuminate audience response not as collective but as individual and subjective. Though necessarily partial, this methodological approach provides interesting ways of constructing and analyzing the subjectivity of visual experience and of "reading" visual performance.[90]

Andrew Ducrow, then manager of Astley's, invited audiences in 1835 to feast their eyes on "Oriental" subjects, including "His excellency Mulvie Mohammad, Ismael Khan, Ambassador to his Majesty the King of Oude, and his wife," who, his posters claimed, would be dressed in "splendid Asiatic attire," spectacularly visible in the box seats occupied by special guests, which, significantly, were raised above and in front of the stalls and the circle.[91] But as a visit one year later by their friend Najaf Koolee Meerza, the Prince of Persia, showed, the gaze moved in two directions. At the amphitheater (and probably from the same box seat his friends had occupied) he peered out into the audience and saw "50,000 ladies with charming faces like the moon, and the ray of their beauty gave a most powerful splendour to the place."[92] (Like the moon, these faces were presumably white.) To Meerza's Persian eye, the sheer concentration of these radiant women was so "astonishing" that it diverted his attention away from the stage, on which stood "an Asiatic emperor in Eastern splendour" illuminated by a fire "the light of which made the whole place look as red as crimson."[93] Meerza's two-way glance— directed toward both the audience and the Eastern spectacle—as well as the audience's (likely) gaze at him and the performance, raises interesting questions about this East-West encounter. How were gender, class, and ethnicity negotiated? If both the prince and the audience enjoyed the effects of power through a gaze signifying possession (he of them) as well as curiosity (they of him), then this was a highly charged encounter whose dialectic tensions were apparent, if not clearly articulated in Meerza's memoir.[94] Moreover, by positioning East and West in the audience and on stage, Astley's and other circuses like it provided a new experience whereby the "exotic Orient" was allied with conspicuous (visual) consumption and metropolitan life in ways that anticipated the Great Exhibition of 1851 and other such displays.[95]

If, like physical attraction, curiosity is in the eyes of the beholder, its arousal said as much, if not more, about the spectator than the subject caught in his gaze. Meerza's account tells us how he constructed feminine whiteness, but how did the women construct his "blackness"? Moreover, what does the Victorian interest in the circus tells us about racial imaginings? How can these be read? While Catherine Hall sees the construction of a "grammar of difference" as central to classifying and containing colonials and the colony, this ordering may be extended to the construction of an imperial gaze, which, like language, was neither inherent nor stable.[96] And where the gape was concerned, this processing became ever more problematic, especially where bourgeois codes of conduct were disrupted by unseemly displays of open-mouthed amazement: when combined, the gaze depicting interest and the gape revealing stunned fascination and bewilderment ran counter to each other. The gape and the gaze may have been constituted together for Meerza (looking out) and members of the Astley's audience (looking up at the prince), raising interesting questions about how this experience fitted into the "vulgar wonder" and "noble curiosity" paradigm. Furthermore, what was being dynamically constructed then and there, and what preexisting knowledge was being reinforced? Only cursory, sideways glances or stares, as well as more direct encounters between these historical actors, provide clues about these racial imaginings, illustrating just how complex the problem was.[97] Thus problematized, the circus might usefully be compared with other popular leisure sites where these encounters occurred, such as Turkish baths.[98]

Dress was an important initial signifier in these instances. On a visit to Regent's Park Zoo, where entrance cost one shilling or was free for members, the Bombay architects remarked in their memoir of 1841 that they had "attracted a very great number round us from the peculiarity of our dress, and we were the objects of very great curiosity . . . as much so perhaps as the winged and four-footed inmates of the place." The juxtaposition of the Indians and the exotic captives highlighted a perceived interrelationship between them, while it furthermore emphasized differences between the men and the curious-minded metropolitans who surrounded them. So perplexed were the latter by the racial origin of the Indians that "it was amusing to hear one call us Chinese, they are Turks says another; no they are Spanish, vociferates a third."[99] In the provinces, where colonial subjects were less commonly sighted, they unsurprisingly captured even greater attention. While touring Maidstone, "we were followed by a dense crowd of persons attracted by our costume, and as our friend knew the governor of the gaol, we went in there to get rid of the pressure; but when we came out, they had increased so very considerably, that we could not see all that our friends wished to shew us." Emerging from the prison showcased their racial difference, which, when highlighted by the brightly colored costumes, became a spectacle. Nor was Maidstone any different from "all the little places through which we passed," where "nearly their whole population . . . poured forth . . . to gaze upon us in our foreign costume."[100] In such encounters, colonial subjects provided visual proof of the colony and were a source of fascination and sometimes anxiety and bafflement, which reflected real tensions between colony and metropole, tensions that were easily translated from a visual "grammar of difference" defined by cultural boundaries and ethnic stereotypes.

When the men visited Astley's circus, these competing impulses became a real problem, resulting in their speedy exit from the gallery of the amphitheater. They advised their "countrymen," for whom their book served as a metropolitan guide, that "never for the sake of economy" should they visit that part of the ampitheater commonly populated by "humbler classes, as well as by rogues, thieves and pickpockets." There, they warned, the foreigner is "often teased and insulted with gross and abusive language by these fellows," adding that "the majority of lower orders in England are very rude in their manners and behaviour towards strangers, whom they do not like to see in their own country."[101] Not only does Nowrojee and Merwanjee's account raise interesting questions about spectators' watching other spectators, as we saw in Meerza's encounter at Astley's, but it also points to the problem of what public role "Oriental" subjects could comfortably occupy in this culture.[102] As subjects in the Eastern spectacle or seated in the box seats, for instance, they were objectified and domesticated, but as paying spectators in the gallery among plebeians their role was obviously different. Public response clearly depended on the social classes of those around them and the context of the encounter: middle-class patrons at the zoo reacted with mannered fascination; a socially mixed group at Maidstone turned into a mob; and at the circus an apparently plebeian audience in the gallery jeered. Excitement that fueled curiosity and a "desire to know" could easily turn into anxiety about strange peoples, their manners, and their customs.

"Human nature everywhere thirsts for novelty, and measures out its favours in proportion to the rarity and oddity of the thing," wrote T. N. Mukharji, who, as the highest-ranking South Asian in the Department of Revenue and Agriculture, became involved with the India Exhibition Commission and was responsible for planning and other public duties at the Colonial and Indian Exhibition in 1886. He specifically noted how audiences flocked to see Hindu and Muhammadan artisans who "wove the gold brocade, sang the patterns of the carpet and printed the calico with the hand." They were met by "stares from eyes of all colours—green, gray, blue and black."[103] This appetite for ornamentalism persisted, intriguing even, or perhaps especially, the pious who sought to improve "the manners and habits of heathendom." On a visit to disseminate the Gospel to performers at Carl Hagenbeck's Ceylon Exhibition in the Agricultural Hall, Joseph Salter, of the London City Mission, was struck by "the solicitations of a nách girl" who was "fantastically dressed and ornamented, with painted lips and cheeks, nose rings, and her caste-mark on her forehead."[104]

Returning the gaze, colonials like Mukharji were fascinated by such fascination. When reading a newspaper at a restaurant at the exhibition site, he became "suddenly aware that he was being looked at" and glanced up at a man and his daughter. The latter, he wrote, "delighted with everything I said, expressed her astonishment at my knowledge of English, and complimented me for the performance of the band brought from my country." The band to which she referred was actually from the West Indies and composed of "Negroes and Mulattos," and her mistake "made me wince," but "I went on chattering for a quarter of an hour," allowing her sufficient means to "brag" about seeing and talking to "a genuine 'Blackie.'"[105] Nor was Mukharji alone in witnessing this kind of racial confusion. In 1896 Rao Nadkarni despaired about the "remarkable" ignorance of the English, who believed "that Indians are no better than negroes," who were "utterly sunk in barbarism."[106] By glancing back, Mukharji and others went from being an object of curiosity to a subject engaged in challenging and destabilizing it—and then writing about it. Mukharji's "wince" may have gone unnoticed by the girl, but as Saloni Mathur argues, "he transforms the exhibition into a space where 'Europe,' too, can be observed."[107]

That mixture of fascination and anxiety evident in the Bombay architects' account of 1841 and that of Mukharji in 1889 arguably motivated a popular desire to see increasingly elaborate and spectacular "Oriental" exhibitions throughout the period. The colonial subject's participation in "the ocular exchange" informs us about what Stuart Hall calls the "circularity of power" and the way meanings are constructed.[108] With respect to curiosities, this was a dynamic process that depended on a shifting visual dialogue between the two observers, although not as equal partners. The social context in which this took place (e.g., the circus, zoo, or colonial exhibition) conditioned the experience, although objectification and exclusion of the "Oriental" was the common outcome.

Curiosity underwent a significant change when the rare, the exotic, and the bizarre moved from the private spaces of the collector's cabinet to the democratic spaces of the street, the fair, and, by the nineteenth century, the circus. This change could not have taken place without access to foreign markets that delivered to London. Animal dealers, in particular, boasted unusual stock and sold to showmen and elites alike. There were six such dealers listed in the *Post Office London Directory for 1840* and thirty-four in 1851, many of whom were located in areas of the City, Clerkenwell, and Southwark and thus near to the dockside.[109] The metropolis attracted ethnic and racial "others" as well, some of whom performed in the ring, while the vast majority of others inspired imitation by white Britons. A critical mass of economic and social forces led to the formation of a new kind of curiosity—in which a desire to know and a desire to gape became intertwined—that was paradoxically born out of the Enlightenment. (As noted earlier, Chevalier de Jaucourt considered the impulses to know and to gape contradictory.)[110] This new way of seeing marked an important moment in the history of curiosity and at its peak in the mid-nineteenth century coincided with British consolidation in India, wars with China, and imperial expansion elsewhere. In spectacles featuring "Oriental" themes, the habits, manners, and belief systems of non-Britons were objectified. Audiences' interests became animated by protoanthropological lessons that fulfilled a popular desire to authenticate knowledge or perceived truths about the "other" (e.g., the mysticism of the Indian, the strength of the black man, the cunning of the Chinese).[111] By constructing knowledge in this way, these spectacles contributed to a wider project of perceiving and ordering colony and metropole and of justifying market expansion that in some cases predated the Great Exhibition of 1851. For onlookers like Nowrojee and Merwanjee in the late thirties and early forties this was a cause of fascination, even bewilderment. If a laissez-faire market, based on Enlightenment principles of progress, enabled these spectacles to flourish, then it also, paradoxically, acted as a barrier to cultural understanding. Based on the cultural encounters represented by visitors to the metropolis, for many Britons (of whatever class) a desire to know and an impulse to gape were never far apart when it came to this kind of visual experience. The overseas market, with its plethora of exotics, both men and beasts, enabled showmen and others to tap into the public mood and gratify this growing, increasingly gluttonous appetite for the hitherto unseen. Like the demand for female acrobats and child prodigies (the subject of chapters 5 and 6), this greed tells us something about the Victorians. Despite or because of moral opinion, popular taste was driven by a desire to see, experience, and possess the sensational and the fantastic, that is, a world far removed from the streets and workshops of Victorian Britain and yet one that was central to them. It was curiosity, driven by mid-nineteenth-century progress and all that it entailed, that propelled this desire forward.

Four

Clown Laughter, Clown Tears

In May 1870 the clown William Mitchell, aged fifty-three, relinquished an engagement with Mr. Ginnett's circus in Leamington. Mitchell felt unwell and returned to his native Nottingham to recover his health. With no means of support and "his friends being few," he found shelter in a workhouse and slept there for nearly six weeks. On 22 June he "raised himself and tried to dress but he was too feeble and fell back on his bed as a corpse."[1] His story is instructive without being unusual. Many such performers were familiar with poverty and, like Mitchell, found their last place of refuge to be the workhouse. Clowns led a paradoxical existence in Victorian society. On the one hand, they were engaged in making merry; on the other, they were beset by problems engendered by their low status in the circus hierarchy. As a consequence, they often found themselves outside institutions and on the periphery of networks that benefited their fellow performers whose skills were more valued. The circus ring was a key site for mocking the social hierarchy and turning it upside down, at least temporarily. But this was no laughing matter given that outside the ring the clown's low social status was reinforced, not challenged.

The long eighteenth century's reformation of manners marked an important turning point in the history of laughter, which had an impact on the circus a century later. Between the Tudor period and the Enlightenment elite laughter became more refined. By the eighteenth century it was considered impolite, even barbarous, to laugh aggressively at the unavoidable misfortunes of others. In short, the household idiot once kept by the Tudor and early Stuart aristocrat was no longer funny.[2] If at the top of the social hierarchy laughter became restrained, it also led to a profound divergence with low, folk humor.[3] Perhaps for this reason Lord Chesterfield said in 1748 that he found "nothing so illiberal and so illbred as audible laughter . . . not to mention the disagreeable noise that it makes and the shocking distortion of the face it occasions."[4] When not controlled, it could be dangerous, even fatal. One contemporary in 1831 recounted a story of a woman who had died of laughter after a visit to Drury Lane. As a consequence of seeing an actor's whimsical performance in *The Beggar's Opera* she was "thrown into hysterics" that continued for several days until she "expired."[5] Nearly fifty years later the philosopher George Vasey called the sound of laughter "not only disagreeable and ridiculous but when imitated the sounds are hideous and idiotic." He observed that "sensible and intelligent persons whose lives are occupied in the important duties of improving their minds . . . are rarely tempted to laugh."[6] More crudely, Fred Karno, the early-twentieth-century entrepreneur and showman who discovered Charlie Chaplin, expressed his hostility to plebeian laughter by describing it as "noise from a hole" similar to farting; both, according to Peter Bailey, belong to "a determinedly orificial culture."[7] More poignantly, Sigmund Freud and, later, Henri Bergson—both influenced by Thomas Hobbes—believed laughter to be connected to superiority and hostility. Laughter is impossible where sympathy is present, they agree.[8] Its physical manifestation—that is, showing teeth—suggests aggression and has something to tell us about the history of mass hatred and fear in the twentieth century.[9] If low and high culture grew further apart in the modern period, as some have suggested, then it would seem that an examination of laughter can shed light on class relations and respectability.

The Victorian circus clown occupied an awkward position within the history of laughter, however. Deflecting attention away from the seriousness of daily life, he played an important, perhaps even essential role by making the crowd laugh. Quoting a fifteenth-century theological apology, Mikhail Bakhtin agrees that "wine barrels burst if from time to time we do not open them and let in some air."[10] In this sense, laughter is the highest expression of free consciousness. According to the historian Keith Thomas, in its most conservative sense laughter is "essentially corrective, uniquely capable of exposing follies and affectations."[11] At the same time, the anthropologist Mary

Douglas holds, it could be socially subversive because it "consists of a victorious tilting of uncontrol against control" and can be seen as the "triumph of . . . unofficial values over official ones."[12] An examination of circus laughter permits an exploration of how liberation and transgression were constructed—and to what end. In short, laughter revealed truth by the very nature of its spontaneous expression. And lest we forget Rabelais's importance, Thomas Love Peacock noted in the 1830s that he was "one of the wisest and most learned, as well as the wittiest of men . . . [who] put on the robe of the all-licensed fool [in order to] convey bitter truths."[13]

Although not as learned, the nineteenth-century circus clown, as the bearer of truth, had a similar role to play in Victorian society. In this age when manners underwent reform, the circus offered the public no freak show (in contrast to that of the American impresario P. T. Barnum), and thus it would be a mistake to see it as continuing a tradition of low folk culture.[14] But was the Victorians' laughter provoked by "innocent amusement" based upon "trivial events . . . of everyday experience," as Donald Gray has suggested?[15] Laughter at the circus could sometimes be characterized in this way, but not universally. In short, circus laughter was neither crude and barbarous nor essentially trivial and innocent. Occupying an ambiguous place somewhere in between these categories, that circus laughter emitted by the crowd, historiographically speaking, serves to complicate "low" and "high," "unofficial" and "official" cultural categories.

The discipline of the law in part accounted for clowning's importance to the circus in the Victorian period. Clowning involved neither script nor words. As we have seen, most circuses (with a few exceptions over the period, such as Astley's and Hengler's) did not receive a license for stage plays, whose broad definition after the passage of the 1843 Theatre Regulation Act included various theatrical genres, including pantomime.[16] Many circus managers appealed, often unsuccessfully, to local magistrates to get the license so that they could present pantomimes, which were popular with the public during the Christmas season and lasted well beyond December. Yet, many were often denied a license on the grounds that they had no stage on which to perform pantomimes. Meanwhile relishing the quasi monopoly over spoken drama, theater managers who had a license enjoyed the new benefits that reform after 1843 delivered. In pantomimes in their houses, dialogue was extended and the harlequinade, or dumb-show element, shortened.[17] By contrast, circus managers often explained in court when faced with "informations" brought by jealous theater rivals that dialogue was incidental to the larger plot acted in the ring, which emphasized harlequin and his fellow clowns. Moreover, many managers redeployed the argument used earlier by the magistrates that without a stage there could be no stage play, over which these authorities otherwise had jurisdiction. The history of complaints against circuses by minor theater managers is a long and bitter one, largely a consequence of the minor theater's new legal legitimacy.[18] Furthermore, given that so many unlicensed circuses set up permanent quarters in provincial cities in the second half of the century and thus coexisted with licensed theaters, the potential for inspection by "theatrical spies" hired by rival managers and the threat of legal action were great.[19] It is in this context that we need to understand and locate the clown's importance in the circus program and understand his comic routine; this was a matter of legal discipline rather than merely artistic choice.

The history of pantomime's development in Britain goes back to the early eighteenth century, when the Licensing Act of 1737 created the ripe conditions for John Rich's silent character, the Harlequin. Joseph Grimaldi, his successor, continued to develop the comic business and earned notoriety for pantomime's popularity; in particular, he earned favor with Charles Dickens, who edited the clown's memoirs.[20] Featuring fairies (many of whom were played by small children, a point taken up in chapter 6), these pieces were derived from nursery fables ("Little Bo Peep," "Mother Goose"), popular legends ("Jack Sheppard," "Dick Whittington"), well-known fairy tales ("Cinderella," "Blue Beard," "Babes in the Wood," "Alladin"), or scenes from classical mythology.[21] Given the important role that fairies occupied in the Victorian imagination, the pantomime's sprite, or "fairy element," gave expression to desires for the fantastic—articulated also in literature and drama and apparent in art and early photography. The Victorians were fascinated and enchanted by fairies, who transported them from one world to the next, as evidenced in British fairy paintings, which flourished from the 1830s to the 1870s, according to Carole G. Silver.[22] Just like Alice, they stepped across a make-believe threshold into a netherworld where shrimps, pearls, sprites, and fairies danced around the ring and created a magical place for the visual imagination.[23]

In a letter of 1878 the Tyneside solicitor Robert Spence Watson wrote to his children describing a scene at a circus in which it was "made quite dark and the white circle was covered with a carpet painted . . . and a beautiful garden of sweetly scented flowers was formed (when the lights were turned up) where the sawdust had been. In the centre was a great flower bed which, at the bidding of a child fairy, opened and disclosed a sweet Little Red Riding Hood lying asleep amongst the roses. The fairy awakened her and told her that she was to entertain her friends and then they came in." She was a good fairy who gently interrupted a peaceful slumber. But the border between consciousness and unconsciousness was blurred as a dreamlike scene then unfolded. Perhaps audiences were meant to witness an event that was taking place within the mind of the sleeping girl; the fairy thus created this illusional world that depicted her dream for the audience. Accompanied by music, the scene then featured "a chorus of children's voices singing 'Little Bo Peep,'" thereby intermingling and overlapping familiar texts. So enchanted by this scene was Spence Watson that he remarked, "It was really a charming sight and the children were almost beside themselves with joy." He added that "one little grand daughter of old Mr. Westmacott's ran up to the barrier and joined wildly in the dancing."[24] Implicit in his account was the laughter of enchantment.[25]

The departure of the fairies signaled a vanishing magical world.[26] Following an elaborate transformation scene, the clown's disorderly world replaced it.[27] The clowns typically entered the ring yelling to the audience, "Hullo! Here we are again!" Although the relationships among the clowns varied and the structure was highly elastic, many circus pantomimes featured Harlequin (the male lover), who pursued Columbine (the ingénue), while Clown (the rival) stood in the way and vied for Columbine's affections, sometimes with the help of Pantaloon (her father).[28] Harlequin has the magic wand, however, and can change the course of events to suit his desires.[29] Set against backdrops depicting everyday streets and the inside of London shops, the display involved chasing, wooing, and general knockabout humor, as well as dancing, scenic trick work, song, and musical accompaniment.[30] At Astley's in the 1840s such scenes were said to elicit "shouts of laughter and perfect hurricanes of applause" and, as one commentator enthusiastically wrote, "unparalleled paroxysms of laughter."[31] In the final scene the lovers find themselves in a splendid place, a temple or palace, and then are transformed back to the characters they were in the first part of the pantomime.[32]

The chaotic nature of the scene, moving from familiar fairy story (or stories) to clown banter, music, and slapstick, and back again, demanded that those "in the know" permit a seemingly messy narrative structure to interfere with rules and boundaries of a known literary text. In the case of *Harlequin Little Red Riding-Hood; or, The Wicked Wolf and the Wirtuous Woodcutter,* for instance, the magic fairy turns Jack, the Woodcutter and Red Riding Hood's suitor, into Harlequin; Red Riding Hood is transformed into Columbine; the Wolf becomes the Clown; and in an act of gender-switching the Mother is turned into Pantaloon.[33] Presenting a "text within a text," or what J. S. Bratton calls "intertheatricality," circus managers relied on audiences to fill in the gaps and complete "circuits of meaning."[34] Not surprisingly, the display's meaning eluded many foreigners. After witnessing such an English pantomime several times, the French circus aficionados H. Le Roux and Jules Garnier noted in 1890 that it made little sense: "It consists of a series of disjointed actions played side by side, accompanied by rapid changes of costume, mad pursuits, and grotesque disguises."[35]

Pantomime thus demanded cultural knowledge on the part of the audience and often had a distinctively national flavor, whatever its former connections to commedia dell'arte.[36] The Shakespearean jester's comic parody of the "national drama" was another form of knowing humor that mocked yet reinforced Britain's literary tradition. Wearing "white tights ornamented with blue or red patches indiscriminately arranged," these clowns "[declaim] passages from Shakespeare and [sing] Irish songs which delight the public in the cheap places."[37] Citing an example of this in his memoirs, the clown Peter Paterson described a gag in which he pretended to have a toothache and then said, "To draw or not to draw, that is the question."[38] The scene relied on the audience's making a connection between Hamlet's contemplation of life and death (the sublime) and Paterson's consideration of his tooth (the ridiculous). The more original the clown's antics, the more appreciative the audience. In 1879 another circus clown and owner, Charlie Keith, wrote that in an age when patrons went to the resident circus more than twice a week, the novelty of all artists—especially the clown—was crucial for doing good business.[39] As Keith's comment suggests, the development and popularity of the resident circus by the late 1870s meant that clowns had to keep up with the times and constantly rethink their acts. At the end of the century, Yorick, the Shakespearean clown, claimed that he kept his jokes fresh by "read[ing] a great deal," importantly drawing an implied distinction between himself and his illiterate fellow clowns.[40] This was humor driven by specialized knowledge, therefore. Le Roux and Garnier noted that "the dialect of Old Tom, and the tirades of King Lear, would not please any audience, except in the United Kingdom," adding that "some other work must be found for foreign engagements."[41]

The pun, specifically designed to address local grievances or subvert the town's social hierarchies, was another style of knowing humor on which clowns relied. On a conundrum night at Ginnett's circus in Exeter in 1887, when local residents entered into a contest for a "handsome" silver-plated teapot, the clown recited the winning entries, which included "Why should the Dean of Exeter be Superintendent of the new Fire Brigade?—Because he generally sleeps in his Close"; and "Why is it unsafe to go into the Cathedral-yard at present?—Because one of the Canons is going off." The justices were also mocked: "Why should the Exeter Bench of Magistrates be convicted of gambling?—Because they have hitherto held an illegal half-crown."[42] If it was to be appreciated by a knowing audience, the joke had to be clever and, depending on the audience and its respectability, in good taste. This balancing act was no easy feat: it involved the clown's ability to reconstitute literary works or reconfigure social boundaries in order to express collective and individual identities and to create a carnival atmosphere—without causing public offence. If the circus manager wanted his troupe to return to a community in following seasons, this was a serious consideration.

Where impolite jokes were cracked and authority derided, the reputation of the circus was sometimes compromised. An 1846 complaint made by the author and London theater manager Frederick Fox Cooper to the Lord Chamberlain's examiner of plays called attention to the clowns and buffoons at "our amphitheatres" who performed scenes in which mocking "royalty is the chief aim . . . and the grossest liberties are taken with it to influence the applause and laughter of the pit and galleries," that is, those who sat in the cheapest seats.[43] Like many managers of minor theaters, who felt threatened by the numbers of patrons circuses attracted, Fox Cooper may have complained out of envy.[44] Whatever his interest, he raised an important legal point. Because the Lord Chamberlain licensed texts and had no control over improvised scenes or artists' gestures, "orificial" sounds, and facial contortions, if his censoring powers extended to circus performances, then they were inadequate; if they did not, then he lacked authority altogether.[45] And since most circuses lay outside the licensor's control, the problem was potentially more serious because there was no official machinery for regulation and inspection except when specific complaints arose. Small wonder that clowns looking for work often reassured prospective employers of their respectability. After finishing an engagement with Myers's American Circus, one "classical jester" advertised in the *Era* in 1860: "If [you] inquire which of all the clowns now travelling is most elegant and concise in language—most chaste in sentiment . . . you will find the answer is Hunter Mantle."[46]

Although the female clown at the circus was less remarked on, the one who performed on the music-hall stage raised a different set of problems. Witnessing Miss Catherine Parks, "a nice looking young woman," attired in pantomime costume on the stage of the London Pavilion music hall, the diarist Arthur Munby noted her "broad grin" and "clumsy dance." She interrupted her "turn" at one point and "apologised to the audience for not standing on her head or doing other clown's tricks, saying 'I being a lady, turn in my toes instead.'" Perhaps her modesty was inspired by the fact that her mother, present behind the scenes, was "arranging the cockscomb and chalking the cheeks of her [other] clown daughter."[47] Clearly, however, the clown's free-spirited, careless physicality conflicted with and transgressed bourgeois codes. Her allusion to the handstand suggests that costumes played an important role in revealing bodies, particularly legs, as in other "feminized spectacles," such as acrobatics and burlesque.[48]

Such stunts as the one Miss Parks alluded to—but did not perform—involved some gymnastic ability, and so the boundary separating clowning from gymnastics was often thin, especially in the circus. The gymnastic clown's stumbling, falling, and collapsing body was seemingly amorphous and usually male. In 1868 Charlie Keith performed as the "India-rubber clown" and was known both for his comic humor and for his ability to "throw somersaults very neatly."[49] In some cases, devices assisted in the scene, as they had nearly two decades earlier when the clown Leclair performed on stilts in an act in which he was said to "pick up his handkerchief" supposedly while "slightly intoxicated."[50] While stilts had long been commonplace, the introduction of innovative mechanisms added to the circus's (and the clown's) novel attractiveness. At Hengler's circus in London in 1885, for instance, "an American riding machine" was introduced into the clown act. This "crane-like apparatus" was fixed in the center of the circus, and an "unsuspecting stranger" (really a disguised clown) was attached to it and then mounted on a horse. The act itself involved the man's riding the horse around the ring at great velocity until suddenly "the rider is snatched from the saddle and . . . then whirls round and round suspended to the arm of the machine, performing as he goes along attitudes of the most mirth provoking kind" (fig. 19). According

THE MAKING OF ACROBATS: THE "AMERICAN RIDING MACHINE" AT WORK.

Fig. 19. Sketch, "The Making of Acrobats: The 'American Riding Machine' at Work," *The Daily Graphic*, 11 February 1892. (By permission of The British Library, Colindale Newspaper Library)

to a witness, "This caused fits of laughter among the spectators," laughter so powerful that it continued "long after the victim has been released."[51]

Whereas in this case the artist's apparent incompetence at riding a horse and his lack of physical coordination provoked laughter, other gymnastic clowns relied on skill and grace. Le Roux and Garnier described one clown who vaulted from a carpet, performing a somersault from a springboard over a wall of horses.[52] It was also common to see a clown riding—flawlessly— on horseback at great speed. The unlikely contrast between the clown's gaudy dress and merry attitude, on the one hand, and his skill, on the other, showed that gymnastic clowning involved more than lighthearted banter. Rather, it paradoxically embodied the sublime (lightness, speed) and the ridiculous (grotesque make-up, dress, and character), as did the Shakespearean clown's act.[53]

In still other cases clowning involved strength—or the appearance of it—as in the case of a mock boxing match between the famous pugilist Tom Sayers and a clown called Brown in Messrs. Howes and Cushing's circus that visited Swansea in 1861. So expectant were Swansea fans that after seeing the posters advertising the "Champion of the Prize Ring" they "literally besieged" the Cameron Arms Hotel upon his arrival there. Later, they reportedly flooded into the circus to watch him.[54] To create the realistic atmosphere of the prize ring in the circus ring, Sayers wore two medals on his breast, along with his prize belt, and when he entered the ring the band played "See the Conquering Hero Comes." His "sham battle" with Brown in the performance was "warmly applauded," one reporter noted.[55] While the real attraction was Sayers, not Brown, the latter provided an important comic element that showcased the former's strength and reputation. Given that an accident occurred during the evening performance in which "the boxes gave way and some sixty or eighty of the audience were precipitated" to the ground—not an untypical occurrence—it is remarkable that the performance did not end. Instead, only one or two scores of people were said to have left; the rest remained for "what they had paid their money to witness," the *Era* reported.[56] It took a rare visit by a prizefighter to elevate the status of the clown in this case and ones like it. Otherwise, he was often used as "filler" between the other acts and thus not taken seriously.

Masks, so important in the business of clowning, both concealed and revealed important aspects about the artist, provoking a mix of admiration and

Fig. 20. Blackface
minstrels, n.d.
(Edward Linley
Sambourne Family
Archive, Royal
Borough of
Kensington and
Chelsea Libraries)

curiosity that inspired laughter. A close connection existed between the harlequin's mask and that of the blackface clown who moved from street to music and concert hall to seaside resort and circus, especially from the early
1860s (coinciding with the American Civil War).[57] According to George F.
Rehin, "Harlequin's mask has been perceived as Negroid or African."[58] For
the Victorians, these blackface clowns both reinforced and confused racial
distinctions; that is, by playing Jim Crow and performing ditties like "Stop
dat Knocking" or "Black-eyed Susan" with "bones" and banjos as instru-
ments they fed a mania for live ethnological displays. When "white niggers,"
that is, white performers whose faces were painted black, appeared, the
power relations embedded in the display were subverted as racial categories
were inverted (fig. 20).[59] One female member from a troupe of Christy Min-

strels described to Munby the ease with which she managed this act of racial switching: "It takes us half an hour to colour, sir . . . an another half hour to wash it off."[60] Another demonstrated to the Reverend H. R. Haweis how "all the black comes off." "'I am not so bad-looking either,'" the clown added, implicitly making an aesthetic judgment that contrasted whiteness and blackness, attractiveness and hideousness.[61] Munby believed that while a man could "blacken his face" and "grin and tremble as a clown," a woman could not. Rather, when "a woman attempts such things, the first thing we think of is her degradation and disfigurement," which marred the ideal of womanhood and turned her beauty into grotesqueness that became a public spectacle.[62] It was likely for this reason that the Victorians saw more male than female clowns in the trade.

With their make-up removed, Munby's interviewee revealed, "we're mostly English, but one or two are American."[63] In some cases troupes like the American Comic Operatic Company, which performed at the Circus Royal in Hull in 1843, went by such names in order to heighten their exotic and "genuine" allure. The company promised a grand Ethiopian entertainment, including "a variety of new songs, refrains, dances, odd sayings, etc."[64] The intermingling of "American" and "Ethiopian" nationalities was seen elsewhere. Two years later at Astley's, for instance, the Southern American Minstrels featured prominently in the circus's posters promising the appearance of "Messrs. Woolcot, Robbins, Parker and Ring in their American Nationalities and Ethiopian entertainment."[65] In contrast to whites (who might be British or American, for instance), black artists were conceived of as culturally monolithic, their identities constructed by the advertisers who promoted them. "American" and "Ethiopian" were merely nationalities that were imposed on them and could change to suit the market and popular taste. Their homogenous exoticism was made explicit by a band of American-Ethiopian serenaders who promised to present the Dundee public in the 1860s with miscellaneous "negro vagaries and strange sayings."[66] Decades later, the conflation of race and nationality became even more bizarre when at Astley's (under Sanger's management) in 1881 the Mohawk Minstrels performed (fig. 21).[67] In short, the appeal of such artists was not their genuine identity as blacks (of whatever national description) but their ability to parody manners and physical traits of the race they professed to represent.[68]

Describing the way in which the minstrel catered to the British public's taste in this regard, the Reverend Haweis said, "English fun is mixed with

Fig. 21. Poster, Sanger's Amphitheatre, 1881. (Theatre Museum, London; © V&A Images)

Negro humour."[69] One Ethiopian street serenader provided Henry Mayhew with examples of the conundrums that he and his fellow singers offered in between the songs:

"Supposing you nigger was dead, what would be the best time to bury you?"
One says, "I shan't suppose."
Another says, "I don't know."
And then I say, "Why, the latter end of the summer."
And one asks, "Why, Jim?"
"Because that's the best time for blackberrying."

A melancholy song such as "Dinah Clare," about a "poor girl that fell into the water-butt and got burnt to death," might follow.[70] The combination of pun and song relating to death might seem a poor recipe for inspiring laughter, but Le Roux and Garnier noted that in England their gags were often melancholy, in keeping with the English temperament.[71] Their jokes blended "common-place aphorisms and sentimental reflections," which, they added, "would not be appreciated in France."[72] Besides performing antics, these minstrels also engaged in general knockabout clowning, such as "violent dances," "a species of gymnastics which resembles the 'chahut' of the lower classes in France. The great split is as familiar to them as the somersaults." A scene of chaotic fun and sentimental frivolity helped to reinforce messages about the performers' perceived lazy, disorderly, emotional, and "childlike" nature, which required colonial subjection.[73] Reduced to his "natural" essence, therefore, the artist was engaged in a process of "fixing difference" between himself and his white audiences, although those "differences" were appropriated and reappropriated depending on the popular taste for Americans, Ethiopians, and so on.[74]

Whereas in America minstrel song and dance addressed issues about slavery and plantation life, in Britain this artistic form spoke to an altogether different set of concerns related to imperialism, civilization, and, to some extent, racial fantasy.[75] After observing the Christy Minstrels, Munby recalled "a grown woman with black face and bosom and unctuous arms playing elegantly upon that highly civilized instrument [the piano]." Meanwhile, those around her played the violin and "bones," while, "curious[ly]," others sang sweetly and tenderly, suggesting that their constructed outward vulgarity clashed with their inner refinement.[76] This juxtaposition of low and high, unnatural and natural, black and white, therefore had meaning that went above and beyond mere curiosity or innocent fun. Rather, it fulfilled a desire to invert characteristics of "civilized" peoples in order to affirm British civility and the benefits of the nation's civilizing project. Spectators were thus implicated as subjects of power along with the black performers, who were subjects to that power and therefore unequal in this exercise, in which meaning was created from representation.[77]

Yet this power relationship became worryingly destabilized, some contemporaries thought, when the blackface clown's relationship with the law was pondered. His mask provided the perfect cover for hiding. When these clowns performed in the open air and in bourgeois metropolitan neighborhoods like Marylebone (as opposed to Lambeth), the noise they were said to emit disrupted codes of civility. The inventor Charles Babbage notoriously launched a stream of complaints against these minstrels and their German and Italian counterparts, though he found that "it is difficult to identify them" before the police because of their make-up, as he told Michael T. Bass, MP, who attempted to take up his cause against street nuisances before the House in 1863–64.[78] A decade earlier Dickens had used the theme of make-up as subterfuge in *Hard Times* when Tom Gradgrind Jr. runs away to Sleary's circus and becomes a comic black servant acting in *Jack, the Giant Killer* in an attempt to hide from the law. (He has robbed a bank in order to pay his gambling debts.) Upon his discovery, his father admits, "If a thunderbolt had fallen on me . . . it would have shocked me less than this!"[79] Tom Jr. has rejected the utilitarianism that defined his father's moral world. His performance in the pantomime, in which he wears "a preposterous coat, like a beadle's," clearly ridicules his father and the law that he has violated.[80]

In general, the clown's ability to satisfy a universal need to "let off steam" raises interesting questions about how the restrain-release mechanism underpinning Victorian laughter worked.[81] While engaged in making merry, the clown raised serious questions about the way in which the attitudes and desires that he mocked were constructed. To varying degrees, this process involved overturning rules and codes underpinning the social order. As Spence Watson pointed out in his 1878 account of a pantomime performance, the wish to retreat into the fantastic netherworld appealed to the young and old and satisfied an escapist urge present in this industrial culture. This impulse found expression in other forms of popular culture, such as photography and literature, on which these pantomimes were based.

There was also laughter that was distinctly not escapist: that inspired by the blackface minstrel, whose performance raised interesting questions about colonial subjection and the civilizing project. If empire was important in this respect, so too was nation, as the Shakespearean clown demonstrated in his parody of the "national drama." Here, both cultural literacy and national identity penetrated the Victorian imagination. In presenting another type of disorder, the knockabout clown employed his or her body by making orificial sounds or rudely gesturing (as at low London circuses in the 1840s), inverting gender signs and meanings (as at the Pavilion in the 1860s), or falling off the back of a horse with the help of an innovative "American" riding machine (as at Hengler's in the 1880s).

In short, these disparate acts, whether escapist or not, engaged with national traditions, moral impulses, and aesthetics in an apparently amusing way for many contemporaries, relieving them from their workaday world. In the course of performances, the clown invited audiences to take pleasure in communal laughter, which was necessary for "letting off steam." The consequences of repressing these impulses were detrimental to the order—and re-order—of things and denied essential truths about the world, as Rabelais believed and Dickens knew.[82]

Although the clown occupied an essential role in the circus, his world outside the ring was paradoxically marked by social isolation, abject poverty, sickness, and melancholy. The seemingly frivolous and decadent world of laughter sharply contrasted with his concerns about finding new engagements and, more generally, keeping body and soul together. The clown's pathos emerged from this combination of contradictory roles—as jolly performer and struggling artist. Anticipating Leoncavallo's *Pagliacci*, Picasso's harlequins in his Blue Period, or the vagabond clown in films by Fellini and Bergman, Mayhew described one such artist as a "melancholy-looking man, with the sunken eyes and other characteristics of semi-starvation, whilst his face was scored with lines and wrinkles, telling of paint and premature age." As one who traded in the laughter of sadness, his shifting moods and pathos were integral to his role in the circus. He told Mayhew, "Many times I have to play the clown, and indulge in all kinds of buffoonery, with a terrible heavy heart. . . . I can't help thinking of the bare cupboards at home; . . . with no food at all either to give to my children or take myself . . . but what's that to the world?" He added, "I would rather starve than ask for parochial relief," a measure of his respectability. But as he said this, Mayhew saw "the tears start from the man's eyes."[83]

Charles Dickens also plays on this theme, again in *Hard Times,* when circus girl Sissy Jupe recalls how her father, a clown, sometimes cried when his audiences failed to laugh at his jokes "and he used to come home despairing." "It was because he grew so scared and trembling, and because he felt himself to be a poor, weak, ignorant, helpless man (those used to be his words), that he wanted me . . . [to] be different from him," she says. However much she tries to sooth his aching soul, her efforts are not enough, and one day he fails to return home, whereupon the abandoned Sissy (her mother is dead) is then sent away to Gradgrind's school. She goes, though still clutching the bottle of nine oils—which never leaves her possession throughout the novel—that she got for her father before his disappearance. This potion, used for soothing the bruises of circus folk "when they get any hurts in the ring," as she says, is symbolic of her desire to cure the poor man of his pain, although he is too far gone, both physically and psychically, to be relieved.[84]

What made the clown's trade so hard? Money—or lack of it—for a start. Mayhew's penny-circus jester told him that famous clowns like Mr. Barry had been reputed to make £10 weekly at Astley's, whereas at smaller penny circuses like Frazier's and Clarke's the lesser-known performer was likely to earn only £2 weekly.[85] Based on a salary list from the late 1870s or 1880s, possibly from Hengler's in Liverpool, the reality was somewhere in between. For instance, the clowns on this list received the following weekly sums: Neddy Volks, £5; W. Matthews, £4 10s.; St. Leo and Test, the gymnastic clowns, £4 each; Prossini, £4; and Fred Lemaine, £3 10s.[86] Compared with the company's trapeze artist, Bonsalo Demon, who earned £15, or the tumblers, George Terts and Fanny, who together earned £25, the clown was indeed the lowest paid on the list.

Like all other artists', his engagement was short term, lasting a week, a month, or a season if he was lucky. For those who were fortunate enough to arrange consecutive engagements with various companies, as the clown Edwin Croueste did between 2 June and 20 October 1878, when, as we saw in chapter 1, he performed with six different troupes for one to five weeks each, it was possible to stave off hardship.[87] In each troupe, Croueste was the head of a "powerful army of clowns," and as stated earlier, he was in such demand that the manager of the Colosseum Circus at Cheltenham sought to engage him in September to perform the following winter season.[88] However fortunate Croueste was, steady employment was generally unreliable.

The clown's chances of continued employment were made more uncertain by competition from other artists who filled clown vacancies on a whim. This was allegedly done during the Christmas season, when the pantomimes required them. In an open letter to the *Era*, Charlie Keith complained bitterly about the "unprofessional practice of low comedians, actors and Music Hall artistes accepting engagements for their own line of business, and often giving their services as clown free or for trifle extra . . . when they feel funny." They did not think they were harming the circus clown, he added, although in fact they were "keeping the legitimate and professed clowns out of engagements and bringing down salaries."[89] Furthermore, once artists secured employment, they typically performed in more than just the role for which they were engaged, thereby depleting the number of vacancies in the company and depriving the jobless of opportunity. From the manager's perspective, it was a way of ensuring that he got the most for his money;[90] it was a strategy Benthamites would have approved. Decades later, however, the tide was said to turn, and circus performers were seen to take jobs away from fellow artists in halls: "Many acrobats, and even equestrians, depend nowadays on the halls," remarked one acrobat turned dancer.[91]

Economic pressures frustrated performers further as they often were expected to provide their own costumes, which drained their small and unsteady incomes. Mayhew's penny-circus clown claimed that he could "make a suit complete, with pumps and all, for 30s to 35s." For this, he wore a "ring dress, with red rings round my trunks, and a fly to correspond. The tights had straight red lines . . . [the] wig was one with a red [cocks]comb."[92] According to Keith, the clown's garments did not last "one quarter of the time of those of a private individual," requiring constant care or replacement. There were other incidental expenses, such as transportation. As discussed in chapter 1, during the second half of the nineteenth century circuses increasingly became fixed in towns and cities, operating alongside the music hall and the theater. As a consequence, the artist traveled independently from one engagement to the next, usually by train, and had to pay for not only travel costs but also lodging. "The fact is," observed Keith, "owing to his continually having to shift about . . . his lodgings, in the course of a year . . . cost considerably more than the rental of a house."[93] While the expense of costumes, transport, and board was a burden that all artists had to bear, the clown's relatively small salary made it more difficult to afford these things.

His peripatetic existence also meant that he had fewer chances of establishing and maintaining communal ties with neighbors, so important in

Clown Laughter, Clown Tears

times of sickness and hardship.[94] The pattern of circus residency made this problem particularly acute since the performer's short-term connections to the community meant that he might pass through a town as a complete unknown. Furthermore, given his limited engagement with the company, he was less likely to be considered as part of a "family" in the way he might have been with a tenting company. Although this problem did not affect the clown alone, he occupied a distinctly low, socially isolated position and needed all the friends he could get, as William Mitchell's case illustrates.

On the other hand, some clowns received both sympathy and material help from their managers. But this was often a matter of luck and good connections, on which no artist could rely. The most common form of help was the benefit night, a traditional practice inherited from the theater, on which the proceeds of the performance were given to a needy member of the company (fig. 22).[95] On such occasions the theater or circus, as well as its amenities and staff, were theoretically provided free by the manager to the beneficiary or a representative of the beneficiary, who then hosted the performance.[96] As in other artisan trades, these efforts by managers were seen to be necessary to foster good working relations, particularly when virtually no friendly society or working men's club provided for these artists.

In March 1857 Astley's manager, William Cooke, hosted a benefit for the ailing clown Tom Barry by granting the free use of his theater and inviting such members of the trade as Harry Boleno and his pantomime friends, Mr. Tanner and his troupe of dogs, and the singer Mr. Ross to perform there.

Fig. 22. Poster detail, Cooke's Royal Circus, 30 August 1843. (Glasgow University Library, Department of Special Collections)

When Barry's illness worsened and the clown died the following week, other managers followed Cooke's example. Pablo Fanque extended the hand of friendship to Barry's widow and held a benefit in her husband's name at his Allied Circus in Bradford. Using the *Era* offices to transmit the money he earned from this event, Fanque enclosed £10 worth of "post office orders . . . being the profits of the benefit. I should have been better pleased had it been more, but this was the close of a very dull season."[97] As Barry's case demonstrated, the manager's desire to alleviate the artist's (and his family's) plight was strongest when the artist died and his family needed financial help with burial costs, outstanding debt, and provision for the future. Trading on the public's sympathy in an effort to rouse help, the manager called attention to the needs of the poor artist's family.

Sometimes the manager found his kindness repaid in times of need. When the Cookes' Portsmouth circus burned down several years later, the family received support from a number of artists, including the clowns Hunter Mantle and Edwin Croueste. At least thirty performers donated their time and demonstrated their sympathy for the loss "of some Valuable Horses, including the celebrated 'Raven,' 'Snowdrop'. . . but also Wardrobe and Properties, &c.," as the bills advertised (fig. 23).[98]

Kindness was also extended to the deceased's family by taking in his children and instructing them in the trade that their father, now dead, was incapable of teaching. This was profoundly important in a trade that typically relied on a system of family apprenticeship. Such acts of benevolence were appreciated by the family of Mr. Charles Watson, the "Hibernian Clown and American Jester," who died at age thirty from consumption after a "long and painful illness," leaving his family penniless. After Mr. Kimbar, of the Theatre Royal Portsmouth, had "generously . . . superintended the funeral arrangements," the circus managers George and John Sanger took on the two sons of the deceased as apprentices.[99] Whatever rivalries there were between circus and theater managers, this benevolent act suggested that solidarity and human compassion were shared between them in times of need.

Provision for the future was also made by a subscription given to the family on a monthly or annual basis. Such an act of "prompt kindness . . . does the [managers] honour," the *Era* remarked in an effort to collect more cash from its readers to help the Watsons. Subscriptions could yield help from abroad as well, as Charlie Keith demonstrated when he was on tour with his Circus Salamonsky in Russia and then Cologne in 1873. After discovering

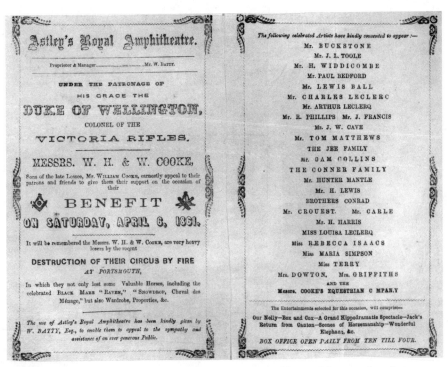

Fig. 23. Bill, Astley's Royal Amphitheatre, 6 April 1861. (Theatre Museum, London; © V&A Images)

that the clown Rochez was ill and faced a life of permanent infirmity, Keith raised money from his company, although he was apologetic that his fellow artists' contributions could not be more: "But some of the givers are foreigners unacquainted with Mr. Rochez, . . . who are ever ready to assist a brother artiste, whatever his nationality."[100] In cases like these, the trade clearly operated as an international fellowship. While Keith himself contributed £1 2s. 6d., the contributions made by fourteen of the members of the company came to £5. When he turned to Hersog and Schumann's circus in Berlin, the company raised a total of £2. Forwarding the money to the *Era* offices, Keith included an open letter in which he reminded all English clowns of their brotherly responsibilities and encouraged them to contribute to Rochez's fund.[101]

Their efforts, he believed, were required because although the poor clown belonged to the trade's friendly society, the General Dramatic, Equestrian and Musical Agency and Sick Fund Association, he received nothing to alleviate his hardship. His was a tragic irony given that such membership was meant to signify "a basic badge of respectability." The organization was founded in 1855 on the progressive principle, common among other such organizations in this period, of "sooth[ing] the hours of sickness, accident and old age while elevat[ing] the profession."[102] Such societies, observed Lord Beaumont, "place within the power of the labouring classes the means of making themselves independent in their old age by means of sacrifices during the earlier portion of their lives" so that they could "look to coming years without the prospect of the workhouse."[103] However noble its aspirations, the association's benefits excluded the likes of Rochez. Keith complained in another open letter to the *Era* that "actors have the greatest and most legitimate claim on its funds" since they formed the majority of the society's members, an observation borne out by the association's subscription lists, as we saw in chapter 1.[104]

By 1879 the situation had become so acute that Keith was compelled to remark in his memoirs, "There are so many [fellow artists] ever ready to receive my proposal to found a similar institution . . . but my vocation keeping me abroad prevents me from giving the matter that attention which it requires."[105] Small wonder that ad hoc welfare schemes continued into the late nineteenth century. While many circus artists encountered destitution and had no connection to a friendly society, the clown was particularly vulnerable. Poorly paid and often socially isolated except at the very top level, he was unlikely to have a nest egg or a community of friends on which he could rely. Furthermore, helping hands—when they were offered—were by no means extended to all. Rather, managers and fellow artists gave aid to those who were popular and generally did not offer it to those lesser and more numerous clowns who escaped their attention.

One of the circus's key functions was to make its audiences laugh. The clown was integral to this process. The way in which he encouraged this response varied, depending entirely on his ability to read his audience, assess popular taste, and deliver something comic. That this process took place in a ring meant that laughter became contagious and the individual's laughter became part of a communal one; the individual's laughing body was in turn consumed by the amorphous laughing body of the audience. This had potentially subversive consequences if ridicule rather than good-natured humor prevailed. Certainly, Fox Cooper's response in the 1840s to low, unmannered laughter that mocked royal authority suggests as much. But the clown's subversiveness could and did prove more subtle than this even at respectable venues. Rather than needing careful control, laughter could paradoxically prop up and poke fun at convention in a perfectly respectable way. The jester who distorted Shakespeare's words, the fool who inverted the town's social hierarchy by reciting conundrums written by locals, the gymnastic clown who fell off a horse's back, the young woman who pointed her toes inward, and the white female singer who painted her face black—all played on the margins of culturally constructed boundaries, in turn revealing important tensions. To be sure, these displays exposed shared areas of anxiety and stress that only the laughter of topsy-turvydom could relieve. That this laughter was variously shared by Dickens, Spence Watson, Munby, and the working-class population that occupied the pit and gallery suggests that the circus occupied a socially complex role; it was neither low nor high culture but "popular" in the widest sense of the word.

Despite the clown's crucial role in the circus, his work was undervalued and underpaid. Many found it necessary to rely on fickle, ad hoc welfare schemes such as benefit nights and subscriptions, from the mid-nineteenth century onwards, when the trade expanded. Artists like William Mitchell, who had no savings nor help networks, ended their lives in workhouses. Thus, often isolated, hungry, and poor, they became a casualty of industrial culture. Their role as both merrymaker and melancholy artist rendered their existence pitiful and yet strangely fascinating—a theme taken up at the turn of the century by painters like Picasso and other observers abroad and at home who were interested in social dislocation. For both contemporary observers and clowns, therefore, laughter was a serious matter indeed that reflected concerns and problems underpinning modern/ist existence.

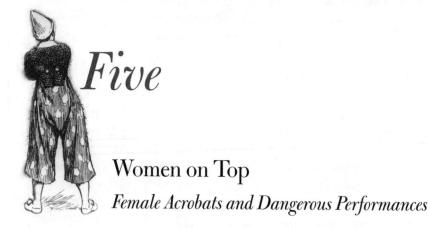

Five

Women on Top

Female Acrobats and Dangerous Performances

In July 1863 Selina Powell, otherwise known as Madame Blondin, performed on a high wire in front of thousands of spectators at Aston Park, Birmingham. Shackled and blindfolded, with a bag over her head, she carefully took her balancing pole in her hands, cautiously felt the rope with her feet, and then, according to one contemporary observer, "stepped upon the swaying cord . . . every eye in the immense multitude being fixed upon her. . . . She had walked just three short steps when—the rope collapsed."[1] The fall, which resulted in her death, might not have stirred so much attention had it not been for the fact that the performer was eight months pregnant.[2] Her performance and subsequent death horrified the nation and sparked a nationwide outcry against "dangerous performances." The short-term uproar over the Madame Blondin case was superseded by three decades of debate linking acrobatics to contemporary concerns about sex, death, the family, childhood, artistic regulation, and commercialized leisure.[3] The case attracted moral reformers and regulators, who drew heavily on the inexhaustible reservoir of public feeling about respectability, on the one hand, and on patrons and artists, who supported "free trade and fair play," on the other.

Discussions about the physically and economically precarious nature of the acrobat's trade that emerged from the 1863 accident gave way to parliamentary debate over the next three decades, resulting in two statutes, in 1879 and 1897, regulating children engaged in dangerous performances (the subject of the next chapter). Important to parliamentary discussions and reform were the changing tastes and values common to London and the provinces. Issues relating to danger, sexual pleasure, and athleticism—three qualities that contemporaries associated with the female acrobat's art—became the focus of public discussions. The accident therefore sheds considerable light on the unrespectablility of Victorian amusement and goes some way toward debunking myths about mid-Victorian rational recreation. In connection with this, it also raises important issues about the representation of the female body in public life. The relationship between female beauty and male desire was one that needed context in order to be defined; at the hall or circus it was often seen as morally dangerous, whereas at the Royal Academy it could be seen as respectable. One response used in the female acrobat's defense, however, related to the benefits of physical education for "ladies," a rationale that borrowed heavily on a wider discourse on masculine muscularity.

Madame Blondin's corpse literally embodied the discourses that juxtaposed sexuality with folkish barbarism and juxtaposed both these issues with the athletic female body. Taken together, beauty, flirtation, the thrill, and the strong female body produced complex responses on the part of the viewer, manifested in the gasp, the gape, and the widening of the eyes.[4] In essence, this kind of spectatorship became an engrossing and embodied experience. Critics bothered by this took their concerns to the London County Council, the Lord Chamberlain's office, and local newspapers. The vibrancy of a consumer culture governed by an "unrefined" and "insatiable" appetite for spectacle, as they saw it, was brought into focus by Madame Blondin's accident. Within a competitive commercialized leisure market in which money was exchanged for visual gratification, she, like other female acrobats, had a unique and spectacular commodity to sell.[5] Once she fatally hit the ground below in her pregnant state, however, she became separated from her more agile counterparts, which unleashed the debate on dangerous performances.

In the wake of Madame Blondin's accident, the Queen addressed the mayor of Birmingham, Charles Sturge, in an open letter. She declared herself horrified that "one of her subjects—a female—should have been sacrificed to the gratification of the demoralizing taste, unfortunately prevalent, for exhibitions attended with the greatest danger to the performers."[6] Aston Park, where the accident occurred, had a special significance for the Queen. Only a few years earlier she had appeared at the official ceremony declaring it open to the public.[7] The monarch therefore expressed to the mayor her hope that "in common with the rest of the townspeople of Birmingham, [you] will use your influence to prevent in future the degradation to such exhibitions . . . and . . . that [the park will] be made serviceable for the healthy exercise and rational recreation of the people."[8] According to the mayor and other patrons of the exhibition, whose support had been solicited by the hosts of the event, the Ancient Order of Foresters, the fête was intended to raise funds in order to pay off the balance and purchase the park for the people of Birmingham.[9] Madame Blondin was simply a feature at an event intended to attract a massive audience drawn from as far as forty or fifty miles away. Announcing "the Female Blondin, Mdm. Genieve, the only real, legitimate performer of Blondin's great feats," the posters had referred to her "unrivalled" and internationally acclaimed namesake in order to stir wide interest on the part of the public.[10]

Regardless of the benevolent circumstances, the result of the exhibition was of greater importance, and agreement with the Queen was widespread, as letters to the editor and newspaper columns in various local and national newspapers in July 1863 made clear. Most condemned managers of acrobatic performers, parks, and other places of public resort and called for a stop to dangerous exhibitions in the future.[11] Among those in agreement with the Queen was Charles Dickens, who sharply criticized the role of the "enterprising Directors" of Aston Park, who he said were to blame for placing the acrobat's life in danger and for making "the low sensation as strong as they possibly could."[12] Although Madame Blondin's accident took place at a park, the controversy had the effect of throwing into sharp relief the ubiquity of such performances at circuses, music halls, and other entertainment places, even the street.

At the ensuing inquest Selina Powell's husband refused accusations about his wife's alleged "murder" and offered his own story, which recalled desperate and pragmatic circumstance. The coroner asked Mr. Powell about his involvement in setting up the rope, which he had always done for his wife, and about whether he had been aware that her crossing it might be dangerous, particularly given her pregnant condition. Powell replied that "she was always strong at such times" and that "she had done it hundreds and hundreds of times," even recently: "three times at Sheffield and once at Islington at a private party," raising interesting questions not only about the family's financial need but also about its views on pregnancy.[13] And if her pregnant condition was visible, her performance at Islington also prompts questions about elite indulgence in folkish barbarism. From Mr. Powell's point of view, there were legitimate reasons for his wife's performance: their earnings from such events were greater than they could expect from any other means; after expenses such as railway costs, their earnings came to £8 or £9 per show. But after the accident the distressed husband, now the breadwinner of the family, which included seven children and an aged mother-in-law, had scarcely any means of support; ropewalking was the trade on which he, his wife, and even their children depended.[14]

Such cottagelike industries, in which all the family members were involved in some aspect of the performance, were not unusual and indeed became more common from the mid-nineteenth century onwards. According to the *Era Almanac,* a yearly theatrical magazine, whose figures provide only an imperfect picture of the state of the trade, there were 66 acrobat troupes in Britain in 1867–68, 90 in 1877, and 98 in 1878.[15] These troupes may have included individuals who described themselves as brothers or other family members but were, in fact, not related, yet these numbers provide a broad outline of the family-oriented nature of the trade. A contemporary of Powell's who likewise enlisted his wife and children to perform on the tight wire told Henry Mayhew, "The family by itself can give an entertainment that lasts an hour and a half altogether. I don't perform myself, but I go about making the arrangements and engagements for them. Managers write to me from the country to get up entertainments for them, and to undertake the speculation." Not only was the business family run but it had been passed down from one generation to the next. "My father was in the profession before me," the manager continued, "and my wife's parents were also performers."[16]

Confirming the unhappy juxtaposition of financial necessity and the lack of alternatives that Powell alluded to during the coroner's inquest, a less famous contemporary ropewalker insisted that those in the trade were generally poor. "One day I may pick up 5s; that's a first rate day for street work. In bad weather I can do nothing. . . . I couldn't undertake to depend on 10s 6d a week if I confined myself to outdoor performances . . . and the jewels and the spangles worn by performers like me are a sort of mockery."[17] When they did not perform on the streets, "you will see them on the road to Epsom, Moulsey, Egham or Ascot even, long before the rush begins, in the grey morning" on their way to seasonal races, where their performances began at

Fig. 24. Gavarni, *Acrobats,* in Albert Smith, ed., *Gavarni in London: Sketches of London Life and Character* (1859). (Author's collection)

Fig. 25. Detail from William Powell Frith, *Derby Day*, 1856–58. (© Tate, London 2004)

eleven and continued until six, Albert Smith observed(fig. 24).[18] The acrobatic family performing in the open air was also the subject of William Powell Frith's painting of 1856–58, *Derby Day*, which similarly captured the image (fig. 25). Not only was it difficult to earn one's daily bread but it was hard to leave the trade, especially if the performer had no other skills and had a family to support. When the acrobat reached old age, the contemporary continued, "you are like a worn out horse, reckoned fit for nothing."[19]

Unhappy predicaments aside, the nagging question why a pregnant acrobat should be seen performing at thirty feet from the ground remained.[20] The desire to see the female acrobat's display, motivated by popular interest in sexuality, athleticism, and danger, continued to drive the market for this sort of display even after Powell's death. Since the female acrobat provoked these overlapping interests, her work was seen as controversial and, to some onlookers, unrespectable. After the accident, commercial display became a moral spectacle.

Confirming the public's desire to see dangerous performances, Charles Sturge, who was implicated in the Selina Powell affair for having his name on the bills as a patron of the exhibition, publicly responded to the Queen's protestations in July 1863 by saying that he had had no idea that a dangerous performance would be attempted and that "there is not in the kingdom an individual who laments more sincerely than myself not only the melancholy accident to which you refer, but the depraved taste for a barbarous species of amusement which unhappily has become popular, not only in the Metropolis, but in all parts of her Majesty's home dominions."[21] Of course, the Selina Powell case was doubly controversial because it involved a woman, and a pregnant woman at that. But, while there was general agreement in Birmingham that Selina Powell should not have been on a high wire while pregnant, opinion concerning the presence of women in general on high wires was highly fragmented. The distinction between her pregnant condition and her sex was important, as the latter fact began to dominate the debate surrounding dangerous performances.

Consistent with Birmingham's civic unity, immediately after the accident a memorial was issued containing 1,416 signatures drawn from all classes, including the "clergy, magistrates, bankers, merchants, manufacturers and others residing in Birmingham."[22] The document stated that exhibitions such as Selina Powell's were "in the highest degree degrading and injurious to the well being of society."[23] Agreeing with the sentiment, William Montague, of The Theatre, Lewes, condemned "such exhibitions where females are placed in jeopardy" and, in a spirit of bonhomie, enclosed "2s.6d. (in stamps) for the children of the late Mrs. Powell," adding that he hoped "many others will follow my example on behalf of the *motherless children*."[24]

While the exact ratio of men to women acrobats is unknown, some contemporaries speculated that the latter outnumbered the former and therefore attracted wider attention. One gymnast argued several years later that it was unfair that "the once celebrated Brothers Chillingowullabadorie [*sic*] . . . are outstripped by the appearance of a flying lady," adding that "anybody that understands the art of gymnastics would look upon these ladies as a mere deception of the art."[25] So bad had the problem become, one observer wrote a decade later, that at the Royal Aquarium the management evidently preferred putting women's lives in peril either because its members believed that there were too many women in the world or because they were cheaper and less troublesome to train than men. What was clear, however, was that "women far oftener than men are to be seen risking their lives to give pleasure to a crowd which is too brutalised to care for any less stimulating amusement."[26] In response to the craze in the sixties, the *Tomahawk* featured a satirical, macabre illustration of this grim and grotesque folly, which it pleaded with female gymnasts to end "before it becomes too late!" (fig. 26).[27]

The performances of female acrobats were controversial not only because of the danger involved but also because of their perceived lewdness. One London County Council inspector remarked that the architecture of the gallery where Zaeo performed necessitated that she hover over the heads of the audience. He added that "it is not altogether desirable to place a female in this indelicate position," providing all with a view of her form.[28] Thus, the female acrobat's costume provoked comment, many observing that it left little to the imagination (fig. 27). In *Fifine at the Fair* (1872) Robert Browning contrasted her costume with the multilayered Victorian petticoats: ". . . as multiplied a coating as protects / An onion from the eye! . . ."[29] Similar to the woman in film whom Laura Mulvey describes as the object of the male spectator's "gaze," the female acrobat was "isolated . . . on display and sexualized."[30] On one occasion the diarist Arthur Munby, who frequented the Oxford Music Hall in London, described "a very pretty English girl, . . . of 18 or 20 years; trim and slight and shapely, standing about 5 feet 4."[31] His idiosyncratic interest in the lives of working women made him acutely sensitive to the female acrobat's moral and physical being.[32] In describing her appearance when performing with two male acrobats he observed: "The only clothing she had on was a blue satin doublet fitting close to her body and having very scanty truck hose below it. Her arms were all bare; her legs, cased in fleshings, were as good as bare, up to the hip."[33]

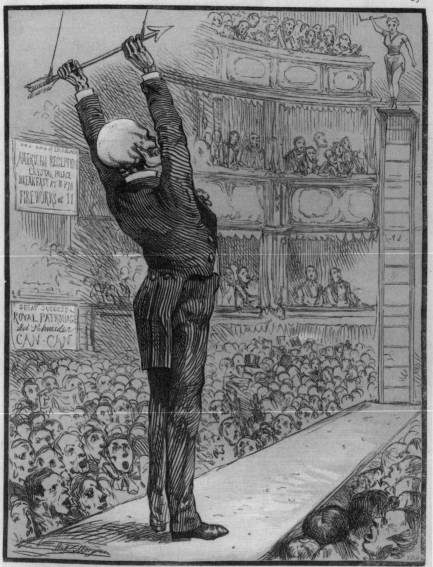

AMUSEMENT FOR THE PEOPLE!

O one of a score of female gymnasts, listen before it becomes too late!   Do not urge the excuse that you work for your husband or children.   Die, and what will your family do?   Become for life a useless cripple, and how will you assist your husband?   Say not that your labour is easy or pleasant, for I solemnly declare to you that in your most confident mood you are trifling with a fatal dart, and have at all times—in the heighth of your triumph—at the moment of your greatest success—grim Death for your playfellow!

[*See Sketch.*

Fig. 26. Sketch, "Amusement for the People!," *Tomahawk,* 18 July 1868. (By permission of The British Library)

Fig. 27. *Carte de visite*, Zazel, ca. 1860s. (Theatre Museum, London; © V&A Images)

Such dress—worn by female dancers as well—inspired the Lord Chamberlain to issue a warning in 1869 to all London's theaters and public places of amusement:

> The Lord Chamberlain has learned with regret that there is much reason to complain of the impropriety of costume of the ladies in the pantomimes, burlesques, etc. which are now being performed . . . he has been most unwilling to interfere in a matter which he considers ought more properly be left to the discretion and good taste of the managers . . . now however, that the question has been taken up by the press and public opinion . . . he feels himself compelled to call it to the serious attention of the managers.[34]

Not coincidentally, a few years earlier the American equestrienne Adah Isaacs Menken had attracted attention for performing in "semi nude" costume in an Astley's production of *Mazeppa* under William Batty's management in which she portrayed the Byronic hero. Managers sympathetic to Batty and others like him later countered such attacks by the Lord Chamberlain and the press by arguing that "short dresses, etc" were worn "to assist rapidity of motion, ease and grace."[35]

Reinforcing the memorandum of 1869, the Lord Chamberlain issued another statement to all theaters in 1874 "urgently repeat[ing] the appeal made to them to assist in abating the . . . growing scandal which has now reached a climax . . . the indecent dances and the immodest dresses which now form so prominent a part of the entertainments at some theatres . . . and once more [asking] their assistance and cooperation in putting a stop to it."[36] No doubt many perceived that the female acrobat's costume enhanced the erotic appeal of her display, particularly when she performed with men. Munby, who belonged to that "certain class" of spectators to which the editorialist in the *Era* referred, witnessed Madame Stertzenbach at St. James's Hall and made diagrams in his diary depicting "her body and loins . . . cased in close fitting spangles, and her legs, up to the very hips . . . naked" (fig. 28). She performed with her husband, who, lying on his back, "held her out or upwards upon her head . . . tossed her about from side to side, placing the sole of his foot actually in the fork between her thighs . . . he then flung her backwards over into a somersault."[37] "The pretty English girl" about whom he wrote at the Oxford Music Hall similarly animated his imagination: "[She slid] down headforemost over the body of one of the men, and then catching her feet under his armpits, and coming upon again by grasping his body between her

Fig. 28. Sketch of Madame Stertzenebach, Munby Diaries, vol. 33, 1865. (Master and Fellows of Trinity College Cambridge)

knees and his leg with her hands, whilst she brought her head & shoulders up by a strong muscular effort."[38]

The female's public visibility was significant not just because of her apparent nudity; she was also, as Peter Bailey has argued, the "bearer of glamour, arguably a distinctively modern visual property and central to orthodox bourgeois notions of sexuality that were fraught with imperatives of release and suppression."[39] Bailey's analysis associates glamour with "magical or fictitious beauty" as introduced by the poetic vocabulary of Sir Walter Scott and can thereby be identified with other definitions concerned with distance, to which the acrobat's art obviously conformed.[40] Distance helped to perpetuate the "magical" qualities surrounding the acrobat and also created an important separation between her and her audience, the expression and consummation of whose desire was necessarily contained by her elusiveness. Browning equated this magic with that of a fairy goddess: "Lo, she is launched, look—fie, the fairy!—how she flees / O'er all those heads thrust back,—mouths, eyes, one gape and stare, . . ."[41] However magical, elusive, and sensual her performance appeared, it took on an added charge in the context of the consumer market in which it took place. In Browning's poem, the father of the trapeze artist, who is master of the troupe, is held accountable for this base commercial opportunism: "The curious may inspect,—his daughter that he sells / Each rustic for five sous. . . ."[42] Yet, Browning's romantic reverie of the fair and the liberated life of these gypsies contrasted sharply with the observations of critics who saw the acrobat's art as a form of female solicitation, differing from prostitution only in being more public.

This view was perhaps most clearly expressed in 1894 by the National Vigilance Association (NVA) purity campaigner Laura Ormiston Chant in her testimony before the Theatres and Music Halls Committee of the London County Council, a body responsible for all matters affecting the licensing of theaters, music halls, and premises used for music and dancing and particularly interested in the Empire Theatre's lax morality, both on stage and in the audience: "We the women of England, in whose name I speak to-day . . . say that [although] these poor girls . . . [who] are shamelessly exposed do not mind it, I say that a civilized community is not to take its standard of decency from those who . . . are not in a position to hold [it at its] highest . . . the amusements of our great city shall be such that young men can go to them without being entrapped and seduced by these sad poor women."[43] For Mrs. Chant and like-minded social reformers, the acrobat was unfavorably associated both with the actress and the dancer, who were traditionally connected to the "low," albeit increasingly commercialized, culture of the theater, and with the prostitute at a time when the inspection of these trades effected legal change and municipal regulation.[44]

The popularity of *tableaux vivants,* apparently naked women who posed as classical statues, complicated such views. These displays relied on the pictorial legitimacy of the female nude as she appeared on canvases exhibited in the Royal Academy or the Parisian salon.[45] But this aesthetic confusion between artistry and indecency was nothing new; it had had an adverse impact on Adah Isaac Menken when she played the title role in *Mazeppa* a generation earlier. Subject to intense scrutiny, the equestrienne had defended herself publicly, stating that "my want of costume, as might be inferred, is not in the least bit indelicate, and in no way more open to invidious comment than the dress worn by Cerito, Rosati . . . I have long been a student of sculpture and my attitudes, selected from the works of Canova present a classicality which has been invariably recognized by the foremost of American critics."[46] That her performances on her American tour received similar scrutiny to that received by her performances in London, however, suggests, at the least, the changeability of opinion about "being stripped to the buff," as one contemporary in Virginia City, Nevada, described her.[47]

No such aesthetic ambiguity existed in the minds of NVA critics in the nineties. By "entrapping" and "seducing" young men for a price, such female performers were thought by some to cater principally to male audiences. The rhetoric of vice was intimately connected to the late-nineteenth-century antisensualist movement, which sought to restructure heterosexual morality. To antisensualists, male enjoyment meant female vice. In this respect, the female acrobat's display was for men's eyes only.[48] The construction consisting of the male gaze and the female object of desire became even more problematic because of Mrs. Chant's presence in the audience. In her testimony before the Theatres and Music Halls Committee she recalled her experiences at the Empire, when "two Frenchmen stood behind the stalls, behind my sister & myself, & wondered that any virtuous woman could look upon such a performance as that upon the stage."[49] Male visitors commented on the flirtatiousness of girls in England (in effect if not in intention), sometimes finding this sort of behavior indecent, sexually shameless, and predatory. As late-nineteenth-century British and American historians have argued, sexual practices and their meanings were becoming increasingly disengaged from procreation, at least among the white middle class, rendering sex a more intimate and nonreproductive practice—a shift that enabled some male spectators to delight in the female acrobat's performance, while provoking those who did not approve.[50]

The problematic connection between sex and the female acrobat became inflamed through the force of advertising when Mrs. Chant's bête noire took the form of an indecent poster of Zaeo at the Royal Aquarium (fig. 29). With upraised arms, smiling, and wearing a tight bodice and apparently no tights, Zaeo appeared on a poster that was distributed throughout London in 1890 and was the focus of a censorship campaign by the NVA.[51] In the view of Chant and others, "real ladies" did not flaunt their physique either in the temporary space of the ring or in the more permanent realm of advertising.[52] The prevalence of the poster in the day-to-day life of Londoners or city and town dwellers in general should not be underestimated. In 1868 Munby noted that "the streets are placarded with posters announcing Fillis's Troupe of Female Acrobats [which] has been engaged at an 'enormous expense,'" adding that "tonight they appear for the first time at the London Pavilion."[53]

The degree to which such images filtered into the consciousness of the passerby poses some interesting questions. As a visual episode in the everyday, these posters created a highly democratic culture through mass advertising in which the important connection between sex and commodification carried highly charged cultural codes. Contemporaries did not have to attend the music hall, circus, or pleasure ground in order to observe them but merely needed to walk down the street. Without necessarily wishing to partake of it, the spectator was integrated into the performance world through his observation of street advertising in the form of the poster-bill, meaning that the commercialized performance world was engaged in performance outside the music hall, park, or circus and inside the imagination of the wider public. That is, these spectacles extended beyond the confines of amusement places and into the street.

In an editorial letter to the *Standard,* "a working man" worried about the moral character of his "young sons" because "the large pictures of women [are exhibited] to the gaze of young men thereby exciting evil passions in them."[54] The problem was worse in London, where while "some house [is] being either pulled down or rebuilt . . . the hoardings at the front are covered with these vile advertisements."[55] Alarming images problematized in visual terms the tension between the public's sense of "moral decency," on the one hand, and the commercial opportunism that exploited the public's voracious appetite for "sensational" exhibitions, on the other; the uncertainty of the former and the prevalence of the latter only served to underline fears of moral disorder in what some defined as a modern-day Babylon.[56]

Fig. 29. Poster of Zaeo, from *The Life of Zaeo*, 1891. (Rare Book and Manuscript Library, Columbia University)

That bills and posters were also distributed and placarded in shop windows and on shop walls reinforced the messages from the sidewalk and thus widened the boundaries of the spectacular.[57] In their discussion of early modern English consumption spaces Nigel Thrift and Paul Glennie rightly pointed out that the social practices of shopping included more than just the exchange of items, extending to social interaction between the shopkeeper and his clientele.[58] Thus, within the culture of commodification the poster played an important role as a focus for conversation or casual observation. Given the uncontrollable nature of this sort of interaction, members of the NVA, as well as others, found a moral imperative and reason for immediate action in their drive to censor posters and to prevent sex from being made into a commodity.

While some viewed the acrobat's art as sexually provocative, others saw it as a sign of female health, even freedom. The unbearable lightness of Zaeo and other artists prompted some to comment on early feminist ideals: "The real 'new woman,'" remarked one journalist in 1898 after seeing the Barnum and Bailey Circus in Bournemouth, "is not the intellectual character depicted by Susan B. Anthony–Cady Stanton School but rather a woman of physical brawn and skill expert . . . on the wheel, in the fields and in the circus ring."[59] Serious training was required to develop these talents, and this was not lost on contemporary observers. During the debate over the Zaeo poster, one person noted, "The first time I saw [it], I was with a friend and said to him, 'that woman, if her pictures do not exaggerate, is a living argument for physical education.'" In this instance, the attractiveness of the acrobat's body and her flirtatious qualities were overshadowed by her athletic strength and skill. The observer added that since she ran "a gymnasium of girls of the clerk and shop assistant class," who were "cribbed, cabined and confined during the day with their bodies," she would have liked to have pictures of Zaeo in order to show her students "the grace, stateliness and strength which may all be acquired by bodily exercise."[60]

The elusive matter of the extent to which the female acrobat saw herself as an object of sexual or athletic interest was addressed in a defensive statement by Zaeo herself. Dismissing the claim of impropriety in her displays, she instead focused on the healthfulness of her work.[61] When asked in a *Daily Graphic* interview whether she thought that severe muscular training was bad for girls' health, she responded,

Bad! Why it is the very best thing in the world for them. Look at me, I was a poor, slender, weakly child, and now I weigh 12st 2lbs. I never have a cold, a cough, a day's illness of any sort! I only eat two meals a day, very simple and sustaining—in my early breakfast and late supper, and never eat or drink between the two. Some day I may open a gymnastic class for girls myself, as I have a feeling that it would help to make young women think how valuable such training is to their future health. But I am glad to see, both on the Continent and in England, much more attention is now being paid to the physical training of our sex.[62]

Zaeo's twelve-stone, two-pound figure and healthy eating program were not in keeping with Victorian constructions of the "delicate" feminine body and the idealized, dainty appetite in etiquette books, works of fiction, and tea-room and restaurant menus.[63] On the other hand, the acrobat's "strong muscular condition" spoke to the ways in which other contemporary discourses concerning physical development translated into a system of discipline, order, and neatness, particularly among boys and girls.[64]

Female gymnastic training such as at Fraulein Wilke's Gymnasium in Croydon and the Orion Gymnastic Club in Hackney mushroomed in the late nineteenth century, complementing similar developments for boys and men.[65] According to the *Gymnast,* a contemporary exercise magazine that advertised a club directory of gymnasiums throughout London and the provinces, there were ten such places in the metropolis that offered "ladies classes" taught by female instructors. Based on these listings, Fraulein Wilke's Gymnasium catered only to women and girls, providing "gymnastic classes for ladies of the Church Institute on Wednesday and Saturday afternoons . . . with special classes for married ladies on Saturday mornings."[66] The appearance of the *Gymnast* magazine and a host of gymnastic manuals, such as William Blaikie's *Sound Bodies for Boys and Girls* (1884) and F. J. Harvey's *Physical Exercises for Girls* (1896), attested to the growth of female training. These and other guides were clear in distinguishing the gender divide, suggesting activities suitable for each sex. According to the 1898 pamphlet *Hints for Gymnasts: Being Sound Advice to Leaders and Teachers,* "The weaker sex will naturally not require such difficult or hard work as boys; it should never be the object of the teacher to make girls under him muscular or 'strong women' but rather sound, healthy women." The pamphlet suggested that "it is best to avoid for girls' classes such exercises as wide straddling or wide lunging movements," a rule easily broken by female acrobats in displays involving splits or balancing on one leg, for instance.[67] To get around the problem, femininity had to be constructed in other ways. Where ease was accompanied by grace, the cultural dilemma now found a resolution, at least in the eyes of some viewers. Watching Zazel perform at the Aquarium in an acrobatic display when she, like Madame Blondin before her, wore baskets on her feet as she walked along the high wire, one witness noted that "she tripped along as nimbly as on *terra firma.*"[68]

The acrobat's success depended upon the performer's negotiating various aesthetic codes that were sometimes in conflict. The tension, for example, caused by the public's approval of her "ladylike" athletic exhibitions, on the one hand, and the controversy surrounding her sexually provocative poses and costume, on the other, made her task of aesthetic negotiation inherently problematic and complex. In the course of her display the acrobat confused respectable and unrespectable aesthetic codes, paradoxically creating market demand. Importantly, the negotiation process in which she was engaged meant that she abandoned both aesthetic extremes and, in exchange, played a game with the audience in which it appeared that she might transgress behavioral boundaries but she stopped short of doing so.[69] For example, although Zaeo and others wore costumes that made them appear nude, they were not really nude, and they did not remove any articles during their performances, as in popular burlesque, to further excite or alarm the audience. The point here is that like the clown, the acrobat was engaged in symbolic play arising from opposing aesthetic impulses on the part of the public that stemmed from community standards, on the one hand, and human interest and desire, on the other.[70]

Despite the acrobat's partial sublimation of her strength to her gender identity, her most striking quality (and that of other athletic performers, such as equestriennes) was her superhuman dexterity. Her attempts to defy gravity placed her in the role of a cultural figure rebelling against static forces, effectively divorcing herself from the outside world.[71] Edgar Degas's celebrated *Miss La La at the Cirque Fernando,* painted in 1879, the same year that the first Dangerous Performances Act was passed, suggested as much. Above the spectators' heads appears Miss La La, who strains herself upwards by clutching a rope in her mouth until she reaches the high wire (fig. 30). Not only does she divorce herself temporarily from the outside world but she further detaches herself from her viewers, as "the bearer of glamour," in this elevated state. In an age of urban expansion, the desire for free, unimpeded

Fig. 30. Edgar Degas, *Miss La La at the Cirque Fernando,* 1879. (National Gallery Picture Library, London)

movement and distance from the thick crowd influenced this cultural connection; and in an age of liberalism, the free-moving individual merited the applause and enthusiasm of the throng below.

There was, however, a fine line between the acrobat's superhuman dexterity and senseless daring, which ultimately depended upon the skill of the performer. One observer noted that at the Adelphi Music Hall in Oldham in 1871 "the Brothers Banvard, executed some daring feats on the trapeze fixed at a height of 20–30 feet . . . and one of the three men fell into the orchestra headforemost." The response of the audience, according to the report, was a single one of "panic" in which "men yelled and women screamed."[72] Another writer suggested that even when the act was performed properly "and the actor only looks as though he would slip from the trapeze, as if he were falling head foremost on the people beneath him and then catches himself with his feet on the horizontal bar," there were generally screams "from the female portion of the audience, and frequently from the sterner sex also."[73]

But for performers such as Blondin, the famous Hero of Niagara, from whom Selina Powell derived the name Madame Blondin, such acts were devised to give the *illusion* of danger (fig. 31). For him, the tension was not between life and death but between illusion and reality. In an interview he recalled that the only time in his career that he had met with an accident had been at the Crystal Palace: "The man who was letting the fireworks did not understand his business and he knocked me off my rope . . . I caught the rope with my legs and I did it so that the public thought it was part of the performance and cried 'Do it again.'" He added that in contrast to amateur performers, "I never lose my presence of mind . . . no matter what takes place."[74] Confirming his coolness, one observer who witnessed Blondin said, "Concern for the performer's safety is depicted on the faces of the spectators. . . . Blondin shows none."[75] However great Blondin's talents, there was nothing illusionary about the practical dangers that were involved in these acts, and this quality captivated the public.

Responding to an attack on his "dangerous profession," Blondin wrote immediately after the Selina Powell incident that "every accident which has befallen rope-walkers is attributable entirely to their want of knowledge and experience of the profession they were engaged in."[76] The comment, however, failed to address the practical problems associated with faulty equipment, as in the Selina Powell case, or the incompetent assistants who interfered with his display at the Crystal Palace. Even so, the proliferation of

Fig. 31. *Carte de visite,* Blondin, n.d. (Theatre Museum, London; © V&A Images)

"amateurs" within the trade gave performers like Blondin reason for reproof. To be sure, a few years earlier Munby had noted in a visit to the Cambridge Music Hall, near Shoreditch Station, that the boxkeeper had informed him that "Zuleilah," the acrobat performing, was "a Miss Foster, a publican's daughter of the neighborhood; that she only became an acrobat 2 or 3 months ago, stimulated, like the rest of them, by the success of La Pereira" (fig. 32). Following this visit, on the same evening at around ten o'clock Munby had stopped into a "Temperance Music Hall," where admission was "only *one penny*" to see "a Jewess" by the name of Little Azella who "is only nine years old." Standing next to Munby, the performer's sister had informed him that the girl performing, whose real name was Betsy Asher, "has only been at it three weeks, besides 8 days, [and] that she practised at home."[77]

The presence of amateurs such as Little Azella in the trade made many "professionals" complain about growing negative publicity.[78] The circus manager Tom Transfield opined on the eve of the first debate of the Dangerous Performances Bill in 1872 that "there were many unprincipled agents who send out these people for the sake of getting the commission and they work at half the salary that genuine artists do." In his view, these "agents" privileged financial gain over physical safety, and this had serious repercussions for the trade.[79] Furthermore, they did this at very little cost to themselves if the "rules and regulations" issued by Hernandez and Stone's circus in the 1840s were typical; they specified that "in case of indisposition [if brought on by accident in the business of the theater or circus] half salaries will be paid for the first week" only, after which any illness was the performer's problem.[80] In later years, better-off performers might turn to insurance companies, which only moderately improved matters. The equestrienne Nellie Reid informed the *Era* in 1885 that after her fall from her horse while performing in the ring, the Accidental Insurance Company gave her three weeks' compensation, amounting to £18. This would have been little reprieve, however, if the injury had been serious and the performer had had to retire indefinitely.[81]

Despite Blondin's defense of the safety of his trade when conducted by "professionals" like himself, there is little doubt that the built-in tension between life and death represented the very essence of the acrobatic art, particularly where there was no net—which was assumed by some to attract larger audiences. In accordance with this observation, a contemporary criticized an early use of nets at Drury Lane in 1853, when Mr. Sands, a famous American ropewalker, performed. An article in the *Sunday Times* stated that

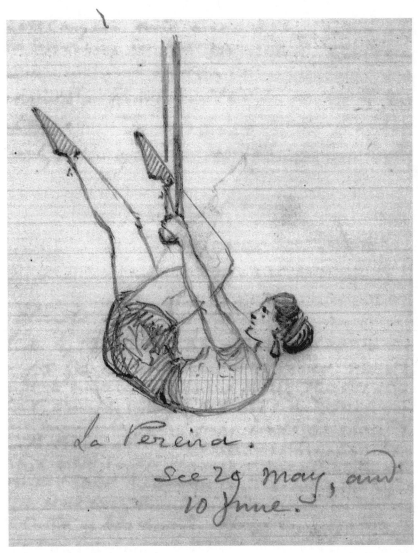

Fig. 32. Sketch of La Pereira, Munby Diaries, vol. 36, 1868. (Master and Fellows of Trinity College Cambridge)

"while a net is fixed underneath in which he must fall if the . . . apparatus fails," it "rather takes away the flavour of the affair . . . the public will scarcely care to see it when they find out that it is not even dangerous."[82] For this reason, Madame Blondin and others like her did not use nets.

Patrons' desire to see the artist defy gravity relates to the blasé attitude, a psychic condition that was unconditionally reserved to the city, according to Georg Simmel.[83] While the rapidity and discord of the metropolis frayed the individual's nerves, effecting his blasé outlook, as Simmel says, it also triggered a desire for the sensational, I would argue. The effect of an audience watching such a display was inimical to Simmel's notion of atomized urban life. Even assuming the subjectivity of individual response, these spectators witnessed a performance that was designed to thrill or prompt fear, effectively challenging the blasé.[84] That the public's ever-increasing appetite for danger was noted by so many observers raises interesting questions about the tension between spectacle for the sake of fun and spectacle for the sake of danger and the frisson arising from this tension for the individual spectator. Contemporaries did not need to stand beneath the wire to appreciate this dilemma; worried politicians in Parliament pondered it as well.

From 1863 to 1897 the attention of both houses was repeatedly drawn to the problem of dangerous performances, and an examination of the debates that followed provides a useful overview of the state of public opinion on the question. The issue transcended party lines in Parliament, and thus the groupings are difficult to trace. That said, the strong influence of the evangelical lobby is clearly visible throughout. However strong the outrage within Parliament, the practical problem of regulation for a government with laissez-faire instincts was also very real. Regulation was often left to backbenchers, and only in the climate of much greater intervention in the 1890s did the government take steps toward direct involvement in remedying the problem of "dangerous performances." The history of attempts at legislation between 1863 and 1897 is thus a story of widespread public sentiment on the matter being expressed in the newspapers and of how this opinion was taken up by a small group of backbench MPs and reforming peers in Parliament. Against this movement was a well-organized employers' and performers' lobby persistently arguing their right to pursue their livelihoods as they saw fit.

Several days after Selina Powell's fall the Liberal Home Secretary, Sir George Grey, faced a series of questions in the Commons regarding the manager's responsibility to his performers. He said that in cases where the performer was in evident danger of losing his or her life, the secretary of state had addressed circulars to the occupiers and owners of places of amusement warning them of the responsibility they incurred and the consequences that might result to them in the case of a performer's loss of life. "In general, he was glad to say such remonstrances had been attended with the desired effect."[85]

Of course, the Home Office and the Lord Chamberlain's office were in a better position to police such activities in London than in the provinces. Some days after the matter was raised in the Commons, Spencer Ponsonby Fane, of the Lord Chamberlain's office, directed an internal memo to William Bodham Donne, who was in charge of regulating the theater, stating that "the Lord Chamberlain desires me to draw your attention to the recent accident to the 'Female Blondin' at Aston Park and to the remarks upon it in Parliament and the Press . . . and desires me to request that you will add this prohibition [of dangerous performances] to the Regulations respecting theatres."[86] Bodham Donne responded that while he would address the prohibition in the list of regulations, he would also watch over the bills and posters of the theaters in the metropolis.[87] But these measures depended heavily upon the cooperation of the theater managers and therefore provided no alternative means of enforcement. By design, regulation was limited to those places over which the Lord Chamberlain had jurisdiction, and therefore halls, parks, and circuses were excluded from his control. This problem led to investigation years later when Sir Richard Mayne, the chief commissioner of the Metropolitan Police, was examined before the 1866 Select Committee on Theatrical Licenses and Regulations. He recalled cases at the Alhambra and the Cremorne Gardens, both in London, where there had obviously been great potential danger: "We were . . . prepared to try the question [against the owner] by action or indictment if he persisted [in allowing the dangerous performances to continue] . . . the proprietor yielded in those cases. . . . But if we had actually been forced to proceed by law, I am afraid our powers would have been . . . rather ineffective."[88]

The inadequacy of legal authority and the heightened awareness about the dangers of the trade that Selina Powell's fall caused thus set in motion the Dangerous Performances Bill. It was introduced three times in Parliament as private legislation, in 1872, 1873, and 1879, the last being the year it passed. Its sixteen-year gestation—which began in the form of a question put before the House several days after Selina Powell's fall in 1863—is largely attributable to the fact that some MPs and Lords, aware of the delicate balance between legitimate moral regulation and tyrannical interference with a worker's right to earn a living, acted reluctantly. Some observers argued that this delay had encouraged more acrobatic accidents to occur. "From the time of the Aston Park accident, some sixteen years ago," J. Kinghorn opined in 1879, "each appalling accident and attendant outburst of virtuous indignation has been followed by [a] bill which has been . . . patted on the back and then when the fitful fever wore off, withdrawn."[89]

Still, some were more supportive of the bill than others, particularly when the subject of children involved in dangerous performances was considered. In 1873 Lord Buckhurst, a Conservative peer and ally of Lord Shaftesbury on this issue, moved that the Dangerous Performances Bill be read for a second time in the Lords and said that while he knew that the Lords did not wish to interfere with legitimate athletic and gymnastic exercises—and in fact neither did he—"he thought these exhibitions by adult performers tended to degrade the public sense. What then must be the case when they were exhibited by young boys and girls? He knew he should be met by the objection that unless the training commenced at a very early age, children could not perform such feats."[90] The concern for both women and children involved in dangerous performances was connected to the fact that these groups were often conflated in parliamentary discussions on issues that related to work; the Royal Commission report on agricultural work in 1868–69, for example, merged the two groups.[91] Soon after, however, the emphasis shifted to children exclusively and thus corresponded to established concerns over the regulation of child labor. Women were dropped from the discussions after Powell's fall (although they were reintroduced fleetingly and unsuccessfully in the 1880s) largely because the antiregulation impulse within Parliament was too strong to include them. Extending the law to protect performing children, however, did untold damage to their trade, many "professionals" argued. The first Dangerous Performances Act, passed in 1879 under Benjamin Disraeli's Conservative government, prohibited children under fourteen from performing acts such as acrobatics, which were deemed injurious to life and limb, and made the parent or guardian who permitted such a performance subject to a fine.[92] In the short term the act infringed on the family's already unstable income, and in the long term it opened the door to further regulation, as we will see.

What was significant about the Selina Powell case of 1863, besides its basic gruesomeness, was the range of issues and concerns that grew from it. The accident prompted many to pause and ask why such exhibitions were popular. The question was a complex one that highlighted the public's appetite for and interest in sex, athleticism, and danger. The tension between what constituted innocent amusement and what defined salacious degradation made the acrobat's trade equivocal in the late nineteenth century. Issues concerning cruelty, sexual immorality, danger, and commodification provided the fuel with which campaigners struggling against acrobatic displays fought their battle. Thus, in the market for spectacle more than just the act of commercial exchange (e.g., money for aesthetic enjoyment) occurred. Underpinning the acrobat's art were meanings and representations that focused the mind's eye and inspired comment and controversy.

As an artist "bearing glamour" and "out of reach of the consumer," the female acrobat had a complex role. While she embodied sexuality, the real danger of her act lay not in her flirtation with the audience but in her life-and-death struggle on the wire. Certainly the growth of the gymnastic schools "for ladies and girls" provided a context in which the acrobat could justify the popularity and perhaps even the respectability of her trade. Yet, given the heights at which she performed, she symbolized the "spectacle," hovering above the public sphere and challenging established moral codes, while encouraging—in the eyes of her opponents—the formation of new ones that undermined rational recreation. Her act was more than just a display; it was a dramatization of sociocultural conflicts in a Geertzian sense.[93] Like all other types of entertainers who experienced the pressure of competition, she found herself forced to accommodate the vagaries of popular tastes in a competitive marketplace, tastes that were beyond the control of legal bodies or moral pressure groups. If the battle was between a moral minority and female acrobats, then the war was between legal—and royal—authority, on the one hand, and a vibrant consumer world controlled by public taste, on the other.

Six

Sensational Imbalance
The Child Acrobat and the Mid-Victorians

While Madame Blondin's accident alerted the public to the perils of the acrobatic trade, the ensuing parliamentary debates about the problem focused on performing children and were linked to the wider issue of child labor. In contrast to their peers in the textile and mining industries, who were affected by the Factory Acts of the 1830s and 1840s, child performers remained untouched by legal controls. This gulf widened when the statutes were further extended in the next generation to include children in other industrial occupations, such as bleaching and dyeing, paper staining, and cartridge making.[1] While the employment of children in the entertainment world was, relative to their employment in these other occupations, not extensive, it was highly visible since these "prodigies" were spectacularly displayed in theaters, music halls, and circuses.[2] The impact that performing in these venues had on the minds and bodies of young children was the kernel of the controversy surrounding them. As anxiety about their public role mounted, so too did that surrounding their training for specific performance trades such as acrobatics, which were considered to be physically taxing by definition.

Despite their public role in the ring, the itinerant status of these children, who traveled with tenting companies or moved from one resident company to the next, obviously made them difficult to trace—a fact that only heightened public anxiety about their work. Much of what we know about the child acrobat was written by spectators and by observers who, preoccupied by morality issues, watched spectators watching the displays. In order to dissect these contrasting "gazes," it is useful to examine how spectators wrote about them within the context of periodicals and newspapers. Moral opinion, outraged by the public's interest in child performers, was hotly articulated in the "waif story," a term used by Anna Davin to describe a strand of writing within "Sunday school literature"; it is also a subcategory of what Margaret Nancy Cutt called "tract fiction."[3] As Davin has shown, these books, published largely but not exclusively by evangelical presses, appeared mainly from the mid-1860s and were influenced by discourses on ragged children, nineteenth-century didactic writing for children, sentimental fiction, and reports by social reformers.[4] They center on poor boys and girls who, due to adult cruelty and neglect, become waifs.[5] Morally lost and spiritually deprived, these children ultimately find salvation in Christ after traveling along a long road marred by brutality and sadness. Child acrobats provided a perfect subject for such literary treatment not only because of the physicality of their work but also because the reading audience, composed mainly of children, recognized them from the street, circus, and theater.

A more sensational offshoot of this genre appeared decades later, in the 1880s, when the campaign to save children from neglect and abuse earned legal and institutional legitimacy. While it is impossible to draw a direct causal link between fiction and political opinion except in cases such as Ellen Barlee's *Pantomime Waifs; or, A Plea for Our City Children* (1884), whose introduction was written by Lord Shaftesbury, it is clear that the two sets of discourses were synchronous during the mid-nineteenth century.[6] To be sure, some parliamentarians were willing to face the challenge of saving the real-life counterparts of those fictional "prodigies." A growing combination of social pressures provoked debate in Parliament over the legitimacy of controlling the acrobatic trade, leading to a heated response from the performance community. The mid-nineteenth century has often been thought of as a period of equipoise; indeed, the historian W. L. Burn considered this age to draw to a close with the advent of the second reform act in 1867.[7] At that time child acrobats remained unprotected, yet a decade later Parliament's long arm had extended to them something of that protection that children in other areas of British life had long felt. In 1879 Parliament passed a statute that fined any parent or guardian who exposed any child under fourteen years of age to "dangerous performances," including acrobatics.[8] The mid-Victorian period, if taken as extending to the early 1870s, was crucial for the escalation of moral panic surrounding child acrobats, which led eventually to legal discipline over them.[9] The speed with which the state came to the rescue of performing children in 1879 would not have been possible without the head of steam generated by journalists, novelists, concerned politicians, and other social observers in the mid-Victorian period. Yet the fact of this reforming zeal implicitly challenges historiographical orthodoxy, which has characterized this period as, in Burn's words, an "age of equipoise."[10]

In a story first printed in *All the Year Round* in 1865 and republished in 1870 under the title *The Unkind Word and Other Stories,* the didactic authoress Dinah Mulock (Mrs. Craik) wrote of a Scottish doctor called Adam Black who recalls a visit to a local circus with his small nieces. They witnessed a trapeze display involving "a mere boy" called Signor Uberto. In anticipation of the boy's appearance in the ring, his nieces asked Black if they might leave since they feared the performance would shock them and be dangerous to the performer. However, the doctor responded that "it was too late. . . . Besides, for myself, I did not wish to leave. That strange excitement which impels us often to stop and see the end of a thing, dreadful though it may be, or else some feeling for which I was utterly unable to account, kept me firm in my place." Quite apart from the attitudes expressed by his nieces, which might bear further consideration if we were to examine the interesting question of children watching other children, Black's observation is significant for its pathos: "I could not help putting myself into the place of the young man, and wondering whether he really did recognize any danger." The "pleasing anguish" that he experienced as a result of entering into the same mental world as the performer kept him firmly in his seat for a reason for which, as he says, he was unable to account. In the performance the boy "mounted, agile as a deer, the high platform at the end of the circus, and swung himself off by the elastic ropes, clinging only with his hands, his feet extended, like one of the floating figures in pictures of saints or fairies." When the other trapeze reached him, the "young man dropped lightly into it, hanging a moment between whiles, apparently as easily as if he had been born to fly." He did this "turn" four times successfully. On the fifth, however, the boy suddenly fell, and Black's "pleasing anguish" turned to horror. "It was so sudden . . . a crash on the mattressed platform . . . from which rolled off a helpless something." As the surprised audience emitted screams, the doctor went to the scene to help the "poor young man." In a moment of silent reflection he blames himself for patronizing the display. "I felt somehow as if I had murdered him, or helped to do it."[11]

Real-life spectators also showed that they were never fully prepared for the worst. And in situations that produced fatal or near-fatal results the spectator's "gaze" turned into the spectator's "gasp," as in the case of a display called the "Leap for Life" by Les Freres Trevannion at the Wellington Circus and Music Hall in Cheltenham in 1869. In it, one of the boys slipped from his brother's grasp and fell 35–40 feet "amidst the shrieks of men, women and children."[12] Such scenes became even more alarming when they involved not only young boys but also small children. Writing to the *Royal Leamington Spa Courier* in 1869, a doctor admitted to having taken his children to a circus at Leamington where they saw "a child advertised as only four years old [who] . . . suspended his frail body at a height of 60 feet from the trapeze. At this elevation, the child was straining his self in a pitiable manner, in going through the 'fearfully dangerous' tricks." The doctor went on to say that if the boy continued these performances, he would be met with "one of those terrible fatalities which are now becoming so common." He recommended that Mr. Henry Austin Bruce, of the Home Office, "take . . . steps as will prevent a repetition of scenes like this 'which no government but an English one would ever dream of permitting for a single night'" (fig. 33).[13] The point was given visual force in a rare photograph of a boy acrobat, El Nino Farini, in the 1860s.

That "these children" were engaged in a trade that was not legally protected and that was mortally dangerous prompted government response, particularly after officials such as Henry Austin Bruce received warnings of these displays, including an article that had appeared in the *Daily News,* reporting that a female performer "carried a child of tender years" strapped to her back as she tiptoed along a tightrope at the Holborn Amphitheatre in 1870.[14] Bruce then contacted the proprietors of the establishment where the performance had taken place, and the child was removed from the exhibition, although the female performer continued her display.[15] However, beyond making these "suggestions," Bruce had little authority in cases such as this. Sir Richard Mayne, the chief commissioner of the Metropolitan Police, concurred and raised this point before the 1866 Select Committee on Theatrical Licenses and Regulations.[16]

Concern was linked not only to sensational stories in the press and else-

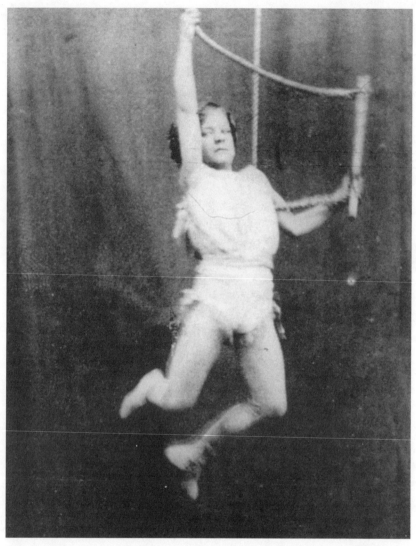

Fig. 33. El Nino Farini, ca. 1860s. (Theatre Museum, London; © V&A Images)

where but also to the perception that the number of children involved in the acrobatic trade was rising. The question of scale is important since many of these children found encouragement for their work within the commercially expanding leisure market.[17] "Nothing fills a house better," one observer noted in 1872, "than juvenile acrobats."[18] As mentioned in the previous chapter, the *Era Almanac* estimated that there were sixty-six acrobat troupes in Britain in 1867–68, ninety in 1877, and ninety-eight in 1878.[19] These numbers were considerably higher than those suggested by the acrobat Jean Battier in 1872, who estimated that "there are about 20 troupes now in England, varying from four to seven in number, and from six to fourteen years of age."[20] Considering the number of acrobats who advertised in the *Era* want ad pages and taking into account the fact that troupes often assumed different names and thereby appear to have inflated numbers in the trade papers, the truth of the figures may have been somewhere in between those in the *Era Almanac* and Battier's estimations. What was important, however, was the perception that the trade was growing. Fueled by stories about performers and by the rise in the number of accidents to child acrobats, critics became more vocal. While the directive for this voice came from no single body, it is notable that evangelical writers of juvenile fiction were particularly keen observers and wove forceful morality tales that gripped the Victorian imagination.

Put simply, the major problem acrobat children posed for evangelicals was that they strayed both from respectable codes of behavior and, more importantly, from religion. Evangelical writers found in them a ready subject for literary salvation, and they found presses such as the Religious Tract Society (RTS) and the Society for Promoting Christian Knowledge (SPCK) willing to spread their message.[21] These writers spun morality tales that combined evangelical concerns about children's religious education with high melodrama and mid-Victorian fantasy and anxiety.[22] Despite the influence that sentimental fiction writers had on waif-story writers, the latter's characterization of the child performer deviated from the former's; for example, in Wilkie Collins's *Hide and Seek* and Charles Dickens's *Hard Times* the circus girls Madonna and Sissy Jupe, respectively, embody "fancy," "imagination," "romance," and "creativity," not the moral impoverishment found in the waif story.[23] That a discrete body of waif stories featured the child acrobat as a subject for rescue is significant not only because many believed that the performer's real-life counterpart was in need of saving but also because the street, the stage, and especially the circus ring provided a provocative fictional venue where a nightmarish world beset by cruelty could be spectacularly witnessed by the reading public, which included middle class and working-class children.[24] To be sure, these books were distributed to Sunday school children as prizes in an effort to encourage and maintain good behavior and reward attendance; they were also on the shelves of "juvenile Theological libraries," libraries in elementary schools, and reading rooms in

served parishes.[25] The contrast between the rational recreation of read-
d the irrationality of performing as it appeared in the waif story could
ve been more stark.

Evangelical concern for these child prodigies is pointedly expressed in
The Little Acrobat and His Mother (1872). As the title implies, the child-
parent relationship is given critical focus in order to explain the child's descent into the performance underworld. Centered on a German acrobat
boy—clearly an exercise in cultural displacement—"who is in the service of
a troupe of travelling gymnasts," it tells a story about "his adventures, hard-
ships, and subsequent deliverance from an evil course of life." The child,
who suffers from physical neglect by his mother, is looked upon with pity
and revulsion by a merchant and his friend, Mr. Werner, the director of an
asylum for "orphans and forsaken children," both of whom have seen the
boy perform: "'How old do you suppose that boy is?' said Mr. Werner. 'I
should say about ten years old,' replied his friend. 'I think he is more than
that; children who lead that sort of life seldom grow. I should like to get him
into my asylum'" (fig. 34).[26]

The imagined effect that institutionalization would have on the boy's
body could only bring desirable ends from Mr. Werner's point of view. Both
Mr. Werner and his companion found the world to which the acrobat boy belonged deeply troubling. At the root of the boy's problem was his mother,
who "was so dirty and idle" and whose heart "was hardened by a long life of
sin," according to the narrator. Not only her physical but also her intellectual
neglect had led to the child's early decline. He was illiterate, not even knowing his real name when Mr. Werner asked him: "'What is your name?' 'Acrobat.' 'I know your profession is that of an acrobat, but what is your Christian
name?' 'acrobat.'" Physical and intellectual neglect translated into moral
degeneracy: "How many sins this poor boy must have committed, and seen
committed, without even knowing that they were sins," Mr. Werner laments.[27]
Upon being "rescued" by Werner and brought into the asylum, Acrobat is
evangelized, which ultimately saves him, as literary convention would have
it, from his strange ways. Acrobat, in turn, eventually attempts to "rescue" his
mother from the darkness of her un-Christian existence, a resolution that
clearly reflected the RTS's moral agenda.

Such waif stories were critical not only of the parents who neglected their
children's early education but also of the audiences that patronized the exhibitions and thereby encouraged the performer's steady, devilish descent.

THE LITTLE ACROBAT.

Fig. 34. Frontispiece from *The Little Acrobat And His Mother*, 1872. (By permission of The British Library)

In *The Mountebank's Children* (1866), published by the SPCK, the performances of the traveling circus are attended by "many idle country people," whose "roars of laughter were heard till late at night." They paid to see Master Frederick and his sister, Milly, a "delicate-looking little girl" and contortionist, whose mother "oils her joints all over everyday, because she is learning to turn her joints backwards." The narrator observes with distress her "throwing her head and arms backwards until she could hold her feet in her hands, and putting her face between her arms, she formed a circle with her body."[28] Interest in Milly heightens when Mossman, her manager, "rolled her over and over . . . with a stick in his hand." Whereas her display sparks awe in the audience, it is meant to provoke pity in the reader. Like Acrobat, Milly is presented as a frail, poorly child whose pitifulness is enhanced by a performance that leaves her "exhausted and panting" at the end of it.[29]

Readers like those attracted to Mrs. Walton's *A Peep behind the Scenes* (1877) were likely large in number. Published by the RTS in 1877, it sold more than 2.5 million copies, popularizing that critical vision of fairground life, spectacle, and performance common in waif stories.[30] Walton's book tells the story of Jessie, a pretty but vain country girl who wants to run away with the circus. So enamored of the silver and gold costumes she sees in a circus procession in her town, she is easily led astray when the troupe's manager approaches her and asks invitingly if "you would like to be dressed like that?"[31] Jessie joins the troupe but finds her dream shattered by unkind treatment and eventually runs away. She finds shelter and comfort in the caravan of a fairground entertainer, Rosalie, whose recent evangelical conversion, in response to her dying mother's last words, makes her the moral guide and central figure of the story. She encourages the girl to believe in Christ, and like the biblical lost sheep, Jessie makes her way home to the mother she abandoned when she ran away. By coincidence, Rosalie's aunt, the wife of a minister, lives in the same village, and Jessie finds work as her servant. Meanwhile, Rosalie decides to leave the world of the fairground and eventually appears on her aunt's doorstep, hungry, tired, and bereaved, only to be greeted by Jessie. The circus and fairground serve as a metaphor for Vanity Fair and its ungodly souls, whom Jessie and Rosalie must encounter in their individual paths toward redemption.[32] Here and elsewhere, the representation of the girl performer converged on Enlightenment assumptions that children were fundamentally innocent and Romantic sensibilities relating to the contemporary "cult of childhood," as well as reformist ideas on the subject of child labor.[33] In these stories, children's straying from their natural, virtuous paths was seen to be the result of corrupt influences beyond their control.[34]

Lord Buckhurst, who later agitated for legal change to protect child performers, said that the public's bad taste was to blame for the continuation of their displays (and accidents), which he said must be "demoralizing" not only to the children who performed them but also to the people who witnessed them.[35] He believed that the crassness of the exhibition, in which the performer's body was twisted and turned, necessarily resulted in his or her degradation and, by extension, that of the audience. In *The Mountebank's Children*, Milly wears a tight bodice and bends into a hoop, showing the audience her frontal anatomy, which, according to the author, could only serve to demoralize her.[36] A later novel, *An Acrobat's Girlhood* (1889), by Hesba Stretton (author of *Jessica's First Prayer*, which sold an impressive 390,000 copies), similarly presented a child acrobat, Trixy, bending herself "backward in a half circle in front of Mr. La Fosse [her manager] on [a] bicycle with her face upside down," an image that horrifies her sister, who witnesses the display.[37] "Yes, the people were shouting and clapping their hands while my poor little sister felt almost [like] dying," she added.[38] Seen from one perspective, the image of Trixy's private rehearsal was worse than Milly's public display if only because the former was beyond the public's moral scrutiny.

Like earlier evangelical writing for children, these stories were meant to "inflate the sordid" by sharply contrasting the grim realities that industrial life produced, such as child labor and cruelty, on the one hand, and "an imaginary world where universal human values and natural justice ordered existence," on the other.[39] In the context of the waif story, the circus ring and its world "behind the scenes," signifying danger and disorder, offered "a system of meaning" that exposed larger insecurities and doubts that underpinned the mid-Victorian age. Oddly, while the RTS and the SPCK struggled to gain public sympathy for the child acrobat (as well as for other waifs and strays), the skill with which the authors depicted mental and physical abuse added a spectacular dimension to their already sensational stories.

What made their physicality more worrisome in both real life and the waif story was that these children were seen to be bound to their managers like slaves and made to rehearse and perform "degrading" tricks that exposed their visibly misshapen bodies.[40] For example, Acrobat's manager forces him "to fast when he was ordered, to twist his body and limbs into all sorts of strange shapes, and sometimes to remain for a long time in the same position, mostly a very fatiguing one."[41] For Shaftesbury, a noted advocate of children's welfare since the creation of the Factory Acts, such static confinement was dangerous, cruel, and "appalling." He recollected "the case of a child, about 14 or 15 years of age, who was in training for the acrobatic business . . . and [stood] on his head for a considerable time, until from its continual practice it had become second nature to him." As a consequence, the development of the acrobat's body became stunted by this training; a "number must become diseased or crippled under the process." Investigating these stories involved "going his nightly rounds" and playing "eyewitness" to incidents of cruelty, as one of Shaftesbury's friends had done. On one occasion, "he heard shrieking and piercing cries, and on going up into the room from whence the sounds proceeded he found seven or eight children, with two or three women standing over them with sticks, beating them . . . because the children would be required in a few days to [perform] at an adjoining theatre."[42] Like many other urban explorers interested in revealing the "frank brutalities" of working-class life, Shaftesbury's unnamed friend moved within an "unchecked" underworld, crafting sensational stories about urban dangers and obscenities that reinforced existing stereotypes about performing children.[43] These observations were well timed, coming at a moment when some politicians in the House of Lords believed that legal action had to be taken for the sake of the child acrobat.

Those peers who supported state intervention faced formidable opposition. Initially, neither the growing number of circus troupes nor the public's increasing awareness of acrobatic training and performance, inspired by Madame Blondin's fall, seemed likely to motivate legal regulation. Indeed, the very lifeblood of the leisure market's expansion was the laissez-faire climate of mid-Victorian Britain.[44] For this reason, Lord Buckhurst, a Conservative peer and ally of Lord Shaftesbury's, faced many dissenting voices in the House of Lords when he introduced a private bill designed to protect the lives and limbs of acrobat children in 1872. Some politicians, such as the Liberal peer, the Earl of Morley, said that while they "did not wish to defend the taste of those who took pleasure in witnessing dangerous exhibitions of this kind," they "did not think bad taste was to be corrected by an Act of Parliament any more than drunkenness." Buckhurst argued that the object of his legislation "was not to interfere with the indulgence of that taste where it was legitimate, but . . . merely to protect young children of tender years from being compelled to take part in acrobatic performances which were danger-ous."[45] His view emerged from a widening belief that state intervention that helped those too weak to help themselves could be justified, as in the case of the child-labor provisions introduced in the 1860s and the compulsory vac-cination of children by an act of Parliament in 1867.[46] Buckhurst's argument was, however, met with derision. In keeping with Morley's Liberal opinion, the Marquis of Salisbury, a Conservative peer, suggested that the bill be ap-plied to jockeys, who also "went through muscular performances for gain [laughter]."[47] The Lords were clearly amused by this problem; as one writer in the *Era* noted caustically, they "have indulged in much laughter," which, he lamented, "is not surprising."[48] Other peers simply believed that the wording of the measure was not precise enough and therefore moved that it be withdrawn.[49]

Another stumbling block was disagreement over the age group that the bill was meant to protect. Buckhurst's interest in the Children's Dangerous Perfor-mances Bill had extended beyond just helping children "of tender years." In its initial form the bill had aimed to protect acrobats up to sixteen years old, in-dicating that the terms *young persons* and *children* were, for the purposes of the statute, conflated. When the bill was reintroduced in 1873, Buckhurst's goals were more modest, and the bill called for protection of children under age twelve. By 1879, when it received the Royal Assent, the age restriction had been raised to fourteen.[50] Significantly, in naming the statute in 1879, the term *young persons* was replaced by *children*. Legal protection of children aged fourteen years and younger had been applied roughly four decades earlier to child la-borers in workshops and factories. The members of a royal commission ad-vising the government in the thirties said that at the beginning of the fourteenth year "the period of childhood . . . ceases and that of puberty is established, when the body becomes more capable of enduring protracted labour."[51] That the 1870s bill aimed to regulate sixteen-, twelve-, and then fourteen-year-olds arguably illustrates the extent to which those politicians supporting it viewed acrobats (at least initially) as different from other laboring children and were thus uncertain as to the age at which they no longer needed protection.[52]

When first introduced in 1872, the bill provoked resistance not only among some politicians but also among members of the acrobatic trade, serving to unite them in a common struggle. Their very livelihoods were at stake: "Should this Bill pass it will throw out [of] employment some hun-dreds of professionals who have no other means of living," said J. H. Ricardo, of the Ricardo Troupe.[53] Many in the trade agreed with him, arguing that because acrobat children often performed with their parents in troupes, the bill would adversely affect "professional" families.[54] Implicit in such arguments was that there was an important difference between legitimate acrobat families and those daredevils who gave the trade a bad name. It was common knowledge, wrote one gymnast who signed himself "Raslus," that recent stories about children falling from ropes had been about novices, not professionals like himself and their families or apprentices: "I do not think it just that because a number of ambitious, untrained boys and girls are permitted to try their 'prentice hands and feet without the experience necessary for gymnastic performances, that we, who have devoted perhaps the better part of a lifetime, and overcome the difficulties, should have to suffer."[55] As professionals, "Raslus" and others did not believe that their trade was dangerous. On the contrary, said the DeCastro Brothers in a letter to the editor of the *Era*, "we take every precaution against danger. On the stage, we have a thickly padded carpet and we are very careful of our boys during the performance."[56] In fact, it was because of their professional status that they took these precautions in order to achieve legitimacy with the public.

Another argument overlooked by the peers was that the trade encouraged performers' self-sufficiency: "[The peers] may have a feeling for the little ones," said one acrobat on the eve of the bill's passage, but the performers' honest living "saves them from crime or the workhouse." He added that as a consequence of his own training, which had begun at the age of three, and since leaving his last master to whom he was apprenticed, "I never knew what it was to want a pound." Concerned about the likely impact of the acrobat's bill, George Austin, of the Austin Troupe, portended that "it will be the means of throwing many a family who are now gaining livelihoods . . . into poverty and want."[57] The trade was ill-prepared to cope with the problem on the eve of the bill's passage due to a fundamental lack of organization. As a consequence, individuals such as the acrobat J. Grovini made pitiable attempts to reverse the tide of change; he offered to contribute his hard-earned one pound "for any expense necessary to suppress the movement," which, he said, was "both unjust and radically ill advised." In agreement with Grovini, George Austin said that he was "quite willing to put some money aside for the expense of a petition," but one was never devised.[58] However noble, such gestures were too little too late.

Besides the short-term effects relating to income loss and popular perception, the proposed law also had long-term consequences for the trade. "How can we have adult acrobats," the DeCastros queried, "without first having the youthful learner?"[59] Furthermore, warned Ricardo, "should this Bill become law, in a few years, there will be no great adult performers in Circuses, Theatres, Music Halls or other places of amusement."[60] This was exactly the effect that advocates of the bill wished the law to have. "If children were not allowed to perform in public," argued the Conservative peer, the Earl of Malmesbury, "their parents would not think it worth while to train them."[61] Ricardo and others feared that without constant practice, those children in training would eventually lose their skills and therefore would not be able to perform in the coming years; their trade was a branch of athletics that required daily practice. Not everyone in Parliament believed, as Malmesbury did, that the law could deter parents from training their children. In a speech during the second debates on the bill in 1873, Shaftesbury argued that the bill, which only related to performance restrictions, would not affect the tortures that occurred in acrobatic training since they "were perpetuated at home and under the secretary of privacy."[62] Many believed, as he did, that parent-managers would find ways to continue their trade even if it meant forcing it underground.

The circus manager George Sanger injected such a view into the debates. He warned that the bill "will not . . . stop the practice. [It] will merely drive it into another channel. We shall then depend on the Continental artists or men [who] will take children from here, teach them across the Channel and bring them back efficient artists after the time of restriction has passed."[63] Sanger hit an important and fragile chord: the itinerant lifestyle of many of these performers made them unlikely candidates for legal control regardless of state intervention. For this reason, Shaftesbury sought the help of existing agencies in order to make these acrobat children answerable to an authority other than their parents. In particular, he enlisted the help of school boards in order to enforce "the compulsory powers" of the Education Act of 1870 to compel acrobat children to attend schools.[64] It was hoped that they, like other child workers, such as flower girls, matchbox makers, errand runners, and "little mothers" might be brought within the grasp of civil society, educated, and reformed.[65] In assuming that the statute would bring acrobat children under the authority of the school system, however, Shaftesbury failed to consider that children who performed with troupes usually did not remain in any community long enough to warrant registration in a local school district. Even if they and/or their parent-trainers performed with a circus that was resident in a town (as many of them were), their engagements were typically no longer than several weeks or possibly a season lasting several months. The problem was discussed in Parliament decades later when George Smith introduced his bill erroneously conflating gypsies and circus performers into the category of "moveable dwellers."

Ultimately, the 1879 act did not prohibit training practices per se since the peers could not agree to regulate all levels of labor in the trade. There was such a thing as "overregulation," it had been argued.[66] In addition, there remained the practical difficulty of how to police private households in which the alleged cruel training took place. The surveillance of homes, if put into law, would intrude on the rights of freeborn Englishmen to the privacy of their homes, a theme taken up in later debates, notably by Henry C. Stephens, of the Liberty and Property Defence League.[67] And as some laissez-faire-minded contemporaries pondered, where would it stop? In its final form the law represented a compromise between the pro- and antiregulationists. It prevented children under fourteen from performing feats that were "dangerous to the life and limb of a child, in the opinion of a court of summary jurisdiction," and further stated that any "parent or guardian, or any person having the custody, of such a child, who shall aid or abet the same, shall severally be guilty of an offence against this Act, and shall be . . . liable for each offence to a penalty not exceeding £10." In addition, the law stated that the court "shall have the power of awarding compensation not exceeding £20, to be paid by such employer [of the place of entertainment] to the child . . . for bodily harm so occasioned."[68]

Of course, the debates over the Dangerous Performances Bill did not end with the passing of the statute. The child acrobat continued to draw the attention of the public and legislators alike, especially since, in the words of Shaftesbury in 1883, the provisions of the act were being "altogether ignored" and "at this time the evil prevailed to a greater extent than it ever did before."[69] Although inadequate from Shaftesbury's point of view, the statute did open the door to further reform; the provisions relating to acrobats in the Acts for the Prevention of Cruelty to Children in 1889 and 1894, brought forward by the Liberal Lord Herschell and the Conservative Wilson Noble, of Hastings, were testament to this fact.[70] By the late 1880s, when the trade was inextricably tied, in the minds of many proregulationists, to other dangerous ones, these anticruelty laws threatened the parent and/or guardian of the performing child with more punitive measures.[71] They also protected other performing children, including pantomime girls, who became the subject of intense concern in this period.[72] Thanks to Jesse Collings, a Liberal from Birmingham, and Conservative Secretary of State Matthew White Ridley, the door to reform widened further when in 1897 the amended Dangerous Performances Act raised the minimum age for participation in displays regarded as "dangerous to life and limb" from fourteen to eighteen for girls and from fourteen to sixteen for boys.[73]

Whether in the ring, in the waif story, or in Parliament, the child acrobat engaged the interests of the mid-Victorian public and in the process drew attention to tensions underpinning the social order. For patrons, the tension was between morbid curiosity and a desire to admire and stare awestruck at the "amazing" prodigy. For reformers, it was between their moral cause and the dominance of the consumer demand for this spectacle. The contentious issues surrounding the acrobatic trade that were brought into focus by these two camps emerged in Parliament, where the conflicts between state interference and individual privacy and between market intervention and laissez-faire politics were played out. Yet, the prospect of legal interference in the affairs of child performers exposed public anxiety, not the peaceful equilibrium that Burn saw in mid-Victorian England.

These "wretched" acrobats, powerless and threatened by the Dangerous Performances Bill, provoked a paradoxical reaction among contemporaries: they became objects of revulsion on the one hand and pitiful subjects who might be saved on the other. While they were similar to other laboring children insofar as the conditions of their work were, in the 1870s, brought before politicians for reform, they were unlike their peers in one essential way: their world was viewed as foreign, gypsylike, and suspect even though the troupes with which they labored belonged to a commercial entertainment market that was embedded in the fabric of Victorian society. Regardless, those stereotypes, supported by sensationalized stories, provided the seeds of discontent in the public mind and in Parliament. The parents and managers of these acrobats, unwilling to observe passively the dismantling of their trade by the legal system, challenged the arguments supporting the Dangerous Performances Bill and drew attention to larger issues about the relationship between the state and the individual. Their protests were, however, insufficient where matters of life and death were concerned, and the Dangerous Performances Act of 1879 was passed. Inadvertently, the mid-Victorian public's desire to see acrobatic spectacles involving children created the conditions for moral panic to reach its sensational pitch. Such anxiety encouraged public debate and was ultimately responsible for creating legal change, which continued until the end of the century. It was a historical paradox that the little acrobat, whose balancing performance relied on maintaining equilibrium, exposed deep cultural and political tensions, not equipoise, in mid-Victorian Britain. The tremors arising from them were to be felt for decades to come.

Conclusion

In Charles Dickens's *Hard Times* Mr. Bounderby distinguishes between industrial Coketown and Sleary's traveling circus when he pompously tells the manager, "You see, my friend," he says, "we are the kind of people who know the value of time and you are the kind of people who don't know the value of time."[1] Even when Sissy Jupe, the circus girl in the troupe, explains that the artists "bruise themselves very bad sometimes" because of constant practice, Bounderby fails to get the point and instead barks, "Serve 'em right . . . for being idle."[2] Dickens's fictional portrayal of Bounderby was mirrored in real-life examples, as we have seen. In the mid-nineteenth century, during a critical moment of commercial organization and transition, the circus was caught in between its perceived vagabond past and the demands of its industrial present. In distinguishing between the two, its members often adopted the language and practice of respectability. Theirs was a trade that was not here today, gone tomorrow, but embedded in the very fabric of industrial society, as they played before the public every week and throughout the calendar year, outside of feast times. The traditional assembly of the circus or circus-like acts at the fair changed over the course of the nineteenth century. While many equestrians, clowns, and acrobats continued to perform at fairs, many more presented their acts inside tents and amphitheaters. These new spaces implied a more complicated existence for the circus, driven by the pressures of commercial and legal demands as well as by productive needs. The new leisure market, which expanded in the second half of the century, was constituted by employment contracts, agents, lavish amphitheaters and modest booths or tents, touring schedules, an expectant but also blasé public, and ubiquitous muddy roads. In such a climate the financial stakes were high, work was hard, and competition was severe. As a consequence, some companies went bankrupt. Integrating itself into the new world of leisure, the circus paradoxically met with suspicion from some observers, who argued that it was gypsylike, wayward, immoral, useless, and derelict. Given how far the trade had moved from its fairground past, it was a bitter irony that these arguments revived traditional antifair prejudices.

While I have been concerned throughout this book with the social history of the circus, that is, with how its members lived and built their trade, I have also been interested in the representation and reception of the acts in the ring. The question how the spectacle was constructed through the observer's gaze and what visual dialogue ensued has been central to this part of the investigation. Approaching my material in this way, I have necessarily been concerned with the subjectivity of vision and have interpreted the acts under discussion from a multiplicity of perspectives, ultimately seeing the circus as a dynamic and densely representative site that interested many, even those who never went. Like the fun-house mirror, the circus reflected a kind of "grotesque realism" that was colorful, ornamental, and, most of all, exaggerated but nonetheless based on a truth about the nineteenth-century world. It did so by representing equestrian dramas of real events and individual feats that featured the human body in a manner that defied nature and, sometimes, social convention. The program may have seemed to be a collection of eclectic eccentricities, but it demanded that contemporaries make sense of each one of them by classifying them as sacred, profane, or something else. This led to a strange blending of visual texts: the nationalist equestrian drama with the exotic animal from some faraway marketplace; the clown's amorphous, laughing body with the female acrobat's physically and morally daring act and the child's "unnatural" bending. The process of defining and ordering these and other exhibitions meant that the circus contributed to a system of knowledge that compelled and fueled the Victorian imagination, which, in this vibrant commercial leisure market, was never idle or satisfied and always curious. It has been this mental process that has concerned me most and has enabled an examination of what the circus meant to contemporaries. Because it was entirely visual, my treatment has involved deconstructing the acts through a variety of interpretive processes as a way of uncovering their meanings, which were never static. In each chapter I have isolated the act at a moment in time when it presented particular problems or generated articulated response from contemporaries. The circus's intersection with cultural, political, social, and economic life has thus been demonstrated along with the historical significance of the act itself.

In general, the circus reveals a strange double life lived by the Victorians. The human body featured in the ring, which went faster, higher, and deeper, encouraged greedy eyes that searched for more—more authenticity, more curiosity, more skillfulness, more daring. The circus thus revealed a shifting and unstable boundary between foreigner-hating and nationalism (the equestrian spectacle); objectification and interest (the "exotic" human or animal); subversion and innocent fun (the clown); lewdness and skillfulness (the female acrobat); and barbarity and fascination with the prodigy (the child performer). It is not enough to say, although it was certainly true, that there were different and conflicting cultural currents in this society. These contradictions at times presented real obstacles to improvement and to post-Enlightenment rationality, both of which the Victorians not only prized but used to define themselves and their world.

The assumption throughout this book has been the existence of a Rabelaisian need for creative release, a universal desire that can be traced throughout any time and place.[3] In Victorian Britain this impulse was constantly negotiated and renegotiated according to new industrial imperatives. The circus—the embodiment of creative release and carnival—responded to these demands and in the process fulfilled this universal desire by appealing to a socially heterogeneous audience. I therefore had to ask why it attracted so many, and I looked for answers in a culturally complex and imaginative tissue where curiosity, a desire for liberation, baroque fascination, intellectual interest, and innocent delight were all bound together. By inviting a wide public to step up, the circus presented a world inside the ring where riches were mixed with vulgarities, sawdust with tinsel. And once revealed, that world evaporated into a fantastic, colorful, gaudy dream that was at once ephemeral and central to the Victorians and their world. The circus was central because it inverted the order of things and, in turn, created something new. It did so, not on holidays, but on virtually every day of the week and in every corner of the kingdom. Its topsy-turvy world, combining the sacred and the profane, coexisted with industrial society yet raised essential questions about the role of carnival culture in Victorian Britain, the answers to which were highly contested.

Appendix

Summary of Major Pieces of Legislation

Vagrancy Act and Related Statutes and Bills

1824: 5 Geo. 4, c. 83, sec. 4. Act for the Punishment of idle and disorderly Persons, and Rogues and Vagabonds, in that Part of Great Britain called England. "That every person committing any offense herein-before mentioned, and after having been convicted as an idle and disorderly person; every person pretending or professing to tell fortunes, or using any subtle craft, means or device, by palmistry or otherwise, to deceive and impose on any of His Majesty's subjects; every person wandering abroad and lodging in any barn or outhouse, or in any deserted or unoccupied building, or in the open air or under a tent, or in any cart or waggon, not having any visible means of subsistence, and not giving a good account of himself or herself . . . every person wilfully, openly, lewdly, and obscenely exposing his person in any street, road or public Highway . . . with the intent to insult any female; every person wandering abroad and endeavoring by the exposure of wounds or deformities to obtain or gather alms; . . . every person apprehended as an idle or disorderly person, . . . shall be deemed a rogue and vagabond . . . and it shall be lawful for any Justice of the Peace to commit such offender to the House of Corrections for a time not exceeding three calendar months."

1877: 40 & 41 Vict., c. 60, sec. 6. An Act to Provide for the Registration and Regulation of Canal Boats used as Dwellings. "A child in a canal boat registered in pursuance of this Act, and his parent, shall for the purposes of the Elementary Education Acts, 1870, 1873, and 1876 be deemed, subject as herein-after mentioned, to be resident in the place to which the boat is registered as belonging, and shall be subject accordingly to any bylaw in force under the said Acts in that place."

1884: 47 & 48 Vict., c. 75, secs. 5–6. An Act to Amend the Canal Boats Act, 1877. (5) "The power to make regulations given to the Local Government Board by the principal Act and this Act shall include power to the Education Department to make regulations with respect to the form of certificates or pass books as to attendance at school to be used by children in canal boats." (6) "The Education Department shall every year report to Parliament as to the manner in which the Elementary Education Acts,

1870 and 1873, 1876 and 1880, are enforced with respect to children in canal boats, and shall for the purpose direct Her Majesty's Inspector of Schools to communicate with the School Boards and School Attendance Committees in their district."

1889–94: Failed attempts by George Smith of Coalville to have the House accept his Moveable Dwellings Bill, modeled on the 1877 and 1884 acts concerning boat people. Required that each van be registered for a limited period and only after approval by the local authority. Children of van dwellers also were to be registered with local school boards.

Licensing

1737: 10 Geo. 2, c. 28. An Act for reducing the laws relating to rogues, vagabonds, sturdy beggars, and vagrants, into one act of Parliament. Section 3 declared that no new plays or additions to old ones were to be acted unless a copy thereof had been sent to the Lord Chamberlain. Section 5 of this act flatly stated that no plays were to be acted but in Westminster or places of His Majesty's residence.

1751: 25 Geo. 2, c. 36. Disorderly Houses Act. Provided for the licensing of all "places of publick entertainment" by magistrates outside the city and by the Lord Chamberlain within the city of Westminster proper. Effectively for a trial period of three years, it proved so successful that it was made a permanent statute in 1755 (28 Geo. 2, c. 19). The intent of the act was to authorize the presentation of, not plays, but "publick entertainment" defined broadly to include musical presentations and equestrian shows. Burletta as it developed combined music and spoken drama, becoming a new theatrical genre that gained widespread popularity. In some cases, spoken dramas were enacted and could be licensed by the magistrate so long as they were performed twenty miles outside the city of Westminster, as according to the 1737 ruling.

1831–32: Select Committee to inquire into law affecting Dramatic Literature. The committee was set up in order to investigate the state of the minor theaters and unlicensed drama. As a consequence, attention was increasingly focused on the fact that despite the 1737 law, plays were performed in theaters other than the patents and thus unlicensed. The question what separated burletta from spoken drama was raised but remained largely unanswerable. According to the report, legislation was necessary to compel secondary London companies and all provincial companies to pay royalties to authors because of the widespread "cribbing" that occurred in the theatrical world. Such a measure was said to inspire playwrights to achieve literary excellence and refrain from "quick translations" of other people's works.

1843: 6 & 7 Vict., c. 68. An Act for Regulating Theaters. In section 1 the patent theaters no longer had the exclusive royal prerogative to perform stage dramas, and therefore restrictions herefore mentioned under 10 Geo. 2, c. 28, were repealed. Section 2 placed on individual theaters the burden to obtain stage play licenses from the Lord Chamberlain. In section 3 the Lord Chamberlain was granted the power to issue stage play licenses to the nonpatent or minor theaters in his jurisdiction of the cities of London and Westminster, boroughs of Finsbury and Marylebone, the Tower Hamlets, Lambeth and Southwark, as well as those places where the royals resided. In addition to settling the question of royal prerogative, section 5 was designed to provide an orderly means of licensing new theaters in areas where magistrates had refused to allow them. Section 23 stated that the words "stage play" included every "tragedy, comedy, farce, opera, burletta, interlude, melodrama, pantomime, or other entertainment of the stage." Far from initiating a new idea, the act implemented and protected existing practices.

1855: 18 & 19 Vict., c. 120. An Act for the better local management of the metropolis. Section 44 established the Metropolitan Board of Works (MBW) as an inspection body that, among other things, had authority over places of public entertainment in the metropolis.

1878: 41 & 42 Vict., c. 32. Metropolitan Management and Building Acts Amendment Act, 1878. Amended the 1855 act and provided greater powers of inspection for the MBW. Sections 11 and 12 enlarged its powers regarding fire safety in theaters, certain music halls, and other places of public entertainment.

Dangerous Performances

1879: 42 & 43 Vict., c. 34. Children's Dangerous Performances Act. An Act to Regulate the Employment of Children in Places of Public Amusement in Certain Cases. The act applied to circuses, music halls, and "other places of public amusement." Section 3 specified that any child under the age of fourteen who had taken part in any public exhibition or performance dangerous to the life or limb of the child was protected. Any parent or guardian in violation was to be fined, the amount not to exceed ten pounds.

1897: 60 & 61 Vict., c. 52. Amendment to 1879 Children's Dangerous Performances Act. An Act to Extend the Age under which the Employment of Young Persons in Dangerous Performances is Prohibited. Clause 1 applied to any male under the age of sixteen and any female under the age of eighteen; clause 2 stated that except in the case of an accident causing bodily harm to any child or young person, no prosecution or other proceeding would be instituted without the consent of the chief of police in the police area where the offense was committed.

Prevention of Cruelty to Children Act

1889: 52 & 53 Vict., c. 44. An Act for the Prevention of Cruelty to, and better Protection of, Children. Section 1 stated that anyone who inflicted cruelty on boys under fourteen and girls under sixteen would be fined no more than one hundred pounds or, in default of payment or in addition to payment thereof, would be sentenced to no more than two years' imprisonment, with or without hard labor. Section 3, clause c, legislated that anyone who procured a child under the age of ten to perform in any street, in any premises licensed to sell drink, in premises licensed according to law for public entertainments, or *in any circus* or in any other place of public entertainment, if found guilty, was liable to pay a fine of twenty-five pounds or, in default of payment or in addition thereto, spend three months in prison, with or without hard labor.

1894: 57 & 58 Vict., c. 41. An Act to consolidate the Acts relating to the Prevention of Cruelty to, and Protection of, Children. Section 2, clause d, stated that any person who was not a guardian with a performing license or parent might be prosecuted for allowing a child *to train* as an acrobat, contortionist, or circus performer or for allowing a child to train for any exhibition or performance that was in its nature dangerous. This applied to boys and girls under the age of sixteen; the punishment was a fine not to exceed twenty-five pounds or, in default of payment or in addition thereto, no more than six months' imprisonment, with or without hard labor. Section 2, clause c, stated that no child under the age of eleven was to be permitted *to perform* in premises licensed according to the law for public entertainments, or *in any circus* or other place of public amusement, even with the parent's or guardian's permission; in other words, children could perform in circuses after the age of eleven, but they could not be trained for specialized fields, such as acrobatics, until they were sixteen. *But this did not apply to places in which children's performance licenses were granted by magistrates.*

1897: 60 & 61 Vic., c. 52. Amendment to 1894 Act for the Prevention of Cruelty to Children, An Act to Extend the Age under which the Employment of Young Persons in Dangerous Performances is Prohibited. See above.

Animals

1822: 3 Geo. 4, c. 71. Martin's Act. An Act to Prevent the Cruel and Improper Treatment of Cattle.

1835: 5 & 6 Will. 4, c. 59. Martin's Act. An Act to consolidate and amend several laws relating to the cruel and improper treatment of animals, and the mischiefs arising from the driving of cattle and to make other provisions in regard thereto. Revisions included bull-running, cockfighting, badger baiting, and other "wicked sports."

1839: 2 & 3 Vict., c. 47. Act for Further informing the Police in and Near the Metropolis. Empowered the Metropolitan Police to enter premises kept for the purpose of baiting or fighting animals and take all persons into custody, according to section 47.

1849: 12 & 13 Vict., c. 92. An Act for the more effectual Prevention of Cruelty to Animals. Section 2 stated that any person guilty of cruelly beating, ill-treating, abusing, or torturing any animal would be liable to pay £5. Section 3 stated that any person who managed any place for the purpose of fighting or baiting domestic or wild animals would be liable to a penalty not exceeding £5 for every day he ran such a place. Section 4 stated that if the damage to an animal was done by someone other than its owner, compensation of no more than ten pounds had to be paid. Section 5 made it illegal for any person to impound or confine or cause to be impounded or confined in any pound or receptacle any animal without provision of wholesome food and water for it. Any person who refused was liable to pay a fine of 20 shillings. Section 29 clarified that the word *animal* referred to any "horse, mare, gelding, bull, ox, cow, heifer, steer, calf, mule, ass, sheep, lamb, hog, pig, sow, goat, dog, cat, or any other domestic animal," thus leaving the treatment of wild animals to be dealt with more thoroughly later in the century. See the following entry.

1900: 63 & 64 Vict., c. 33. An Act for the Prevention of Cruelty to Wild Animals in Captivity. Section 1 stated that the term "animal is to mean any bird, beast, fish, or reptile which is not included in the 1849 Act." Section 2 declared that "any person shall be guilty of an offence who, whilst an animal is in captivity or close confinement, or is maimed, pinioned, or subjected to any appliance or contrivance for the purpose of hindering or preventing its escape from such captivity or confinement shall, by wantonly or unreasonably doing or omitting any act . . . cause or permit to be caused any unnecessary suffering to such animal; or cruelly abuse, infuriate, tease, or terrify it, or permit it to be so treated." Section 3 added that the fine for those acts would be no more than five pounds and that in default of payment, the punishment would be imprisonment, with or without hard labor.

Notes

Archival Abbreviations

BCL   Birmingham Central Library
BL   British Library
CFA   Circus Friends Association
EC   Earl's Court Exhibition Centre
FRC   Family Records Centre, London
ML   Minet Library, Lambeth Archives Department
NYPL New York Public Library, Lincoln Center
PRO   Public Record Office
RSPCA Royal Society for the Prevention of Cruelty to Animals
SLS   Southwark Local Studies Library
TM   Theatre Museum, London
TCC   Trinity College Library, Cambridge
TW   Tyne and Wear Archives, Newcastle

Introduction

1. Although the phrase *speaking to the eye* relates to the public's interest in the illustrated press, I use it here to indicate a wider cultural fascination with the visual. It comes from an article in the *Economist* that was reprinted in the *Illustrated London News*, 24 May 1851, 451–52, cited in Nead, *Victorian Babylon*, 57; for Nead's discussion of visual discourses in relation to the streets, see 57–62.

2. This theme relating to "fancy" runs throughout Dickens's works and is commented on by Dickens's readings manager (see Dolby, *Charles Dickens* [1885], 21 [the year of publication will be given for primary sources only]). See also Philip Collins, "Queen Mab's Chariot"; Schlicke, introduction to *Dickens and Popular Entertainment;* and Simpson, "*Hard Times* and Circus Times," 131. Cf. Leavis, *Great Tradition,* 256–57, where Leavis questions the accuracy with which Dickens depicts the circus in *Hard Times,* finding it more gaudy and sentimental than graceful and skillful. Although, as Leavis admits, such a critique misses Dickens's wider point about the circus on the margins of industrial society, historically speaking Leavis is right: the circus did rely on skill).

3. On theatricality and nineteenth-century spectatorship, especially in London,

see Bailey, *Popular Culture and Performance*, esp. the introduction; Winter, *London's Teeming Streets;* Epstein Nord, "City as Theatre"; Altick, *Shows of London;* and Michael R. Booth, "The Metropolis on Stage," in Dyos and Wolff, *Victorian City*, vol. 1. For an example relating to France, see Schwartz, *Spectacular Realities*, which treats the relationship between urban experience and modern life through visual representation.

4. On freak shows, see, e.g., Bogdan, *Freak Show;* Altick, *Shows of London;* and Thomson, *Freakery*.

5. Dickens, *Hard Times* ([1854] 1966), 8.

6. See Cunningham, *Leisure in the Industrial Revolution;* and in agreement with this thesis, Golby and Purdue, *Civilisation of the Crowd*, esp. ch. 3.

7. Unless otherwise indicated, I use the term *manager* to imply owner (since owners were often managers and *vice versa*).

8. On these changes, see Walvin, *Leisure and Society*, 63; Cunningham, *Leisure in the Industrial Revolution*, 13–14; and Best, *Mid-Victorian Britain*, 137–40. For a historiographical overview of these and other writings on leisure, see Bailey, "Politics and Poetics," 132.

9. For more on changes to the circus program, see Assael, "Circus and Respectable Society," ch. 1.

10. See Speaight, *History of the Circus*. Although the view of when the modern circus was born has been revised, see Kwint, "Astley's Amphitheatre," 16.

11. See Dibdin, *Memoirs*, 34. These amphitheaters included Ryle's Ride in Bath (1772), Jones's in Dublin (1785), Swann's Amphitheatre in Birmingham (1787), the Circus in Edinburgh (1788), Astley's Equestrian Theatre Royal in Dublin (1788), the Circus Riding School in Bristol (1792), the New Circus in Manchester (1793), and the Olympic Circus in Liverpool (1798) (see Kwint, "Astley's Amphitheatre," fig. 1.4).

12. Kwint, "Astley's Amphitheatre," 26, 36.

13. Thomas Frost, *Circus Life* (1875), 52, 68 (quotation), 64, 68–69.

14. Grant, *Great Metropolis* (1836, reprint, 1838), 1:71. Grant noted that the "extraordinary feats of horsemanship are performed within the ring, and the imposing spectacles exhibited on the stage" (72).

15. Poster for *The Battle of Waterloo*, 22 April 1824, London III, Astley's, Playbills, 171, no. 68, BL. On this production, see Saxon, *Enter Foot and Horse*, 140; and on the duration of production runs, see Stephens, *Profession of the Playwright*, 185.

16. Clipping, 28 August 1854, Astley's Files, Mander and Mitchenson Collection.

17. Kwint, "Legitimization of the Circus," 109.

18. Ibid. The prices for the gallery and upper gallery appear on posters from the period.

19. Lynch, *Box, Pit, and Gallery*, 200. The notice "no remuneration to place-keepers required" appears on Astley's posters from the period. In other theaters, and possibly in Astley's as well, the patron's servant was invited to hold his employer's place in the theater. On traders and libraries, see, e.g., poster, Astley's, 13 December 1847, Poster Collection, Illinois State University, Normal, Milner Library.

20. Jim Davis and Emeljanow, *Reflecting the Audience,* 8, 12–13. See also clipping, "Astley's," ca. 1825, 944/747, Fenwick Collection, TW.

21. Edward Dutton Cook, *Book of the Play* (1876), 2:189–90.

22. See, e.g., Golby and Purdue, *Civilisation of the Crowd,* 82–83. Cf. Howkins, "Whitsun in Nineteenth Century Oxfordshire"; and Douglas A. Reid, "Interpreting," in Storch, *Popular Culture and Custom,* 125–53.

23. Walvin, *Leisure and Society,* 116. For more on fairs' institutional legitimacy, see Cunningham, *Leisure in the Industrial Revolution,* 174; and Stallybrass and White, *Politics and Poetics of Transgression,* 34.

24. "The Three Ring Business," *Era,* 13 January 1894, 13.

25. Thomas Frost, *Circus Life* (1875), 79.

26. Gresswell, *Bright Boots* (1956), 28. Fred Gresswell was born in the early 1890s.

27. Cf. Peter Bailey, "Custom, Capital, and Culture in the Victorian Music Hall," in Storch, *Popular Culture and Custom;* Cunningham, *Leisure in the Industrial Revolution;* Benson, *Penny Capitalists,* ch. 7.

28. Goffman, *Presentation of Self,* esp. ch. 1. See also Roy Porter, "History of the Body," 211.

29. See Georg Simmel, "Freedom and the Individual," in Simmel, *On Individuality and Social Forms,* 222, first published as "Das Individuum und die Freiheit," in *Brücke und Tür,* ed. Michael Landmann and Margarete Susman (Stuttgart: Koehler, 1957).

30. This arrangement compares with that in the music hall (see, e.g., Peter Bailey, "A Community of Friends: Business and Good Fellowship in London Music Hall Management, c. 1860–1885," in Bailey, *Music Hall*).

31. Typical of this trend are Speaight, *History of the Circus;* Saxon, *Enter Foot and Horse;* and Coxe, *A Seat.*

32. Kwint, "Astley's Amphitheatre"; idem, "Legitimization of the Circus."

33. See, e.g., Walvin, *Leisure and Society,* 57, 114–15; and Cunningham, *Leisure in the Industrial Revolution,* 32–35, 173–75. For a wider discussion on the industrial/rural dichotomy, see Griffin, "Popular Culture in Industrializing England," 623.

34. On this point and new directions, see Bailey, "Politics and Poetics," 146, 150–60.

35. See Stallybrass and White, *Politics and Poetics of Transgression,* 3–4.

36. Bakhtin, *Rabelais and His World.* Writing in Stalinist Russia in the 1930s, Bakhtin advanced an idea that was particularly poignant. After the war, he had to "defend" his dissertation before the State Commission on Degrees. This was not a formal academic exercise, as Michael Holquist has observed (ibid., xx). It was not published in Russia until 1965.

37. Natalie Zemon Davis, *Society and Culture,* 103.

38. Bakhtin, *Rabelais and His World,* 33.

39. See Philip Collins, "Dickens and Popular Amusements," 16.

40. Bakhtin, *Rabelais and His World,* 19. For a discussion of what Bakhtin meant

by "grotesque realism," see Stallybrass and White, *Politics and Poetics of Transgression,* 8–9.

41. Bakhtin, *Rabelais and His World,* 19.

42. See, e.g., Donajgrodski, *Social Control;* and Malcolmson, *Popular Recreations.*

43. See Hoggart, *Uses of Literacy,* for an important example of a literary subgenre in this field.

44. Gareth Stedman Jones, "Class Expression versus Social Control?" *Languages of Class,* 88.

45. For an analysis of the complex cultural interconnections between high and low, see Levine, *High Brow/Low Brow.*

46. Ibid.; Stallybrass and White, *Politics and Poetics of Transgression,* 19.

47. Interdisciplinary studies on the artist as spectacle or the object of the gaze include Debord, *Society of Spectacle;* Bailey, "Parasexuality and Glamour"; Mulvey, "Visual Pleasures and Narrative Cinema"; Schwartz, *Spectacular Realities;* and Thomson, *Freakery.*

48. On cultural ordering and understanding, see Thomson, "Narratives of Deviance and Delight," 89; and Foucault, *Order of Things,* ch. 5.

49. See Elias and Dunning, *Quest for Excitement,* 81–84.

50. On the question of looking and feeling, see Halttunen, "Humanitarianism and the Pornography of Pain." See also Mulvey, "Visual Pleasures and Narrative Cinema"; Walkowitz, *City of Dreadful Delight;* Radway, "Reception Study"; and Gledhill, "Pleasurable Negotiations," in Storey, *Cultural Theory and Popular Culture.* The area of film studies has been vital in advancing reception studies; see, e.g., Stacey, *Star Gazing,* and Gamman and Marshment, *Female Gaze.*

51. An early and influential historical study of the pluralized self is Bailey, "Will the Real Bill Banks Please Stand Up?"

52. On individualism, subjectivity, and the modern condition to which my discussion relates, see Georg Simmel, "The Metropolis and Mental Life," in Simmel, *On Individuality and Social Forms,* 324–39, first published as "Die Grosstadt und das Geistesleben" in *Die Grosstadt, Jahrbuch der Gehe-Stiftung* 9 (1903); see also Debord, *Society of Spectacle.*

53. Thomson, "Narratives of Deviance and Delight," 82.

54. The playwright and theoretician Bertolt Brecht resisted the idea of a fixed perceptive process and instead believed in the ideological basis of the viewer and that of the play, which were not necessarily in agreement. This interaction constituted performance, which Brecht believed was always ideologically situated (see Bennett, *Theatre Audiences,* 30; and Stuart Hall, "Spectacle of the 'Other'").

55. See Canetti, *Crowds and Power,* 27–28.

56. See Turner, *Forest of Symbols,* 45–47.

57. Pace Burn, *Age of Equipoise.*

58. Cunningham, *Leisure in the Industrial Revolution,* 187.

59. See also my article about divided Liberal attitudes towards street musicians in London in the 1860s, "Music in the Air."

60. On social exploration into "unknown lands," particularly those conducted by Henry Mayhew, see, e.g., Humphrys, *Travels into the Poor Man's Country;* Keating, *Into Unknown England;* E. P. Thompson, "Mayhew and the *Morning Chronicle,*" in Thompson and Yeo, *Unknown Mayhew;* and Gareth Stedman Jones, "Labours of Henry Mayhew."

61. Henry Mayhew, *London Labour* (1861), 90–151.

62. On the spread of disease by gypsies, see Behlmer, "Gypsy Problem"; and Mayall, *Gypsy Travellers in Nineteenth Century Society.*

63. On the closure of the fair, see Howkins, "Whitsun in Nineteenth Century Oxfordshire"; and Malcolmson, *Popular Recreations.* For a different chronological and geographical treatment of the problem, see Stanley Cohen, *Folk Devils and Moral Panics.*

64. On bourgeois hysteria in response to the carnivalesque, see Stallybrass and White, *Politics and Poetics of Transgression,* ch. 5.

65. See Hall, "Spectacle of the 'Other,'" 236.

66. See Cannadine, "Context, Performance, and Meaning."

67. Bakhtin, *Rabelais and His World,* 11; Natalie Zemon Davis, *Society and Culture,* 103. For another interpretation of a second or double life, see Schama, "Unruly Realm."

1. The Rise of the Victorian Circus

1. William Henry Cooke to Caroline Heginbotham, 7 May 1857, William Cooke Papers, iv 157/1, ML.

2. Heginbotham to Cooke, 21 May 1857, ibid.

3. Ibid.

4. Ibid.

5. Cooke to Heginbotham, 22 May 1857, ibid.

6. Caroline's father, Charles, was the keeper of the British Hotel, at 27 Cockspur Street in Charing Cross, according to the *Census Return for England and Wales,* 1851, St. Martin in the Fields, HO 107/1481/27, Family Records Centre, London (FRC). According to the *Post Office London Directory for 1855,* he also ran the European Coffee House, at 2 Mansion House in the City. Two years later it lists him as running the Corn Exchange Tavern, in Mark Lane in the City, a business he passed on to his son, Charles, according to the *Census Return for England and Wales,* 1861, East London, RG 9/226/96, FRC. Given that her father is nowhere mentioned in the letters, he must have died before the engagement.

7. Cooke to Heginbotham, 19 May 1857, William Cooke Papers, iv 157/1, ML.

8. Ibid.; "William Cooke's Celebrated Equestrian Provincial Company from Astleys," *Era,* 10 May 1857, 1; "Cooke's Circus," *Peterborough Weekly News and General Advertiser,* 30 May 1857, 6.

9. Cooke to Heginbotham, 11 June 1857, William Cooke Papers, iv 157/1, ML.

10. Cooke to Heginbotham, 22 May 1857.

11. Ibid.

12. Hunt, *Life Story* (1936), 13.

13. Charles W. Montague, "Recollections of an Equestrian Manager," *Chambers's Journal*, 24 January 1880, 51.

14. Jones, *Unfinished Journey* (1937), 51.

15. Timbs, *Curiosities of London* (1855, reprint, 1868), 13. Typical of the crossover between street and stage, Wildman, the bee exhibitor, displayed his feats at Astley's circus as well in this year (clipping 65, 1772, Astley's Scrapbooks, vol. 1, Th.Cts. 35, BL).

16. Pepys, *Diary*, vol. 9, *1668–69* (1971, reprint, 2000), 293.

17. See David Bindman, *Hogarth*, 88–89.

18. "Bartholomew Fair," 1833, C 26.5–26.51, Noble Collection, Guildhall Library, Corporation of London.

19. Ibid.

20. Ibid.

21. "A Peep at Bartholomew Fair," ca. 1841, ibid.

22. Charles Mackie, "December 1809," *Norfolk Annals* (1901), 1:78.

23. Poster, Lloyd's Circus, 3 August 1822, Noble Collection, Guildhall Library, Corporation of London.

24. Poster, Messrs. O. Brown and Chaff, Bell Street, Marylebone, 1831, A. H. Coxe Collection (Blythe House, Olympia), TM.

25. Clipping, Cattle Market, Canterbury, 7 August 1838, Circus Scrapbooks, vol. 1, Th.Cts. 50, BL.

26. Cunningham, *Leisure in the Industrial Revolution*, 25.

27. Quoted from Esquiros, *English at Home* (1861), 1:347.

28. See, e.g., City solicitors, "Report of the Markets' Committee Relative to Bartholomew Fair," 2 July 1840, Noble Collection, Guildhall Library, Corporation of London.

29. See Assael, "Music in the Air"; see also Griffin, "Sports and Celebrations," which takes a different line on this.

30. These figures are based on a decennial sample collected from the *Era* for the 1847–48 to 1897–98 seasons. For each year the figures are for the period from October to October, corresponding with the end of the tenting season or the start of the winter, or residency, season. These data are for only those companies that called themselves circuses or equestrian companies.

31. "Genealogical Table of the Cookes," *Sawdust Ring* 3, no. 8 (1936): 22.

32. See above, n. 30; see also Assael, "Circus and Respectable Society," appendix tables A1 and A2.

33. *Confessions of a Dancing Girl* (1913), 58. The author trained as an acrobat before becoming a dancer.

34. The percentage is based on hard figures I have for tenting alone and tenting combined with residency during the summer season. But it does not take into account unknown or bankrupt troupes. Even so, there is no reason to suspect a deviation from the general pattern. The percentage of troupes that spent time on the road during the

summer was 61 percent in 1867–68, 50 percent in 1877–78, 30 percent in 1887–88, and 23 percent in 1897–98.

35. Although my sample covers some of these circuses (like Henry Cooke's), not all companies that split into two were reported in the *Era*. Memoirs give some impression of this pattern of division (see Paterson, *Behind the Scenes* [1859], 98).

36. "Wakefield," *Era*, 16 December 1860, 12.

37. "Theatrical and Concert Halls in the North of England," ibid., 16 September 1866, 14.

38. See *Era*, 1850–70. I have counted the number of amphitheaters, as well as companies, detailed above. It should be noted that whether these buildings were semipermanent or permanent structures is often difficult to discern.

39. Patent 753, C. H. Keith, 16 February 1882, in Rees and Wilmore, *British Theatrical Patents*, 48.

40. "Southport," *Era*, 6 January 1878, 18.

41. Bailey, *Music Hall*, x.

42. "List of Fires," *Era Almanac*, 1868, 48–49.

43. "Great Fire at Portsmouth," *Era*, 10 March 1861, 12.

44. "Fall of a Gallery at Hengler's Circus, Sheffield," *Sheffield Daily Telegraph*, 22 October 1872, 7; "The Accident at Hengler's Circus," ibid., 23 October 1872, 3; *Census Return for England and Wales*, 1871, Sheffield, RG 10/4681, 53; RG 10/4684, 59, 62; RG 10/4689, 53; RG 10/4676, 98; RG 10/4678, 56, FRC.

45. "Accident at Hengler's Circus," *Sheffield Daily Telegraph*, 23 October 1872, 3.

46. "The Fatal Accident at Hengler's Circus," *Sheffield and Rotherham Independent*, 28 November 1872, 3.

47. Cf. Bailey, *Leisure and Class in Victorian England*, 156.

48. See Metropolis Management and Building Acts Amendment, 1878, 41 & 42 Vict., c. 32, esp. clauses 11 and 12. The concern about fire was particularly acute after the widely publicized Brooklyn Theater disaster two years earlier, in which nearly three hundred persons had died. A parliamentary paper was produced on the subject and followed by a Select Committee report on the Metropolitan Fire Brigade that reinvited questions already raised in Parliament and with the Lord Chamberlain about the degree to which London theaters were vulnerable to such accidents, but the emphasis was clearly metropolitan and focused on theaters, Astley's included, though there was a trickle-down effect for provincial amphitheaters (see Parliamentary Papers [hereafter cited as PP], *Papers Relating to the Burning Down of the Brooklyn Theatre*, 1877, vol. 68; PP, *Select Committee on Constitution, Efficiency, Emoluments and Finances of Metropolitan Fire Brigade*, 1877, vol. 14; and PRO, LC/7/16, Memoranda from the Lord Chamberlain's office, 21, 23 December 1876. See also PP, *Hansard Parliamentary Debates*, 3d ser., 1877, vol. 232, cols. 128–29). There was, to be sure, much confusion about the MBW's and the Lord Chamberlain's regulatory roles (PRO, LC/7/25, 15, 22 September 1879; see also Assael, "Circus and Respectable Society," 89–91). For George Sanger's lament over Astley's loss, see Sanger, *Seventy Years a Showman* ([1908] 1966), 164.

49. See above, n. 44.

50. See above, n. 30. These figures were derived by multiplying the number of weeks each company performed in the town by six (since most troupes performed on every day of the week but Sunday) and then multiplying this figure by two (since most troupes performed during the afternoon and evening) (see reviews titled "Manchester" in *Era,* 1847–48 to 1857–58).

51. See Bailey, *Music Hall,* x.

52. "Newsome's Circus," *Carlisle Examiner,* 27 January 1866, 3.

53. "The Circus and Ourselves," ibid., 3 February 1866, 3.

54. Keith, *Circus Life and Amusements* (1879), 40.

55. "Hyde," *Era,* 29 January 1898, 23, brackets in the original.

56. "Hyde," ibid., 5 February 1898, 21.

57. See, e.g., the reviews entitled "Hyde" in the *Era* on the following dates: 12 February 1898, 21; 19 February 1898, 25; 5 March 1898, 22; 12 March 1898, 26; 26 March 1898, 22; 2 April 1989, 26; 9 April 1898, 24; 16 April 1898, 22; 23 April 1898, 26; 30 April 1898, 22; 7 May 1898, 23; 14 May 1898, 23.

58. See the following reviews in the *Era:* "Sunderland," 2 June 1878, 7; "Lincoln," 9 June 1878, 8; "Nottingham," 30 June 1878, 9; "Southport," 4 August 1878, 7, and 11 August 1878, 7; "Guernsey," 18 August 1878, 6, 25 August 1878, 7, 1 September 1878, 7, 8 September 1878, 7; and "Scarborough," 22 September 1878, 8, 29 September 1878, 9, 6 October 1878, 9, 13 October 1878, 8, 20 October 1878, 8. His engagements with each troupe might have been longer than suggested here since it is possible that the *Era* did not report on every detail about their length.

59. "Southport," ibid., 4 August 1878, 7, and 11 August 1878, 7.

60. "Wanted," ibid., 15 September 1878, 19.

61. *Era,* 3 October 1858, 1.

62. "Picco Notice," ibid., 14 June 1857, 10; see also "Picco, the Blind Minstrel," ibid., 10 August 1856, 10. While Gay claimed that there was a binding contract between him and Picco, the court ruled that "Picco could not be compelled" to consent to it "for he was no party" initially to the said contract. Although it was not mentioned in the press report, whether the Italian-speaking minstrel understood the terms of the agreement may have played a role in the outcome of the case.

63. "General Dramatic, Equestrian, and Musical Agency," ibid., 22 July 1855, 1.

64. *Dramatic, Equestrian, and Musical Sick Fund Association Almanac,* 1857; "General Dramatic, Equestrian, and Musical Agency and Sick Fund Association," *Era,* 13 July 1856, 10. See also Crossick, *Artisan Elite in Victorian Society,* 176. Nothing was said in the *Almanac* about different fees for men and women.

65. "Inauguration of the Burial Ground of the Dramatic, Equestrian, and Musical Sick Fund in the Necropolis Cemetery at Woking," *Era,* 13 June 1858, 11. For more on the burial plan, see Assael, "Circus and Respectable Society," 121–23.

66. See, e.g., *Era,* 12 October 1856, 1.

67. Keith, *Circus Life and Amusements* (1879), 140.

68. Stub for £2 2s., General Dramatic, Equestrian, and Musical Agency and Sick

Fund Association, dated 30 March 1859, signed by John W. Anson, William Cooke Papers, iv 157/8, ML.

69. According to her diary, she rode three times that season (see Caroline Cooke's 1858 diary, first week in January, ibid., iv 157/6, ML).

70. The figures are based on a sample collected from the *Dramatic, Equestrian, and Musical Sick Fund Association Almanac,* 1858, 1859, 1862, 1863, 1864, 1867. See also Assael, "Circus and Respectable Society," table 3.2.

71. Salary list, Cooke's circus, Portsmouth, 1861, Company Files, TM; Henry Mayhew, *London Labour* (1861), 144.

72. Salary list, Royal Surrey Theatre, 6 October 1861, Surrey Theatre Files, SLS.

73. James B. Jeffreys, *Story of the Engineers* (1946), 121–44, cited in Robert Q. Gray, *Aristocracy of Labour,* 51.

74. Mitchell and Deane, *Abstract of British Historical Statistics,* 472–73. The Rousseau price index stood at 115 in 1861 but only 84 in 1899.

75. "The Equestrienne and Her Trick Act," *Era,* 1 July 1893, 16.

76. Ibid. Cf. salary list, Cooke's circus, Portsmouth, 1861, Company Files, TM.

77. Mitchell and Deane, *Abstract of British Historical Statistics,* 472–73. The index for 1893 was 82.

78. "Scene in a Salford Circus," *Era,* 4 November 1893, 16.

79. *Confessions of a Dancing Girl* (1913), 58–59.

80. Salary list, Cooke's circus, Portsmouth, 1861, Company Files, TM.

81. Caroline Cooke's 1858 diary, second week of January, William Cooke Papers, iv 157/6, ML.

82. "Hull," *Era,* 28 June 1857, 11.

83. Peter Paterson, "Town and Country Circus Life," *All the Year Round,* 16 November 1861, 186.

84. "William Cooke, Junior," *Era,* 20 April 1862, 12.

85. Printed card of William Cooke [ca. 1850s], Astley's Royal Amphitheatre and National Riding School, William Cooke Papers, iv 157/7/2, ML.

86. See above, n. 30; see also Assael, "Circus and Respectable Society," table 2.5.

87. Tower of Varieties and Circus, Birmingham, employment contract, n.d., to commence on 9 October 1899, box RP 76/1549, A. H. Coxe Collection (Blythe House, Olympia), TM. Other circuses also adopted this policy; see, e.g., Barnum and Bailey Circus, employment contract for Alfred Clarke Jr., bareback rider, 8 September 1897, ibid.

88. Alhambra Blackpool Ltd., employment contract, 24 January 1899, ibid.

89. Barnum and Bailey Circus, employment contract for Alfred Clarke Jr., bareback rider, 8 September 1897, ibid.; Barnum and Bailey's circus, program, April–November 1898 season, Barnum Files, EC; Watkins, "Barnum and Bailey in the World," 19, ibid.

90. "Barnum and Bailey in Nottingham," *Nottingham Daily Express,* 10 June 1898, 8.

91. Barnum and Bailey Circus, employment contract for Alfred Clarke Jr., bare-

back rider, 8 September 1897, box RP 76/1549, A. H. Coxe Collection (Blythe House, Olympia), TM.

92. Watkins, *Four Years in Europe* (1901); On the demands of touring with British troupes, including gritty details, see Paterson, "Town and Country Circus Life," *All the Year Round,* 16 November 1861, 181–86; idem, *Behind the Scenes* (1859), 10–14, 76–77, 93–94, 98–101; idem, *Glimpses of Real Life* (1864), 195; Ballantine, *Life of David Roberts, R.A.* (1866), 7; Keith, *Circus Life and Amusements* (1879), 27–29, 32, 43, 49; and John Morrison, "Poet, Musician, and Traveling Showman," *Caledonia,* January–February 1895, 69–75, 164–71.

93. See, e.g., Barnum and Bailey Circus, employment contract for Alfred Clarke Jr., bareback rider, 8 September 1897, rule 13, box RP 76/1549, A. H. Coxe Collection (Blythe House, Olympia), TM.

94. "Barnum and Bailey," *Record,* 25 October 1898, 3.

95. Dickens, *Hard Times* ([1854] 1966), 32.

96. PP, *Select Committee on Regulation of Public Houses, Hotels, Beershops, Dancing Saloons, Coffee Houses, Theatres and Places of Public Entertainment,* 1852–53, vol. 37, p. 372, line 6408.

97. "Mr. Newsome's Circus," *Era,* 15 October 1865, 11. The paper mistakenly referred to Madame Newsome's circus as Mr. Newsome's.

98. "Complimentary Dinner to the Brothers Cooke," ibid., 3 February 1878, 7.

99. Theatre Regulation Act, 1843, 6 & 7 Vict., c. 68, sec. 23.

100. Astley's Amphitheatre was an exception since it held a stage play license from the Lord Chamberlain from 1843 (see ch. 2).

101. See below, ch. 4, n. 18; and Theatre Regulation Act, 1843, 6 & 7 Vict., c. 68, sec. 23. For examples of these nervous applications and theatrical jealousies, see "Circuses and Dramatic Licenses," *Era,* 3 December 1892, 12, and other cases in n. 102 below.

102. Theatre Regulation Act, 1843, 6 & 7 Vict., c. 68, sec. 11. A cursory glance through the entertainment section of the provincial and national papers in this period reveals numerous legal cases against unlicensed circuses by licensed ones and theaters. See, e.g., "Information against the Proprietor of Hengler's Circus," *Era,* 14 April 1861, 11, concerning a case in Sheffield, a continuing problem spot for unlicensed circuses. See also "Traveling Theatre," ibid., 16 November 1862, 6, concerning a portable theater covered by canvas; "Theatre versus the Circus," ibid., 4 January 1863, 5; "Charge of Performing a Pantomime without a Licence," ibid., 13; "The Theatre versus the Circus," *Stockton Herald, South Durham and Cleveland Advertiser,* 27 January 1865, 3; and "Stockton: Alleged Infringement of Act Relating to Stage Plays," *Darlington Telegraph,* 28 January 1865, 2. On legal definitions of pantomime, see "The Case against the Alhambra," *Era,* 15 January 1865, 14. For further cases relating to the circus, all in the *Era,* see "Performing Stage Plays without a License," 28 March 1869, 13; "April—Powell's Circus," 2 January 1870, 2; "What Is a Stage Play?" 29 January 1871, 12; "Important Circus Case," 18 June 1892, 15; and "Stage Play at Circuses," 17 December 1892, 12. It is significant that many of these cases were brought to court

during the Christmas season, extending to January, when both the circus and the theater commonly presented pantomimes. The decisions in these cases were mixed; some were dismissed due to lack of proof regarding what actually took place in the performance. See also Assael, "Circus and Respectable Society," 82–86.

103. Quarterly minutes, Newcastle Town Council, 589/35, 5 August 1868, 371, Newcastle Common Council Minutes, TW.

104. Ibid., 6 September 1876, 349–54.

105. Town Improvement Committee Minutes, Newcastle, 589/517, 12 June 1878, 185, TW.

106. "Newcastle upon Tyne," *Era,* 23 February 1879, 9, and 16 March 1879, 18. According to an announcement in the *Era* the following month, the amphitheater was to reopen after Easter under different management, indicating that the Cookes' troupe had left (see "Newcastle upon Tyne," ibid., 14 April 1879, 18).

107. On complaints against street entertainers, see Assael, "Music in the Air."

108. See correspondence between the Home Office and local vestries and police divisions dealing with complaints, e.g., PRO, HO A33890/12, 22 February 1884; HO A33890/14, 2, 3 March 1884; HO A33890/4, 11 March 1884; HO A33890/23, 5 May 1884; HO 45 A33890/31, 22 February, 1 March 1889; HO 45 A33890/30, 28 March 1889; HO 45 A33890/25, 6 November 1889.

109. PRO, HO 45 A33890/14, T Division Special Report, 2 March 1884.

110. Ibid.; quotation from PRO, HO 45 A33890/14, G Division (Finsbury), 2 March 1884.

111. PRO, HO 45 A33890/14, G Division (Finsbury), 2 March 1884.

112. PRO, HO 45 A33890/23a, 20 May 1889.

113. See, e.g., PRO, HO 45 6453/1, correspondence between the Home Office and the Metropolitan Police, 13 March 1857; HO 45 6453/4, 27 March 1857; and HO 45 6453/6, 8 April 1857.

114. "Van Dwellers' Association," *Era,* 30 January 1892, 17.

115. PP, *Select Committee on Temporary Dwellings Bill,* 1887, vol. 13, p. 4, line 48.

116. *Census Return for England and Wales,* 1861, Manchester, RG 9/2943, 114, FRC. The Sangers' Manchester amphitheater on Portland Street was recorded as a fixed site in a report in the *Era,* 27 January 1861, 3.

117. *Census Return for England and Wales,* 1861, Liverpool, RG 9/2671, 70, FRC. We know, based on newspaper reports, that Hengler's company performed in a permanent structure (see, e.g., "Liverpool," *Era,* 20 October 1861, 11, in which it is mentioned that improvements were made to the building from the previous season).

118. *Census Return for England and Wales,* 1871, Crewkerne, RG 10/2407, 26, 29, 31, 36, 68b, 69b, 70, FRC.

119. See Assael, "Circus and Respectable Society," 130–32.

120. "Van Dwellers' Association," *Era,* 27 January 1894, 7, and 26 January 1895, 20.

121. "Van Dwellers' Association," ibid., 21 January 1893, 18; 28 January 1893, 8; 4 February 1893, 15; 27 January 1894, 7.

122. Cooke to Heginbotham, 28 May 1857, William Cooke Papers, iv 157/1, ML.

123. "Cooke's Circus," *Peterborough Weekly News and General Advertiser*, 30 May 1857, 6.

2. *The Spectacular Hero*

1. Linda Colley has pointed to an absence in the historiography of cultural representations of British national identity (see Colley, *Britons*, 8).

2. J. S. Bratton, "British Heroism," in Bratton, Cave, and Pickering, *Acts of Supremacy*, 22–23.

3. This estimate is based on titles referring to the Napoleonic Wars in Nicoll, *History of English Drama*, 4, pt. 2, "A Hand List of Plays, 1800–1850."

4. Colley, "Whose Nation?" 109; idem *Britons*, 304. For a discussion of plays with nationalist themes in the Georgian theater, see Gillian Russell, *Theatres of War*, introduction.

5. For Lord Acton's phrase, see Bann, *Romanticism*, xi. On "historical-mindedness," see Semmel, "Reading the Tangible Past."

6. On the popularity of the heroic image in art, see Hichberger, *Images of the Army*, 6. There is evidence that females participated in this cult of heroism as well (see Colley, *Britons*, 272–73).

7. Yarrington, *Commemoration of the Hero*, x–xii.

8. Cannadine, "Context, Performance, and Meaning," 116.

9. Lin, "Extending Her Arms," 5. Although the navy is outside the scope of this discussion, nautical dramas like *The Battle of Trafalgar* also commanded popular audiences in theaters and some circuses (see, e.g., Jim Davis, "British Bravery").

10. See Jordan and Rogers, "Admirals as Heroes," 201.

11. Historians like E. P. Thompson, according to Geoffrey Best (see Best, review of *The Making of the English Working Class*, 278; and, in response, E. P. Thompson, *Making of the English Working Class* [reprint, 1980], 916). On the romantic radical hero, see Belchem and Epstein, "Nineteenth Century Gentleman Revisited"; and Gareth Stedman Jones, *Outcast London*, 77. See also the corrective offered by Colley, "Radical Patriotism in 18th Century England," in Samuel, *Patriotism*, vol. 1; and by Cunningham, "Language of Patriotism").

12. But while Northrop Frye has argued that myths are "very seldom located in history," those represented in the circus clearly were (see Frye, "Myth, Fiction, and Displacement," 31; and Behrendt, *History and Myth*, 18–19, 26).

13. Henry Barton Baker, *London Stage* ([1889] 1904), 385. According to Baker, Astley had no fewer than nineteen amphitheaters.

14. On military pageantry as entertainment and for some reflections on equestrian entertainment, see Myerly, *British Military Spectacle*, 139, 144.

15. Henry Barton Baker, *London Stage* ([1889] 1904), 389.

16. Clipping 217, 7 October 1781, Astley's Scrapbooks, vol. 1, Th.Cts. 35, BL.

17. Clipping 1129, 27 August 1789, and P. Astley to Mr. Pownal, 4 December 1786, both in ibid.

18. See Astley, *Description and Historical Account* (1794); and idem, *Remarks on the Profession* (1794).

19. See Derek Forbes, "Water Drama," in Bradby, James, and Sharralt, *Performance and Politics in Popular Drama*, 91–108, on the impact of these spectacles on minor theaters like Sadler's Wells. However, the patent theaters, such as Drury Lane, did not respond to the trend until the 1820s, when the manager Robert Elliston employed Andrew Ducrow, Astley's most well known horseman (see Saxon, *Enter Foot and Horse*, ch. 4. For later examples, see poster, Cooke's, Great Windmill Street, Haymarket, 1831, Circus Scrapbooks, vol. 1, Th.Cts. 50, BL).

20. See, e.g., poster, 1841, Bridges's Circus Royal, East Redford (featuring scenes from the "The Lilliputan Buonaparte"), Circus Scrapbooks, vol. 1, Th.Cts. 50, BL; and poster, Cooke's, 1844, Glasgow Green (featuring the "Life of Napoleon," in six scenes), ibid. Later, William Cooke's traveling circus presented an incident from *The Battle of Waterloo* (see *Portsmouth and Naval Gazette*, 20 July 1850, 5). For a discussion on *tableaux vivants*, see Meisel, *Realizations*, 47.

21. Grant, *Great Metropolis* (1836, reprint, 1838), 1:71.

22. Ibid., 1:72.

23. Philippe Bordes, "Representation of the Hero," in Delon, *Encyclopedia of the Enlightenment*, 1:645; Adam Ferguson, *Essay on the History of Civil Society* (1767, ed. 1995), 28. See also Ferguson, *Essay on the History of Civil Society*, in Ashfield and de Bolla, *Sublime*, 253–61.

24. Ferguson, *Essay on the History of Civil Society* (1767, ed. 1995), 29.

25. Dechamps, "Les défenseurs de Napoléon," 27–28.

26. See Eric C. Walker, "Wordsworth, Wellington, and Myth," in Behrendt, *History and Myth*, 109.

27. Colley, *Britons*, 298–99.

28. Colley, *Captives*, 344–46.

29. On the founding of these institutions during the wars, see Lin, "Extending Her Arms," esp. ch. 3.

30. Colley, "Whose Nation?" 114.

31. Carlyle, *Past and Present* (1843, reprint, 1902), 236.

32. Carlyle, *On Heroes* (1841, reprint, 1908), 222.

33. A bill to increase military expenditure passed in 1852 was proof of the widespread "panic" over invasion (see Spiers, *Army and Society*, 76, 91).

34. Of course, there were several wars of expansion in this period: in Nepal (1814–16), in India (the First Mysore War, 1766–69; the Second Mysore War, 1780–84; the Third Mysore War, 1789–92; the Fourth Mysore War, 1799; the First Maratha War, 1779–82; the Second Maratha War, 1803–5; the Third Maratha War, 1817–18), and in Burma (the First Burmese War, 1823–26).

35. On Benjamin West and his protégés, see Abrams, *Valiant Hero*, 202; on the relationship between high art and patriotic reverence for officer heroes, see Colley, *Britons*, 194–95.

36. Greig, *The Farrington Diary*, 4:155, cited in Abrams, *Valiant Hero*, 206.

37. Hichberger, *Images of the Army*, 26. See also *Dictionary of National Biography* (1887), s.v. "Abraham Cooper"; "Abraham Cooper," in Mitchell, *Dictionary of British Equestrian Artists*, 165; and Guy Paget, "Abraham Cooper, R.A., 1787–1868," *Apollo*, September 1949, 78.

38. On the relationship between panorama and historical paintings, see Altick, *Shows of London*, esp. 136–62, 174–83, 188–97. On the panorama's increasing popularity, see Booth, *Victorian Spectacular Theatre*, 5–6; and Joss Marsh, "Spectacle," in Tucker, *Companion to Victorian Literature and Culture*, 279.

39. Abrams, *Valiant Hero*, 139, 225n30, 192. On Carver, see Laffan, *Sublime and the Beautiful in Irish Art*, 94–95; and for more on this artistic cross-fertilization, see Altick, *Shows of London*, 184–85.

40. For instance, the landscape painter David Cox was a principal scene painter in Birmingham and later at other theaters, including Astley's (see Booth, *Victorian Spectacular Theatre*, 9–12). For a more detailed discussion of the relationship between the Royal Academy and stage painting, see Altick, *Shows of London*, 195.

41. Thomas Smith, *Recollections of the British Institution for Promoting the Fine Arts* (1860), 73.

42. J. E. Marston, *The Life and Campaigns of Field-Marshal Prince Blucher of Wahlstatt* (1815), cited in Hichberger, *Images of the Army*, 27.

43. *Examiner*, 25 February 1816, 124–25, cited in Hichberger, *Images of the Army*, 27.

44. On Madame Tussaud's, see Pilbeam, *Madame Tussaud*, esp. 109–15.

45. Clippings, Vauxhall Gardens, ca. 1827, ML, and Astley's, 1824, Astley's Files, TM.

46. Poster for *The Battle of Waterloo*, 22 April 1824, London III, Astley's, Playbills, 171, no. 68, BL; regarding the production, see Saxon, *Enter Foot and Horse*, 140. On the duration of theater runs in general, see Stephens, *Profession of the Playwright*, 185. The play was not censored by the Lord Chamberlain's office in 1824 since Astley's did not require a dramatic license. It was not until the following year, when the Theater Royal Hull wished to perform it, that the play crossed the desk of the examiner of plays.

47. See Kwint, "Legitimization of the Circus," 109; Kwint estimates that Astley's auditorium could hold about two thousand by about 1800. Cf. Grant, *Great Metropolis* (1836, reprint, 1838), 1:72.

48. Howard, *London Theatres and Music Halls*, 15, 55, 66. At the start of the century, Drury Lane could hold 3,611 (see Pyne and Combe, *Microcosm of London* [1808–11], 1:230). In the thirties, James Grant said that while it could hold 3,060 people, 5,000 were known to have been crammed into it (Grant, *Great Metropolis* [1836, reprint, 1838], 1:43).

49. See Moody, *Illegitimate Theatre in London*, 31–33, 41–47, 74–78; and Michael Baker, *Rise of the Victorian Actor*, 27–28. Much debate ensued in the press about the "decline of the national drama" and about the Theatre Royal Drury Lane's and the Theatre Royal Covent Garden's presumed resemblance to low-brow minor theaters and circuses (see, e.g., clipping, *National Magazine*, 19 October 1833, 1, Theatre

Buildings Files, TM; "The Decline of the Drama," *Times* [London], 9 December 1837; "Decay of the Drama," ibid., 15 January 1837; and, reflecting on the long-term damage wreaked by Drury Lane, "Why Have the Theatres Decayed?" *Era,* 12 January 1851, 12, and Edward Dutton Cook, *On the Stage* [1883], 2:203–4).

50. J. W. Rogers Jr., of the Theater Royal Hull, applied for a license from the Lord Chamberlain to perform Amherst's play, which was given on 25 April 1825 (see Add. MSS 42871 [4]: 155–56, BL). Cooke's circus, resident in Manchester in 1850, presented a full-length version of the play (see advertisement, *Manchester Examiner,* 20 February 1850, 1; see also poster 174, Bowery Theater, New York, 18 December 1840, Circus Scrapbooks, vol. 2, Th.Cts. 50, BL). On the interconnectedness between New York and London theatrical trends, especially with respect to Andrew Ducrow, see McCullough, *Living Pictures,* 8, 11–13.

51. Poster for *The Battle of Waterloo,* 22 April 1824, London III, Astley's, Playbills, 171, no. 68, BL.

52. Hill, *Playing About* (1840), 1:234.

53. "Royal Amphitheatre," *Drama; or, Theatrical Pocket Magazine,* April 1824, 103.

54. John Coleman, "A Gossip about Astley's," *Graphic,* 18 March 1893.

55. For a later study of boyhood imaginings and heroism see, Dawson, *Soldier Heroes,* esp. 22–26, 56, 80–83.

56. Gillian Russell, *Theaters of War,* 98, 111, 116–19.

57. Clipping 1571, [ca. 1824], Astley's Scrapbooks, vol. 3, Th.Cts. 37, BL. This was not the only instance when Wellington was spotted in Astley's audience by appreciative patrons, some of whom belonged to the military (see also clipping, 7 July 1829, Astley's Files, TM). His visit probably coincided with one of the many anniversary performances of *The Battle of Waterloo* that Astley's presented to the public.

58. "Royal Amphitheatre," *Drama; or Theatrical Pocket Magazine,* May 1824, 201; clipping 1571, [ca. 1824], Astley's Scrapbooks, vol. 3, Th.Cts. 37, BL.

59. Baer, *Theatre and Disorder,* 177, 185. See also E. P. Thompson, *Making of the English Working Class.*

60. Voskuil, "Feeling Public," 249. See also Gillian Russell, *Theatres of War,* ch. 5, relating to military audiences in the theater.

61. Skelley, *Victorian Army at Home,* 210–11. On the returning soldier and the late-nineteenth-century music-hall sketch, see Dave Russell, "'We carved our way to glory': The British Soldier in Music Hall Song and Sketch, c. 1880–1914," in MacKenzie, *Popular Imperialism and the Military,* 72; see also Gash, "After Waterloo," 147, 150.

62. Colley, *Britons,* 339.

63. See Briggs, *Age of Improvement,* 214. On this moment of high tension after Waterloo, see Colley, *Britons,* 339, 440n2; and Gash, "After Waterloo," 150–52.

64. Hobsbawm, *Nations and Nationalism,* 85.

65. A' Beckett, *Green Room Recollections* (1896), 33.

66. See, e.g., Bridges's circus bill 5, 1838, Circus Scrapbooks, vol. 1, Th.Cts. 50, BL.

67. Poster, Batty's Circus, Newcastle, 8 September 1838, 944/828, Fenwick Collection, TW.

68. Poster, T. Cooke's Circus, Glasgow, 13 March 1844, Ephemera Collection, E/74, Special Collections Department, University of Glasgow Library.

69. Advertisement, *Manchester Examiner*, 20 February 1850, 1.

70. For a broader discussion, see Colley, *Britons*, 322–23, 334–35.

71. Hobsbawm, *Nations and Nationalism*.

72. Andrew Roberts makes the point that before Waterloo they were hardly equals in status or experience: Wellington was merely a knight of the Bath in 1804, when Napoleon was proclaimed emperor. In contrast to Napoleon's, therefore, his power was entirely circumscribed by Parliament. Moreover, Wellington fought fewer battles, although he won all of them (see Roberts, *Napoleon and Wellington*, xxxvii).

73. Pears, "Gentleman and the Hero," 224.

74. For later examples of these themes, see J. S. Bratton, "Theaters of War: The Crimea on the London Stage, 1854–5," in Bradby, James, and Sharralt, *Performance and Politics in Popular Drama*.

75. Amherst, *Battle of Waterloo*, act 1, sc. 3.

76. Clipping, Astley's Files, 1824, TM.

77. Amherst, *Battle of Waterloo*, act 2, sc. 6.

78. On dramatic posturing, see Meisel, *Realizations*, 6, 42; and Rede, *Road to the Stage* (1827), 78–79, 83–85.

79. See McWilliam, "Melodrama and the Historians," particularly his discussion about radicalism and melodrama.

80. Amherst, *Battle of Waterloo*, act 2, sc. 2.

81. Ibid., act 3, sc. 2.

82. *Thespian Preceptor* (1811), 25.

83. Amherst, *Battle of Waterloo*, act 2, sc. 6.

84. Clipping, Vauxhall Gardens, ca. 1827, Surrey Theatre Files, SLS.

85. Poster, Surrey Theatre, 9 May 1814, "Britons at Bordeaux; or, The Downfall of Tyranny," ibid. The defeat had occurred just two months earlier, showing the speed with which these scenes were re-created for the stage.

86. Ibid.

87. Amherst, *Napoleon Bonaparte's Invasion of Russia*, 3 (program of scenery), 25 (act 2, sc. 4).

88. On apocalyptic enactments, see Meisel, *Realizations*, 170. On reviewers' reflections on J.M.W. Turner and metamorphosis, see *Blackwood's* 52 (July 1842): 26, cited in Meisel, *Realizations*, 186.

89. According to Allardyce Nicoll, the play by William Dimond was called *The Hunter of the Alps* and was performed at the Haymarket in 1804; the play by John Walker, *Napoleon; or, The Emperor and the Soldier*, was performed at Sadler's Wells in 1828.

90. Walker and Dimond, *Napoleon, the Hunter of the Alps* (1828), Add. MSS. 42957: 10, BL.

91. Louis James, "Inverted Emblems for Albion: Wellington and Napoleon on Stage," in Samuel, *Patriotism*, 3:246.

92. *Catalogue of the Napoleon Museum* (1843), vi.

93. Bulwer-Lytton, *Lady of Lyons,* act 2, sc. 1, 32. The comment is meant to underline the theme of the play, namely, that France no longer has its princes, although the Lady of Lyons, Pauline, is in search of a husband who belongs to this extinct class. Deceived by a vengeful former suitor, she marries Melnotte, the son of a gardener, who redeems and elevates himself by joining her cousin's regiment.

94. *Napoleon's Glory; or, Wonders in Saint Helena,* a burletta in one act, Lord Chamberlain's license dated 8 December 1840, Add. MSS 42957 (28): 815–815b, BL.

95. See Bratton, "Theaters of War."

96. The manuscript states that the play was the property of William Batty, manager of Astley's, who probably hired a hack writer to write it, an adaptation from C. A. Somerset's French five-act spectacle. It received a dramatic license from the Lord Chamberlain in March 1852, the month before it was performed (*Bonaparte in Egypt* [1852], Add. MSS 52931 [C], BL).

97. Clipping 1423, 18 April 1852, Astley's Scrapbooks, vol. 3, Th.Cts. 37, BL.

98. Poster, Astley's, 24 May 1852, Astley's Files, TM.

99. *Bonaparte in Egypt* [1852], Add. MSS, 52931 (C): 16, 31, 49, 72, BL.

100. Poster, Astley's, 24 May 1852, Astley's Files, TM; clipping, 17 April 1852, ibid. See also the discussion in ch. 1, above, on stage play licensing. Astley's was issued a license in 1843 under the Theatre Regulation Act, adding to its legitimate status in the theatrical world, as Marius Kwint has argued (Kwint, "Legitimization of the Circus").

101. On plays concerning the French Revolution set in other historical periods, see Jeffrey Cox, "The French Revolution in the English Theatre," in Behrendt, *History and Myth,* 33–52.

102. Egypt was not colonized until 1882, after the repression of the nationalist Arabi Rebellion. It received protectorate status from Britain in 1914.

103. See Altick, *Shows of London,* 342–49.

104. See Cannadine, "Context, Performance, and Meaning."

3. Victorian Curiosity

1. *Oxford English Dictionary,* 2001, s.v. "curiosity"; on conceptual and linguistic origins of the term, see Kenny, *Curiosity in Early Modern Europe World Histories,* esp. ch. 1.

2. Daston and Park, *Wonders and the Order of Nature,* 306.

3. See Pomian, *Collectors and Curiosities,* 53–60; Giuseppe Olmi, "Science—Honour—Metaphor: Italian Cabinets of the Sixteenth and Seventeenth Centuries," in Impey and MacGregor, *Origin of Museums;* and Shelton, "Cabinets of Transgression."

4. See Altick, *Shows of London,* 23; and Whitaker, "Culture of Curiosity."

5. Tait, *Catalogue of the Waddesdon Bequest,* 7.

6. Chevalier de Jaucourt, "Curiosité," in Denis Diderot and Jean le Rond D'Alembert's *Encyclopédie; ou dictionnaire raisonné des sciences, des arts, et des metiers,* 4:578, cited in Daston and Park, *Wonders and the Order of Nature,* 328.

7. Handbill, 8 March 1786, C 26.51/T1786, Noble Collection, Guildhall Library, Corporation of London.

8. Altick, *Shows of London,* 32.

9. See Gallagher and Robinson, "Imperialism of Free Trade." According to P. J. Marshall, in the years 1850–70 the empire provided approximately 20 percent of British imports (see Marshall, "1783–1870," in Marshall, *Cambridge Illustrated History of the British Empire,* 25).

10. Marshall, "1783–1870," 22. On trends in late-eighteenth-century Paris, see Robbins, *Elephant Slaves and Pampered Parrots,* esp. 85–93.

11. See, e.g., 6 & 7 Vict., c. 68, sec. 14, which allowed the Lord Chamberlain to forbid any old or licensed play "whenever he shall be of opinion that it is fitting for the preservation of good manners, decorum or of the public peace so to do."

12. According to section 23 of the Theatre Regulation Act, the licensing powers were restricted to "stage plays" and thus, as John Johnston rightly points out, many circus acts, such as juggling, were outside his jurisdiction (see Johnston, *Lord Chamberlain's Blue Pencil,* 30). However, as we saw in chapter 2 and will see later in this chapter, plays were performed at circuses.

13. See Goodall, *Performance and Evolution,* esp. 11–13.

14. Nadkarni, *Journal of a Visit to Europe* (1903), 136. Nadkarni despaired of the ignorance of the English people who thought of Indians as "no better than negroes" (ibid., 380).

15. Bolt, *Victorian Attitudes towards Race,* 10.

16. My use of the term *ornamental* differs from David Cannadine's in *Ornamentalism* insofar as I am concerned with visual experience and ways of "seeing" difference. For a good, basic description of how cultural historians cope with this concept, see Stuart Hall, "Spectacle of the 'Other.'"

17. See n. 1 to the introduction.

18. I use the term *colonial* here to include objects of the imperial gaze, both inside and outside the official British Empire.

19. Dickens, *Old Curiosity Shop* ([1840–41] 1997), 304.

20. Nowrojee and Merwanjee, *Journal of a Residence . . . in Great Britain* (1841), 107.

21. Ram, *My Trip to Europe* (1893), 64.

22. "A Novel Circus Sale in Oldham," *Oldham Chronicle,* 8 October 1898, 3.

23. See, e.g., Daston and Park, *Wonders and the Order of Nature,* which relates this skepticism to the Enlightenment, although its origins were as early as collecting itself; see also Daston, "Marvelous Facts," 90.

24. Daston and Park, *Wonders and the Order of Nature,* 321.

25. *Morning Chronicle,* reprinted in "A Glimpse at Low Life," *Derby Mercury,* 5 June 1850, 4 (although it does not appear in Henry Mayhew's *London Labour*). See also *Public General Acts,* Act for the More Effective Prevention of Cruelty to Animals, 1849, 12 & 13 Vict., c. 92, sec. 3.

26. Nowrojee and Merwanjee, *Journal of a Residence . . . in Great Britain* (1841), 105; see also "Theatrical Olla," *Era*, 27 January 1839. The appearance of wild animals at one of the patent theaters coincided with and fueled "the decline of the drama" debate that took place in many London papers in this period; see above, ch. 2, n. 49.

27. Clipping, [ca. August 1844], Astley's Files, TM.

28. Howison, *Foreign Scenes* (1825), 1:217–18.

29. Poster, 1844, Ephemera Collection, E/71, Special Collections Department, University of Glasgow Library.

30. Robinson, *London Theatre*, 173.

31. See ch. 2; see also Colley, *Captives*, 264–66.

32. Poster, 6 December 1855, MWEZ + n.c. 7842, Scrapbook, NYPL.

33. See Ritvo, *Animal Estate*, ch. 5.

34. Cf. the Brahmin procession described in Graham, *Journal of a Residence in India* (1812), 35.

35. On general trends driven by London capital, see B. R. Tomlinson, "Economics and Empire: The Periphery and the Imperial Economy," in Andrew Porter, *Oxford History of the British Empire*, 72.

36. Clipping, 4 September 1796, Astley's, Fillinham Collection, 1889.b.10/6, BL.

37. Poster, Wombwell's, September 1829, Noble Collection, Guildhall Library, Corporation of London.

38. On street obstruction, see Winter, *London's Teeming Streets*, 6–7.

39. Doss, *Reminiscences, English and Australasian* (1893), 96.

40. "Shipping Wild Animals in the London Docks," *Illustrated London News*, 21 May 1864, 496; see also Ritvo, *Animal Estate*, 244–45.

41. "Maccomo, the Lion King and the Tiger," *Era*, 24 June 1866, 12.

42. "A Chat with Carl Hagenbeck," ibid., 11 May 1895, 16.

43. "Hughes's Mammoth Establishment," ibid., 7 November 1847, 9.

44. "Wild Beasts under the Hammer," ibid., 14 April 1872, 12.

45. "A Strange Trade," [ca. 1860–90s], Scrapbook Collection, 604, Liverpool, 82, CFA.

46. "A Circus Sale," June 1899, ibid., 22. The number two thousand seems highly inflated if only circus proprietors were present. More likely, it included fairground showmen who ran booths of various descriptions.

47. "Lion Tamers at Work," MWEZ + n.c. 7842, 28 July 1888, Scrapbook, NYPL.

48. On organ-grinders and other street musicians who tended to have monkeys, see Assael, "Music in the Air."

49. See Assael, "Circus and Respectable Society," table 2.5. For example, in 1887, 19 percent of companies went bust, and in 1897, 16 percent, compared with only 3 percent in 1877. Throughout these years the number of companies grew from 32 (1877) to 47 (1887) to 74 (1897).

50. See Harrison, "Animals and the State."

51. RSPCA, *1880 Annual Report*, 90; *1882 Annual Report*, 85. In these two cases

the RSPCA was successful in attaining prosecutions against the tamers. For a longer discussion of animal protection, see Assael, "Circus and Respectable Society," ch. 6.

52. "Alleged Cruelty to Lions," *Era,* 24 March 1894, 17; letter to the editor, ibid., 31 March 1894, 17; "The Aquarium Lions," ibid., 26 May 1894, 9.

53. See, e.g., S. L. Bensusan, "The Torture of Trained Animals," *English Illustrated Magazine* 15 (April 1896): 25–30; and "The Training of Child Acrobats," ibid. 16 (October 1896): 41–45.

54. "Are Trained Animals Tortured?" *Era,* 9 May 1896, 19.

55. "The Alleged Animal Torturing—To the Editors of the *Era,"* ibid., 16 May 1896, 16. See also "The Alleged Animal Torturing," ibid., 18 April 1896, 17; "Alleged Animal Torturing," ibid., 25 April 1896, 16; and letter to the editor, ibid., 9 May 1896, 19.

56. See, e.g., RSPCA, *1896 Annual Report,* 206; *1900 Annual Report,* 104.

57. On later frustrations with the law, see PP, *Select Committee on Performing Animals,* 1921, vol. 7, and 1922, vol. 5.

58. "Bartholomew Fair," 1833, C 26.5–26.51, Noble Collection, Guildhall Library, Corporation of London.

59. "For an America That Loved Freaks"; Watkins, *Four Years in Europe* (1901); official program, "The Barnum and Bailey Greatest Show on Earth at Olympia," Kensington, London, 1898, Barnum Files, EC; Reiss, *Showman and the Slave,* ch. 2. There were more variations on the theme of real imperial subjects (see, e.g., Ben Shephard, "Showbiz Imperialism: The Case of Peter Lobengula," in MacKenzie, *Imperialism and Popular Culture*). On deception in nineteenth-century America, see James W. Cook, *Arts of Deception.* For a study of the reception of Barnum's freaks in Victorian New York, see idem, "Of Men, Missing Links, and Nondescripts: The Strange Career of P. T. Barnum's 'What is it?' Exhibition," in Thomson, *Freakery.*

60. There are certainly earlier examples of freaks shown in assembly rooms (see Bernth Lindfors, "Ethnological Show Business: Footlighting the Dark Continent," in Thomson, *Freakery;* and Goodall, *Performance and Evolution,* 33).

61. "The Noble Savage," *Household Words,* 11 June 1853, 337–39.

62. Poster, Royal Aquarium, 1883, Theatre Buildings Files (Royal Aquarium), TM.

63. See Gilman, "Black Bodies, White Bodies."

64. Dr. John Shortt, "On the Domber," *Journal of the Anthropological Society of London* 2 (1864): clxxxix–cxci.

65. On the music hall, see John M. MacKenzie, "Empire and Metropolitan Cultures," in Andrew Porter, *Oxford History of the British Empire,* 277–79. The complexity of Britain's tactics in the period before 1870 makes it difficult to justify calling it an informal empire. I employ the term *colonial authority* to refer, among other things, to its policy of free trade, sometimes through forceful tactics (see Marshall, "1783–1870," 33).

66. Posters, Astley's, 23, 30 November, 7, 14, 21, 26 December 1857, 4, 11, 18, 25 January, 1, 8 February 1858, Astley's Files, TM.

67. C. A. Somerset, "The Storming and Capture of Delhi!" act. 3, sc. 4, 23 November 1857, Add. MSS 52969 (K), BL. For a literary treatment of these events, see

Brantlinger, *Rule of Darkness*, 202–3, 206; Paxton, "Mobilizing Chivalry"; and Sharpe, *Allegories of Empire*.

68. Cf. Colley, *Captives*.

69. "Norwich," *Era*, 27 September 1857, 12.

70. Somerset, "Storming and Capture of Delhi!," act 3, sc. 4.

71. I am not entirely convinced by Anne McClintock's psychoanalytic reading of such colonial spectacles as fetishistic (see McClintock, *Imperial Leather*, 123), although there was, to be sure, an important element of fantasy underpinning them.

72. Poster, Astley's, 5 April 1858, Astley's Files, TM.

73. On postcards and their imperial significance, particularly during "the frenzy" between 1890 and 1918, see Saloni Mathur, "Wanted Native Views: Collecting Colonial Postcards of India," in Burton, *Gender, Sexuality and Colonial Modernities*, esp. 104–5.

74. Geertz, *Negara*, 136.

75. See ch. 4.

76. J. H. Stocqueler, "The Bombardment and Capture of Canton," 5 April 1858, Add. MSS 52973 H, BL; Bolt, *Victorian Attitudes towards Race*, 199–200; Forman, "Peking Plots."

77. See Bratton, "Theaters of War."

78. J. Barber, *The Rajah of Nagpore; or, The Sacred Elephant of the Pagoda*, 26 January, 23 February 1846 (dated by the Lord Chamberlain), Add. MSS 47991:298–350, BL. See also posters, Astley's, 2, 9, 16, 23 February, 2, 9 March 1846, Astley's Files, TM; and "Astley's," *Era*, 15 February 1846, 5.

79. Bolt, *Victorian Attitudes towards Race*, 167–68.

80. Barber, *Rajah of Nagpore*.

81. Patricia Murphy, "The Fissure King: Parody, Ideology, and Imperial Narrative," in Wagner-Lawlor, *Victorian Comic Spirit*, 24.

82. See program, Astley's, 1878, Astley's Files, TM; Cooke's route book, 1858, William Cooke Papers, ML; and clipping, "The Doom of Old Drury Lane," [ca. 1862], Theatre Buildings Files (Drury Lane), TM.

83. See Brendan Gregory, "Staging British India," in Bratton, Cave, and Pickering, *Acts of Supremacy*.

84. Ibid., 152–53.

85. Cannadine, "Context, Performance, and Meaning," 121.

86. See Gregory, "Staging British India"; see also Cannadine, *Ornamentalism*.

87. See Judd, *Empire*, 8.

88. Bernard Porter, *Lion's Share*, 116; P. J. Marshall, "1870–1918: The Empire under Threat," in Marshall, *Cambridge Illustrated History of the British Empire*, 54–55.

89. Cannadine, "Context, Performance, and Meaning"; see also Bernard Porter, *Lion's Share*, 117–18.

90. See Nead, *Victorian Babylon*.

91. Poster, "Astley's," 9 October 1835, Microfiche Collection, Playbills and Programmes from London Theatre, 1801–1900, Victoria & Albert Museum Library.

92. Meerza, *Journal of a Residence in England* (1839), 2:107, 124. This visit was made in the summer of 1836. His remark that there were fifty thousand ladies is an exaggeration: in this period the amphitheater likely seated from two thousand to twenty-five hundred people, as James Grant observed (Grant, *Great Metropolis* [1836, reprint, 1838], 1:72).

93. Meerza, *Journal of a Residence in England* (1839), 2:107.

94. Cf. interactions between Indian flaneurs and Victorian bourgeois women later in the century (Burton, *At the Heart of the Empire,* ch. 4, esp. 174). Lynda Nead rightly corrects the tendency among cultural historians to construct the urban gaze as exclusively male (see Nead, *Victorian Babylon,* 73).

95. On imperial commodity spectacle, see McClintock, *Imperial Leather,* 59.. See also Richards, *Commodity Culture in Victorian England,* ch. 1; Hoffenberg, *Empire on Display;* and Peter H. Hoffenberg, "Equipoise and Its Discontents: Voices of Dissent during the International Exhibitions," in Hewitt, *Age of Equipoise?*

96. Catherine Hall, *Civilising Subjects,* 17–18; idem, *Cultures of Empire,* 20. See also Pratt, *Imperial Eyes.*

97. On the stare, see Thomson, "Narratives of Deviance and Delight."

98. Jean Ingres's painting *Le Bain Turc* (1862) reveals this trend.

99. Nowrojee and Merwanjee, *Journal of a Residence . . . in Great Britain* (1841), 34.

100. Ibid., 298, 299.

101. Ibid., 110.

102. On the "Indian eye" that returned the imperial gaze, see Burton, "Indian Travellers in *Fin-de-Siècle* London."

103. Mukharji, *Visit to Europe* (1889), 99; see also Hoffenberg, *Empire on Display,* 52–56.

104. Salter, *East in the West* (1896), 149, 143.

105. Mukharji, *Visit to Europe* (1889), 105.

106. Nadkarni, *Journal of a Visit to Europe* (1903), 380.

107. Mathur, "Living Ethnological Exhibits," 508–9.

108. Stuart Hall, "Spectacle of the 'Other,'" 261.

109. *Post Office London Directory for 1840; Post Office London Directory for 1851.*

110. See above, n. 6.

111. On commodity racism, see McClintock, *Imperial Leather;* and McLaughlin, *Writing the Urban Jungle,* 17–18.

4. Clown Laughter, Clown Tears

1. "Death of a Circus Clown," *Era,* 3 July 1870, 6.

2. Thomas, "Place of Laughter," 81. See also Gregory, *Nature of Laughter,* 9–11; see also Minois's more recent *Histoire du rire,* which covers up to the present day.

3. Thomas, "Place of Laughter," 80.

4. Quoted in ibid.

5. "Death by Laughter," in *Cabinet of Curiosities* (1831), 248. Curiously, she was said to be the widow of a minister.

6. Vasey, *Philosophy of Laughter and Smiling* (1875), 115, 97–98.

7. T. Staveacre, *Slapstick* (London, 1987), 67–78, quoted in Bailey, *Popular Culture and Performance*, 196–97.

8. See Freud, *Wit and Its Relation to the Unconscious* (1905); Gay, *Cultivation of Hatred*, ch. 5; and Bergson, *Laughter* (1911). Hobbes linked it with superiority and "vainglory" (see Monro, *Argument of Laughter*, ch. 8).

9. Bremmer and Roodenberg, *Cultural History of Humour*, 2.

10. Bakhtin, *Rabelais and His World*, 75.

11. Thomas, "Place of Laughter," 77–81.

12. Douglas, "Jokes," 297; see also idem, *Purity and Danger*, ch. 7.

13. Quoted in Gay, *Cultivation of Hatred*, 372–73.

14. With reference to Barnum, see, e.g., Linda Frost, "'Living Curiosities' and 'The Wonder of America.'" For the standard work on freakish exhibitions, see Bogdan, *Freak Show*.

15. Donald J. Gray, "Uses of Victorian Laughter," 146. Although he points to "serious" and "holiday" (or innocuous) laughter, he says that the latter prevailed over the former.

16. See ch. 2, n. 46; see also 6 & 7 Vict., c. 68, sec. 23, which exempts booths or shows, with which the circus was sometimes confused.

17. See Mayer, *Harlequin in His Element*, ch. 9, esp. 309–10, 312–13, 316–17, for an account of structural changes to the pantomime in minor theaters after 1843.

18. "Informations," as they were called, were launched against circuses, usually by theater managers with stage play licenses, throughout the century. If found guilty, the circus manager could be penalized according to section 10 of the 1843 Theatre Regulation Act. To take but one example that erupted in a newspaper debate, see letters to the editor, *Sheffield Daily Telegraph*, 1 January 1863, 3, and 2 January 1863, 2, 3; "What Is a Pantomime?" *Sheffield Times*, 3 January 1863, 5; "Information against Messrs. Sanger," *Supplement to the Sheffield and Rotherham Independent*, 3 January 1863, 11; and "Theatre versus the Circus," *Era*, 4 January 1863, 5, and 28 January 1863, 10. Nor was the situation much different later in the century (see, e.g., "Important Circus Case," ibid., 18 June 1892, 15, involving a performance of *Cinderella* at Walsall that was prohibited on the grounds that the managers held no stage play license; cf. ch. 1, n. 102).

19. See, e.g., "Circuses and Dramatic Licenses," *Era*, 3 December 1892, 12.

20. See Mayer, *Harlequin in His Element*, 4–7, 9; Moody, *Illegitimate Theatre in London*, 210–12; and Dickens [Boz, pseud.], *Memoirs of Joseph Grimaldi* (1838).

21. Mayer, *Harlequin in His Element*, 29, 28–31.

22. See Silver, *Strange and Secret Peoples*, 3, although she associates this developing interest with the Romantics and earlier literary movements. On transcendence and the meaning of this genre couched in Freudian terms, see Bettelheim, *Uses of Enchantment*.

23. Fairy plays such as W. S. Gilbert's *The Wicked World* revealed fundamental

criticisms of gender relations and thus shared characteristics with serious drama (see Carolyn Williams, "Parody, Pastiche, and the Play of Genres: The Savoy Operas of Gilbert and Sullivan," in Wagner-Lawlor, *Victorian Comic Spirit,* 12).

24. Robert Spence Watson to his children, describing a visit to Backworth, 213/26, June 1878, Mable Spence Watson Letters, TW.

25. Pace Carolyn Williams, "Parody, Pastiche, and the Play of Genres."

26. See Tracy C. Davis, "Employment of Children."

27. Booth, *Theatre in the Victorian Age,* 199.

28. For a more detailed discussion, see Mayer, *Harlequin in His Element.*

29. Booth, *Theatre in the Victorian Age,* 198–99.

30. See Welsford, *The Fool,* ch. 13.

31. See "Astley's," *Era,* 11 January 1846, 5; and clippings, 6 January 1844, Astley's Files, TM.

32. See Mayer, *Harlequin in His Element.*

33. Tom Hood, *Harlequin Little Red Riding Hood; or, The Wicked Woolf and the Wirtuous Woodcutter,* in Scott, *Drawing Room Plays* (1870), 48.

34. J. S. Bratton, "Jane Scott the Writer-Manager," in Tracy C. Davis and Donkin, *Women and Playwriting* (Bratton's emphasis is different but nevertheless applies to what I am discussing here); Bailey, "Musical Comedy and the Rhetoric of the Girl," reprinted in Bailey, *Popular Culture and Performance,* quotation on 185.

35. Le Roux and Garnier, *Acrobats and Mountebanks* (1889, trans., 1890), 297.

36. Billington, *Social History of the Fool,* 89.

37. Le Roux and Garnier, *Acrobats and Mountebanks* (1889, trans., 1890), 279–80.

38. Paterson, *Glimpses of Real Life* (1864), 113.

39. Keith, *Circus Life and Amusements* (1879), 40.

40. "Twenty Years in the Circus," *Era,* 1 June 1895, 16.

41. Le Roux and Garnier, *Acrobats and Mountebanks* (1889, trans., 1890), 280.

42. "Ginnett's Circus: Conundrum Night," *Evening Post,* ca. 1887.

43. PRO, LC/1/25, Frederick Fox Cooper to the Lord Chamberlain, 18 April 1846.

44. Fox Cooper's experience as manager at the City of London Theatre may have turned him from "poacher into gamekeeper" (see Frederick Renad Cooper, *Nothing Extenuate* [1964], 114).

45. See 6 & 7 Vict., c. 68, sec. 12.

46. "A Word to Equestrian Managers," *Era,* 26 August 1860, 1. Banishing any hints of vulgarity from his acts had long been a concern to the clown (see Moody, *Illegitimate Theatre in London,* 87, 214–15, 225, for a discussion of Grimaldi, respectability, and censorship).

47. Munby Diaries, 15 January 1862, vol. 12, TCC.

48. On female acrobats and their costumes see ch. 5; on women's legs on the New York stage, see Robert C. Allen, *Horrible Prettiness,* 95–96.

49. "Plymouth—St. James's Hall," *Era,* 17 May 1868, 13; and 3 May 1868, 13.

50. "Cirque National at Drury Lane," *Illustrated London News,* 6 January 1849.

51. "Hengler's Cirque," *Era,* 25 December 1885, 10.

52. Le Roux and Garnier, *Acrobats and Mountebanks* (1889, trans., 1890), 284.

53. I use the term *sublime* here to mean a lightness of being that defied gravity and therefore use it in a different sense than in ch. 2.

54. "Swansea," *Era*, 17 February 1861, 14. Tom Sayers continued to perform with Howes and Cushing's circus (see "Birmingham," ibid., 28 July 1861, 11).

55. "Swansea," ibid., 17 February 1861, 14.

56. Ibid.

57. Rehin, "Harlequin Jim Crow," 687, 691–96; idem, "Blackface Street Minstrels," 28. The blackface appeared earlier than this, however.

58. Rehin, "Harlequin Jim Crow," 693.

59. Henry Mayhew, *London Labour* (1861), 191.

60. Munby Diaries, 13 January 1862, vol. 12, TCC.

61. Rev. H. R. Haweis, "Street Music in England," *Good Words*, 1 October 1868, 604, reprinted in Haweis, *Music and Morals* (1871), 570.

62. Munby Diaries, 28 December 1861, vol. 11, TCC.

63. Ibid., 13 January 1862, vol. 12.

64. Poster, Circus Royal, Dock Green Hull, 29, 30 August 1843, MWEZ + n.c. 7842, Scrapbook, NYPL.

65. Poster, Astley's, 30 December 1845, Astley's Files, TM.

66. Poster, ca. 24 December 1866, Printed Ephemera, ML.

67. Poster, Astley's, 4 June 1881, Astley's Files, TM.

68. Featherstone, "Blackface Atlantic," 241–42. My point contrasts with J. S. Bratton's argument that English audiences were disappointed when the Ethiopian serenader turned out to be a fake (see Bratton, "British Audiences and Black-Faced Acts," 131).

69. Haweis, "Street Music in England."

70. Henry Mayhew, *London Labour* (1861), 202. Although this example is taken from the concert hall, the circus probably featured the same songs and themes since performers often traveled between the two venues.

71. Rehin describes the combination of pun and song relating to death as "merry and mournful" in "Harlequin Jim Crow," 34.

72. Le Roux and Garnier, *Acrobats and Mountebanks* (1889, trans., 1890), 282.

73. See Pickering, "John Bull in Blackface," 198; and Featherstone, "Blackface Atlantic," 236–37. On a similar point related to racial taxonomy, see Ritvo, *Platypus and the Mermaid*, 121–30.

74. Cf. Stuart Hall, "Spectacle of the 'Other,'" 249.

75. Featherstone, "Blackface Atlantic," 248–49. A similar point is made in Bratton, "British Audiences and Black-Faced Acts," 129. See also Toll, *Blacking Up*.

76. Munby Diaries, 28 December 1861, vol. 11, TCC.

77. Stuart Hall, "Spectacle and the 'Other,'" 263.

78. Charles Babbage to M. T. Bass, esq., 13 July 1864, in M. T. Bass, *Street Music in the Metropolis: Correspondence and Observations on the Existing Law and Proposed Amendments* (1864), 19; see also Assael, "Music in the Air," 186.

79. Dickens, *Hard Times* ([1854] 1966), 215–16. Before discovering Tom's crime, Sleary takes him in because his family has given Sissy Jupe a home (see ibid., 214–22).

80. Ibid., 215.

81. See Babcock, *Reversible World,* 22.

82. Bakhtin, *Rabelais and His World,* introduction, esp. 48–49, and ch. 1.

83. Henry Mayhew, *London Labour* (1861), 119–20.

84. Dickens, *Hard Times* ([1854] 1966), 45, 46, 31, 222, 20.

85. Henry Mayhew, *London Labour* (1861), 134.

86. Salary list, Liverpool, ca. late 1870s or early 1880s, Scrapbook Collection, Liverpool, CFA.

87. See the comparative discussion of salaries in ch. 1. For Croueste's engagements, see the following reviews from the *Era:* "Sunderland," 2 June 1878, 7; "Lincoln," 9 June 1878, 8; "Nottingham," 30 June 1878, 9; "Southport," 4 August 1878, 7, and 11 August 1878, 7; "Guernsey," 18 August 1878, 6, 25 August 1878, 7, 1 September 1878, 7, and 8 September 1878, 7; and "Scarborough," 22 September 1878, 8, 29 September 1878, 9, 6 October 1878, 9, 13 October 1878, 8, and 20 October 1878, 8. His engagements with each troupe might have been longer than suggested here if the *Era* did not report on every detail about their length, which is possible.

88. "Wanted," ibid., 15 September 1878, 19.

89. "A Clown's Lamentations," ibid., n.d., quoted in Keith, *Circus Life and Amusements* (1879), 103.

90. "Theatrical Trial," *Era,* 1 March 1859, 6. This custom of having performers fill more roles than they had been engaged to fill persisted throughout the century.

91. *Confessions of a Dancing Girl* (1913), 58.

92. Henry Mayhew, *London Labour* (1861), 143, 141.

93. Keith, *Circus Life and Amusements* (1879), 43.

94. See, e.g., Davin, *Growing Up Poor.*

95. See Bailey, "Community of Friends." On women, see Tracy C. Davis, *Actresses as Working Women,* 58–68; and idem, "Victorian Charity." For a general discussion of the benefit system, see Troubridge, *Benefit System in the British Theatre.*

96. Bailey, "Community of Friends," 41.

97. "The Late Tom Barry," *Era,* 19 April 1857, 12.

98. Bill, "Astley's Amphitheatre," 6 April 1861, Astley's Files, TM.

99. "Death of an Equestrian Clown," *Era,* 21 July 1861, 10.

100. "Funny Little Rochez, the Clown," ibid., 12 October 1873, 7.

101. Ibid.

102. *Era,* 9 July 1855, 10.

103. Quoted in Cordery, "Friendly Societies," 53.

104. "To the Equestrian, Gymnastic, And Music Hall Professions An Artistes' Benevolent Fund and Institution," *Era,* n.d., quoted in Keith, *Circus Life and Amusements* (1879), 140.

105. Keith, *Circus Life and Amusements* (1879), 140.

5. Women on Top

1. "Shocking Death of the Female Blondin," *Birmingham Journal*, 25 July 1863, 7. This discussion includes circus acts performed in public parks and other such places. As the introduction states, an isolated consideration of the circus would create an unbalanced view of a trade that was fluid and whose performers appeared in a variety of popular venues.

2. Some accounts suggested that she was actually seven months pregnant. Her husband stated at the coroner's inquest, that he was not sure how long she had been "in the family way" (see "The Accident to the Female Blondin," ibid., 5).

3. For the purposes of this discussion, the term *acrobat* is used, not in its strict nineteenth-century sense, which implied performers "who throw somersaults and do feats on the ground," but in a wider sense to include gymnasts who, according to contemporaries, "did such tricks in the air." For a contemporary look at acrobatics versus gymnastics, see "The Making of Acrobats: An Interview with Zaeo," *Daily Graphic*, 13 February 1892, 5.

4. For an early, influential study on individual subjectivity, see Bailey, "Will the Real Bill Banks Please Stand Up?"

5. I use *spectacle* or *spectacular form* to refer not only to display but also to the many meanings underlying it. The tensions between life and death and between the subversion of respectable codes of conduct and the heroic defiance of social conventions— embodied in the acrobat's display—were, in the context of commercialized leisure, a product of a Victorian consumer demand for "spectacle." *Spectacle* also refers to something out there and above, something that cannot be touched and that is showcased, for example, by a ring or a proscenium (see Bailey, "Parasexuality and Glamour").

6. "Letter from the Queen to the Mayor of Birmingham," *Era*, 2 August 1863, 11.

7. MS 744, Aston Hall, "Aston Park: Proposed Address from the Managers to the Queen's Most Excellent Majesty," speech delivered on 15 June 1858, BCL, Archive Division.

8. "Letter from the Queen to the Mayor of Birmingham," *Era*, 2 August 1863, 11.

9. Bunce, *History of the Corporation of Birmingham* (1885), 197–201; *Aston Hall*, ch. 1.

10. "The Accident to the Female Blondin," *Birmingham Journal*, 25 July 1863, 5.

11. See "Sad Death of Madame Genieve, the Female Blondin," *Era*, 26 July 1863, 11; "Public Meeting at Town Hall," *Birmingham Journal*, 25 July 1863, 7; "Shocking Death of the Female Blondin," ibid.; "Tragedy at Aston Park," ibid., 5; "Shocking Death of Another Female Blondin," *Times* (London), 22 July 1863, 12; "Shocking Death of Another Female Blondin," *Bell's Life in London*, 26 July 1863, 3; and "Fatal Accident to a Female Blondin," *Stockton Herald, South Durham and Cleveland Advertiser*, 24 July 1863, 3.

12. Dickens, *Uncommercial Traveller* ([1860] 1877), 244.

13. "The Accident to the Female Blondin," *Birmingham Journal*, 25 July 1863,

5. Whether the guests at the private function knew she was pregnant is not known. During the autopsy the surgeon found that the unborn baby had died even before Selina Powell left home for the fête, or at least before she ascended the rope.

14. Ibid. It was not unusual for a husband to manage his wife's career. This may not have been the only reason why Mr. Powell did not take part in the performances, however: the reporter for the *Birmingham Journal* said that he was a "crippled husband."

15. *Era Almanac,* 1867, 69; 1877, 83; 1878, 84.

16. Henry Mayhew, *London Labour* (1861), 148, 149.

17. "A Glimpse of Low Life," *Derby Mercury,* 5 June 1850, 4.

18. Albert Smith, *Gavarni in London* ([1849] 1859), 4–5.

19. "A Glimpse of Low Life," *Derby Mercury,* 5 June 1850, 4.

20. "The Tragedy at Aston Park," *Birmingham Journal,* 25 July 1863, 5; "Fatal Accident to a 'Female Blondin,'" *Stockton Herald, South Durham and Cleveland Advertiser,* 24 July 1863, 3. While both these papers agreed that the rope was thirty *feet* from the ground, the *Times* reported that it was thirty *yards* "above the green" (see "Shocking Death of Another Female Blondin," *Times* [London], 22 July 1863, 12).

21. "The Female Blondin Catastrophe," *Era,* 2 August 1864, 11.

22. PRO, HO 45 7472, "Memorial of the Undersigned Clergy, Magistrates, Bankers, Merchants, Manufacturers, and Others Residing in Birmingham," 1 August 1863. On civic unity there, see Asa Briggs, "Birmingham," *Victorian Cities.*

23. PRO, HO 45 7472 "Memorial of the Undersigned Clergy, Magistrates, Bankers, Merchants, Manufacturers, and Others Residing in Birmingham," 1 August 1863.

24. Letter to the editor, *Era,* 2 August 1863, 11.

25. "The Gymnasts of the Period," letter to the editor, ibid., 19 September 1869, 7.

26. "A Cruel Sport," *Saturday Review,* 7 February 1880, 173–74.

27. "Amusement for the People!" *Tomahawk,* 18 July 1868, 24.

28. Quoted in Tracy C. Davis, "Sex in Public Places," 12.

29. Browning, *Fifine at the Fair* (1872), st. 12, pp. 132–33; see also Columbus, *"Fifine at the Fair."*

30. For a psychoanalytic treatment of the voyeuristic-scopophilic look that relates to women in film, see Mulvey, "Visual Pleasures and Narrative Cinema," 13.

31. Hudson, *Munby, Man of Two Worlds,* 286, entry for 11 June 1870.

32. This was a variation on a wider emphasis on working-class women in Munby's diaries (see Rick Allen, "Munby Reappraised"; see also McClintock, *Imperial Leather,* 102–3).

33. Hudson, *Munby, Man of Two Worlds,* 286, entry for 11 June 1870.

34. PRO, LC/7/16, Viscount Sidney to the Managers of the Theatres in the Jurisdiction of the Lord Chamberlain, 28 January 1869.

35. "Music Halls," *Glowworm and Evening News,* 2 February 1869, 2.

36. PRO, LC/7/16, Lord Chamberlain's Memorial, 21 December 1874.

37. Munby Diaries, 25 April 1865, vol. 33, TCC.

38. Hudson, *Munby, Man of Two Worlds,* 286, entry for 11 June 1870.

39. Bailey, "Parasexuality and Glamour," 149, 152.

40. Ibid., 152.

41. Browning, *Fifine at the Fair* (1872), st. 11, pp. 115–16.

42. Ibid., pp. 120–21.

43. Quoted in Donohue, "Empire Theatre," 59; see also LCC Theatrical Committee Papers, Empire Theatre of Varieties, 1889–1904, London Metropolitan Archives Library, LCC 10,803.

44. See Tracy C. Davis, *Actresses as Working Women;* idem, "Spectacle of Absent Costume"; as well as idem, *Economics of the British Stage,* 122–30, for a slightly different emphasis related to Mazeppa's absent costume and the economics of enjoyment. On wider links to the spectacle of women, see Walkowitz, *Prostitution and Victorian Society.*

45. Tracy C. Davis, "Spectacle of Absent Costume," 328; on pictorial legitimacy, see Nead, *Female Nude.*

46. Clipping, "Adah Isaacs Menken," 3 September 1864, Biographical Files, TM.

47. Quoted in McCullough, *Living Pictures,* 64.

48. Mulvey, "Visual Pleasures and Narrative Cinema"; E. Anne Kaplan, "Is the Gaze Male?" in Snitow, Stansell, and Thompson, *Power of Desire.* See also Gordon and Dubois, "Seeking Ecstasy on the Battlefield," 7; Gay, *Cultivation of Hatred;* and Bristow, *Vice and Vigilance.*

49. Cited in Donohue, "Empire Theatre," 59; see also Bland, "'Purifying' the Public World."

50. Mason, *Making of Victorian Sexuality,* 117; Walkowitz, *City of Dreadful Delight,* 5–6.

51. Tracy C. Davis, "Sex in Public Places"; idem, *Actresses as Working Women,* 120.

52. *Vigilance Record,* December 1890, 123, Women's Library. Through the office of the London County Council, which was in charge of licensing the Aquarium, the NVA made its appeal. The London County Council, in turn, made it a requirement for the Aquarium, if it wished to renew its license, to withdraw the poster.

53. Munby Diaries, 9 November 1868, vol. 36, TCC.

54. Quoted in S.R., *Life of Zaeo* (1891), 81. On the title page of this biography appears "with no apologies whatever to the Vigilance Society" a clear attempt to offer a counterargument to the one made by Mrs. Chant and others (cf. Ginisty, *Mémoires d'une danseuse*).

55. ESB, letter to the editor, *Standard,* 2 May 1890, reprinted in S.R., *Life of Zaeo* (1891), 87–88.

56. See Nead, *Victorian Babylon.*

57. The term *bill-posters* was often used instead of *bill* or *poster.*

58. Glennie and Thrift, "Consumers, Identities, and Consumption Spaces." See also bill, "Usher v. Powell" (on the back of which is written, "These to be put in shop windows"), Circus Scrapbooks, vol. 2, Th.Cts. 50, BL.

59. *Bournemouth Guardian,* 20 August 1898, 6, commenting on the female acrobats in Barnum's tenting troupe in Britain.

60. CWB to Captain Molesworth, of the Royal Aquarium, 28 May 1890, recorded in S.R., *Life of Zaeo* (1891), 123–24.

61. For another angle on representation, the acrobat's body, and "risky practice," see Fensham, "'Making-Real' the Body."

62. "The Making of Acrobats: An Interview with Zaeo," *Daily Graphic,* 13 February 1892, 5. The interview was, in part, a response to the controversy surrounding Amye Reade's two novels dealing with child acrobats. For a lengthier discussion of the controversy and the novels, see Assael, "Circus and Respectable Society," ch. 5.

63. See Michie, *Flesh Made Word,* ch. 1. Weakness and pallor became signs of beauty in the overrefined, and eating was connected to the Fall, Michie argues.

64. See Springhall, *Youth, Empire, and Society,* chs. 3–4. For a consideration of the negotiation between Britishness and imperial culture, see Samuel, *Patriotism,* vol. 2.

65. Graf, *Hints to Gymnasts* (1898), O1; see also Strehly, *L'Acrobatie et les acrobates* (1904). On female sport and training, see Fletcher, "Making and Breaking of a Female Tradition"; and, in a wider study, Holt, *Sport and the British,* 117–34.

66. See *Gymnast* 3, no. 33 (1 April 1894): 193–94.

67. Graf, *Hints to Gymnasts* (1898), 20.

68. "Zazel at the Aquarium," *Era,* 29 April 1877, 4.

69. On transgression, see Stallybrass and White, *Politics and Poetics of Transgression,* 21–33. See also Bakhtin, *Rabelais and His World,* chs. 3, 5; and Flaherty, "Reading Carnival."

70. Turner, *From Ritual to Theatre.* Turner places particular emphasis on the role leisure played in the industrial world in order to invert, parody, satirize, lampoon, burlesque, or subtly put down its central values. For a nineteenth-century view of the body and how this relates to Turner's inversion thesis, see Marcus, *Other Victorians;* see also Helen Day, "Female Daredevils," in Gardner and Rutherford, *The New Woman and Her Sisters.*

71. Where superhuman dexterity stops and pain begins is an interesting question addressed in Scarry, *Body in Pain.*

72. "A Serious Trapeze Accident," *Aberystwyth Observer,* 4 February 1871, 2.

73. "Horrifying Accident in a Music Hall," *Era,* 12 February 1871, 12.

74. "Blondin Interviewed," 10 September 1873, Theatre Scrapbook, BCL, Archive Division.

75. Account of 1859 quoted in *Wonderful! Wonderful! Wonderful!!!* [ca. 1860?], 10.

76. "High Rope Performances," *Era,* 16 August 1863, 11.

77. Hudson, *Munby, Man of Two Worlds,* 254–55, entry for 7 September 1868.

78. I do not use the term *professionals* to refer to educational qualifications or membership in elite clubs and associations. It is used here to separate the skilled performer, whose training usually began in childhood, from the unskilled performer, who lacked this background.

79. Letter to the editor, *Era,* 14 July 1872, 4.

80. "Rules and Regulations," Hernandez and Stone's circus, 1849, Astley's Files, TM.

81. Clipping, *Era*, [ca. 1885], Scrapbook Collection, 604, Liverpool, CFA.

82. Clipping, *Sunday Times*, 16 March 1853, Production Files (Drury Lane), TM.

83. Simmel, "Metropolis and Mental Life," 329.

84. Ibid.

85. *Hansard Parliamentary Debates*, 3d ser., vol. 172 (1863), col. 1282.

86. PRO, LC/1/128, LC Out letters, Spencer Ponsonby Fane to William Bodham Donne, 29 July 1863.

87. PRO, LC/1/127, LC In letters, Donne to Fane, 1 August 1863.

88. PP, *Select Committee to inquire into the Working of Acts for Licensing and Regulating of Theatres and Places of Public Entertainment*, 1866, vol. 16, p. 43, line 1054.

89. "The Acrobat's Bill," *Era*, 1 June 1879, 3.

90. *Hansard Parliamentary Debates*, 3d ser., vol. 105 (1873), cols. 1242–43.

91. See PP, *Royal Commission on Employment of Children, Young Persons and Women in Agriculture*, 1868–69, vol. 13.

92. *Public General Statutes*, Children's Dangerous Performances Act, 1879, 42 & 43 Vict., c. 34, sec. 3.

93. See Geertz, "Deep Play: Notes on the Balinese Cockfight," in Geertz, *Interpretation of Cultures*.

6. Sensational Imbalance

1. Best, *Mid-Victorian Britain*, 136.

2. See Tracy C. Davis, "Employment of Children."

3. Davin, "Waif Stories"; Cutt, *Ministering Angels*. See also Avery, *Childhood's Pattern;* Bratton, *Impact of Victorian Children's Fiction*, ch. 3; Davin, *Growing Up Poor*, 91, 162; and Jan, *On Children's Literature*.

4. Davin, "Waif Stories"; Bratton, *Impact of Victorian Children's Fiction*, 84. This shift was especially noticeable after the repeal of the stamp tax in 1855 and the duty on paper in 1861 (see Lang, "Children's Champions").

5. Davin, "Waif Stories." There are, however, earlier examples in children's fiction of performing children who are waifs; see, e.g., Charlotte Adams, *Stolen Child* (1838). Discussions of adult cruelty toward children assumed greater importance in the waif novel of the 1880s, when the campaign to save children from neglect and abuse earned legal and institutional legitimacy (see Assael, "Circus and Respectable Society," ch. 5; and Bratton, *Impact of Victorian Children's Fiction*, 94–95).

6. Lord Shaftesbury had a previous rapport with waif-fiction writers and their publishers (see Bratton, *Impact of Victorian Children's Fiction*, 85).

7. Burn, *Age of Equipoise*.

8. *Public General Statutes*, Children's Dangerous Performances Act, 1879, 42 & 43 Vict., c. 34, sec. 3.

9. Burn, *Age of Equipoise*, 8. My idea of "instability," as compared with Burn's notion of "equipoise," is connected to discussions of "moral panics" in Cohen, *Folk Devils and Moral Panics;* and Walkowitz, *City of Dreadful Delight*.

10. On the mid-Victorian mind and the plurality of ideas, see Kitson Clark, *Making of Victorian England;* Houghton, *Victorian Frame of Mind,* ch. 7; Hamilton Buckley, *Victorian Temper;* and Himmelfarb, *Victorian Minds.*

11. "In the Ring," *All the Year Round,* 28 January 1865, 20, 21.

12. "Alarming Trapeze Accident," *Era,* 21 March 1869, 5.

13. *Royal Leamington Spa Courier,* 3 July 1869, 6.

14. *Hansard Parliamentary Debates,* 3d ser., vol. 199 (1870), col. 1961; "The Exhibition at the Holborn Amphitheatre," *Era,* 20 March 1870, 13.

15. *Hansard Parliamentary Debates,* 3d ser., vol. 199 (1870), col. 1961. On female acrobats, see Assael, "Circus and Respectable Society," ch. 4; Tracy C. Davis, "Sex in Public Places"; and, from the perspective of the stage, idem, *Actresses as Working Women.*

16. PP, *Select Committee to inquire into the Working of Acts for Licensing and Regulating of Theatres and Places of Public Entertainment,* 1866, vol. 16, p. 43, line 1054. See ch. 5, n. 86, and the quotation preceding that note in the text.

17. For a more general discussion of the commercialized leisure market, see Bailey, "Custom, Capital, and Culture."

18. "Juvenile Acrobat Bill," *Era,* 21 July 1872, 12.

19. *Era Almanac,* 1867, 69; 1877, 83; 1878, 84.

20. Letter to the editor, *Era,* 21 July 1872, 12.

21. Davin, "Waif Stories"; Bratton, *Impact of Victorian Children's Fiction;* Lang, "Children's Champions."

22. On mid-Victorian narrative fantasy, see Cohen, *Lewis Carroll;* see also Knoepflmacher, "Balancing of Child and Adult," 501. On melodrama, see "Sensational Novels," *Quarterly Review* 226 (1863): 482–514; Brooks, *Melodramatic Imagination;* Booth, *English Melodrama;* and McWilliam, "Melodrama and the Historians."

23. Simpson, "*Hard Times* and Circus Times," 131; Philip Collins, "Dickens and Popular Amusements"; Schlicke, "Dickens in the Circus"; idem, *Dickens and Popular Entertainment;* idem, "Circus," 102.

24. Dickens and Collins deal with the subject of saving the circus girl in a different way from waif novelists. Dickens sees Jupe's exit from Sleary's troupe and into Gradgrind's schoolroom as a descent into a cold, utilitarian Benthamite world; Collins treats Madonna's release from Jubber's circus in slightly more critical terms. In neither case, however, does the child performer have to deal with the poverty, spiritual decay, and irreligion found in waif novels.

25. Bratton, *Impact of Victorian Children's Fiction,* 17–19.

26. *Little Acrobat and His Mother* (1872), synopsis in backmatter catalogue D, p. 3; text p. 20.

27. Ibid., 6, 10, 22.

28. *Mountebank's Children* (1866) 6, 7, 10, 17–18.

29. Ibid., 18.

30. Cited in Raymond Toole Stott, *Circus and Allied Arts,* 2:290. Walton's book was translated into Spanish as *Entre Bastidores O'hasta Hallarla* in 1910.

31. Walton, *Peep behind the Scenes* (1877), 112–13. The vanity that Jessie displays is similarly treated in Charlotte Adams's *Stolen Child* (1838), in which a young girl who dances publicly is abducted by a showman impressed by her gracefulness.

32. The ending of this story is similar to that of Frances Stratton's *Nan, the Circus Girl* (1898), in which fourteen-year-old Nan finds salvation after running away with Mr. Johnson's Travelling Circus.

33. Coveney, *Image of Childhood*; Pattison, *Child Figure in Literature*.

34. Mrs. Walton's emphasis was slightly different, as indicated, although the man who approaches Jessie and asks her to join the circus is represented as a corrupting agent who leads her into a life of sin.

35. *Hansard Parliamentary Debates*, 3d ser., vol. 212 (1872), col. 619.

36. *Mountebank's Children* (1866), 18.

37. Stretton, *Acrobat's Girlhood* (1889), 52; Patricia Demers, "Mrs. Sherwood and Hesba Stretton: The Letter and the Spirit of Evangelical Writing of and for Children," in MacGavran, *Romanticism and Children's Literature*.

38. Stretton, *Acrobat's Girlhood* (1889), 52.

39. Lang, "Children's Champions," 20.

40. The idea that children were bound to their masters like slaves was later developed by Amye Reade in *Ruby* (1889, reprint, 1890) and *Slaves of the Sawdust* (1892), although not in the waif-story genre. Rather, Reade's work was more closely allied to W. T. Stead's exposé on child prostitution in 1885.

41. *Little Acrobat and His Mother* (1872), 8. For a discussion of "interiority" in connection with this story, see Steedman, *Strange Dislocations,* ch. 6, esp. 103–4.

42. *Hansard Parliamentary Debates*, 3d ser., vol. 212 (1872), col. 622.

43. In a different way, O. G. Rejlander depicted children belonging to the urban poor through photography in this period (see da Costa Nunes, "O. G. Rejlander's Photographs").

44. On mid-Victorian laissez-faire principles, see Burn, *Age of Equipoise,* 161–231; and Bailey, "Custom, Capital, and Culture."

45. *Hansard Parliamentary Debates*, 3d ser., vol. 212 (1872), col. 620, 618.

46. Harris, *Private Lives, Public Spirit,* 196; see also Hoppen, *Mid-Victorian Generation,* 96.

47. *Hansard Parliamentary Debates*, 3d ser., vol. 212 (1872), col. 1504, brackets in original; "Acrobat Bill," *Daily Telegraph,* 22 July 1872, 2.

48. "A Plea for Acrobats," *Era,* 14 July 1872, 4.

49. *Hansard Parliamentary Debates*, 3d ser., vol. 212 (1872), col. 1505; "Acrobat Bill," *Daily Telegraph,* 22 July 1872, 2.

50. *Public General Statutes*, Children's Dangerous Performances Act, 1879, 42 & 43 Vict., c. 34, sec. 3; see also *Bills, Public, etc.,* "Acrobat's Bill," 1872, bill 173.

51. Quoted in Cunningham, *Children and Childhood,* 140.

52. On the distinction between childhood and adolescence, see Gillis, *Youth and History.*

53. "Infant Acrobats," *Era,* 14 July 1872, 4.

54. Letter to the editor, ibid., 21 July 1872, 12.

55. Ibid., 27 November 1870, 12.

56. "Infant Acrobats," ibid., 7 July 1872, 12.

57. "Children's Dangerous Performances Bill," ibid., 20 July 1879, 4.

58. "Children's Dangerous Performances Bill," ibid., 6 July 1879, 4; 20 July 1879, 4.

59. "Infant Acrobats," ibid., 7 July 1872, 12.

60. "Infant Acrobats," ibid., 14 July 1872, 4.

61. *Hansard Parliamentary Debates,* 3d ser., vol. 216 (1873), col. 1244.

62. Ibid.

63. "A Plea for Acrobats," *Era,* 14 July 1872, 4.

64. *Hansard Parliamentary Debates,* 3d ser., vol. 216 (1873), col. 1244.

65. Best, *Mid-Victorian Britain,* 178. The phrase "little mothers" is taken from Davin, *Growing Up Poor,* esp. ch. 5.

66. *Hansard Parliamentary Debates,* 3d ser., vol. 212 (1872), col. 620.

67. See, e.g., "Moveable Dwellings Bill," *Era,* 4 February 1893, 16; and Assael, "Circus and Respectable Society," 205–7.

68. *Public General Statues,* Children's Dangerous Performances Act, 1879, 42 & 43 Vict., c. 34, sec. 3.

69. *Hansard Parliamentary Debates,* 3d ser., vol. 282 (1883), col. 1462.

70. See *Public General Statues,* An Act for the Prevention of Cruelty to Children, 1889, 52 & 53 Vict., c. 44, sec. 3, clause c. See also ibid., 1894, 57 & 58 Vict., c. 27.

71. Amye Reade's *Ruby* (1889, reprint, 1890) and *Slaves of the Sawdust* (1892), mentioned earlier, provided fuel for this argument (see above, n. 40).

72. Cf. Tracy C. Davis, "Employment of Children."

73. An Act to Extend the Age under which the Employment of Young Persons in Dangerous Performances is Prohibited, 1897, 60 & 61 Vict., c. 52, sec. 1. For a fuller discussion, see Assael, "Circus and Respectable Society," ch. 4, sec. 3.

Conclusion

1. Dickens, *Hard Times* ([1854] 1966), 23.

2. Ibid., 20.

3. Bakhtin, *Rabelais and His World;* see the discussion above, in the introduction, and see also Bailey's ruminations on the carnivalesque and the intellectual opportunities that studies on it can offer (Bailey, "Politics and Poetics," 155).

Bibliography

Primary Sources

Manuscript, Scrapbook, and Cuttings Collections

Birmingham Central Library (BCL), Archive Division
Baths and Parks Committee Minutes
MS 744, Aston Hall
Newspaper Cuttings
Theatre Scrapbook

Bodleian Library, Oxford
Johnson, John, Collection

Brighton Reference Library
Clippings on the Circus

British Library (BL)
Astley's Scrapbooks. Th.Cts. 35–37 (3 vols.).
Babbage MSS
Circus Scrapbooks. Th.Cts. 50 (2 vols.: vol. 1, Blondin–Gantiez; vol. 2, Ginnett–White).
Dramatic Biography. Th.Cts. 75–76.
Egerton MSS (Covent Garden)
Eyre, Samuel. Theatrical Programme. Fillinham Collection. 1889.b.10/6.
Henry's Conjuring Entertainments. Playbills, 364.

Huskisson Papers
Kemble Papers
Knight, G. W., Collection. Playbills, 481.
Leeds. Playbills, 321.
Leeds. Playbills, 1878d.19(11).
London III. Astley's. Playbills, 171.
London III. Carr-Glyn Collection. Playbills, 352–63.
London III. Hengler's. Playbills, 432.
London III. Liberty and Property Defence League, 8139a.47(1), 8277ee.48.
London III. London Theatres. Playbills, 433.
London III. National Canine Defence League, 8425s, 07295.d.31.
London III. Programmes, 1880.b.31.
Lord Chamberlain (Add. MSS)
Manchester. Playbills, 251, vol. 2.
Marsh, John, MSS
Nottingham. Playbills, 1888.c.18.
Place Papers
Playbills, Programmes and Theatre Cuttings. Playbills, 251.
Playbills, Programmes and Theatre Cuttings. Playbills, 434–35.

Squire, William Barclay, Collection. Playbills, 342–45.

Streatfeild, W. E., Collection. Th.Cts. 14–34.

Surrey Zoological Gardens. Th.Cts. 51–58.

Theatres. Cuttings from Newspapers. Th.Cts. 68–70.

Theatrical Notices from Newspapers. Th.Cts. 7–13.

Zoological Gardens. Playbills, 323.

Butler Library, Columbia University

Special Collections

Central Reference Library, Islington

Agricultural Hall

Highbury Barn

Cheltenham Art Gallery and Museum

Playbills

Circus Friends Association (CFA)

Scrapbook Collection, Blackburn

Scrapbook Collection, Liverpool

Croydon Local Studies Library

Local Board of Health Minutes

MSS on History of Croydon

Earl's Court Exhibition Centre (EC)

Barnum Files

Buffalo Bill Files

Family Records Centre, London (FRC)

Census Return for England and Wales, 1851–91

Guildhall Library, Corporation of London

GR 331, Bartholomew and Frost Fairs

Noble Collection

Playbills E, G, R–Z

Highbury Library, Islington

Agricultural Hall Clippings

Highbury Barn Clippings

Holborn Local Studies Library

Metropolitan Board of Works Minutes of Proceedings

Illinois State University, Normal, Milner Library

Poster Collection

Lancashire Record Office, Preston

DDCm box 26, Shuttleworth, Dallas, Crombleholme Collection

Liverpool Public Library

Council Proceedings

JUS 347 Licensing Records

Liverpool Royal Society for the Prevention of Cruelty to Animals Minutes (1871–95)

Miscellaneous Theatre Programmes, 1877–1917

Watch Committee

London Borough of Lambeth, Archives Department & Minet Library (ML)

Astley's Files

Cooke, William, Papers

Entertainment License Plans
Printed Ephemera
Vauxhall Gardens

London Borough of Marylebone Library
Ashbridge Collection

London Metropolitan Archives Library
Archives of the London County Council (LCC)
Archives of the Metropolitan Board of Works (MBW)

Mander and Mitchenson Collection
Circus Collection (3 boxes)

Museum of the City of New York
Circus Files

National Society for the Prevention of Cruelty to Children
Annual Reports, 1885–1900

New York Public Library, Lincoln Center (NYPL)
Circus Files
Scrapbook
Stead Collection

Public Record Office (PRO)
Home Office (HO/45)
Lord Chamberlain (LC/1, LC/7)

Richmond Record Office
Vestry Minutes Books

Royal Borough of Kensington and Chelsea Libraries
Sambourne, Edward Linley, Family Archive
Scrapbooks (2 vols.)
Vestry Minutes

Royal Society for the Prevention of Cruelty to Animals (RSPCA)
Annual Reports, 1844–1901
General Council Minutes

South Islington Finsbury Library
Biography
Grimaldi
Miscellaneous Poster Box
Phelps
Playbills
Programs
Views

Southwark Local Studies Library (SLS)
Astley's
Playbills, Miscellaneous
Press Cuttings 791.3Ast, 791.3Loc
Surrey Gardens
Surrey Theatre Files

Surrey County Record Office
Performing Animals Register, 1925

Theatre Museum, London (TM)
Astley's Files
Biographical Files
Circus Files
Company Files
Coxe, A. H., Collection (Blythe House, Olympia)
Miscellaneous Files
MSS Files, 1793–1842
Production Files
Theatre Buildings Files

Trinity College Library, Cambridge
(TCC)
Munby Diaries

Tyne and Wear Archives, Newcastle
(TW)
Fenwick Collection
Finance Committee Minutes, Newcastle
Gateshead Common Council Minutes
Newcastle Common Council Minutes
North Shields Common Council Minutes
South Shields Common Council Minutes
Spence Watson, Mable, Letters
Town Improvement Committee Minutes, Newcastle
Wood Collection

University of Glasgow Library,
Special Collections Department
Ephemera Collection

Victoria & Albert Museum Library
Microfiche Collection, Playbills and
    Programmes from London Theatre,
1801–1900

Victoria Local Studies Library
Local History Collection, Prints/
    Theatres
Rate Books, 1880–89

Women's Library, London
Metropolitan University
National Vigilance Association
    Records

Printed Primary Sources

NEWSPAPERS

Aberystwyth Observer
Ashbourne Chronicle
Bath Courier
Belfast Evening Telegraph
Belfast Newsletter
Bell's Life in London
Birmingham Daily Mail
Birmingham Daily Post
Birmingham Journal
Bournemouth Guardian
Bradford Observer
Bury Free Press
Cambrian
Cardiff Times and South Wales Weekly
    News
Carlisle Examiner
Carmarthen Journal and General Advertiser for the Principality

Cheltenham Looker-on
Cork Examiner
Coventry Standard
Croydon Advertiser and Surrey County
    Observer
Daily Chronicle
Daily Graphic
Daily Telegraph
Darlington Telegraph
Derby Mercury
Dover Chronicle and Kent and Sussex
    Advertiser
Entr'acte
Era
Evening Post (Exeter)
Evening Standard
Express
Field
Glowworm and Evening News
Graphic

Guardian
Hampshire Advertiser
Hereford Journal
Independent
Leeds Intelligencer
Licensed Victuallers' Mirror
Liverpool Mail
Manchester Courier
Manchester Examiner
Mirror
Morning Advertiser
Morning Herald
Morning Post
Newport Gazette
Nottingham Daily Express
Oldham Chronicle
Peterborough Weekly News and General
    Advertiser
Portsmouth and Naval Gazette
Quiver
Royal Leamington Spa Courier
Sheffield Daily Telegraph
Sheffield and Rotherham Independent
Sheffield Times
South Wales Daily Star
Stage
Stockton Herald, South Durham and
    Cleveland Advertiser
Supplement to the Sheffield and Rother-
    ham Independent
Sussex Agricultural Express and County
    Advertiser
Times (London)
Western Daily Press
Yorkshire Chronicle
Yorkshire Gazette

PERIODICALS

Academy: A Weekly Review of Literature,
    Science, and Art
Alden's Illustrated Family Miscellany
    and Oxford Monthly

All the Year Round
Animal World
Athenaeum
Band Of Mercy Almanac
Caledonia
Chambers's Journal
Child's Guardian
Clown of London
Dog's Bulletin
Drama; or, Theatrical Pocket Magazine
Dramatic, Equestrian, and Musical Sick
    Fund Association Almanac
English Illustrated Magazine
Entr'Acte Annual
Era Almanac
Fraser's Magazine
Gymnast
Household Words
Illustrated London News
Jewish World
Journal of the Anthropological Society of
    London
King Pole
Leisure Hour
National Magazine
Oxberry's Dramatic Biography
Pall Mall Gazette
Pearson's Magazine
Penny Illustrated Paper
Players
Punch
Quarterly Review
Record
Saturday Review
Sawdust Ring
Showman
Sketch
Spectator
Theosophical Review
Tomahawk
Windsor Magazine
Variety Artistes' Illustrated Magazine
Vigilance Record

PARLIAMENTARY PAPERS (PP)

Hansard Parliamentary Debates
Select Committee Reports

Report and Proceedings of Standing Committee C on Performing Animals, 1923,
  vol. 8
Report and Proceedings of Standing Committee D on Performing Animals, 1921,
  vol. 7
Select Committee on Bill to Consolidate Laws Relating to Improper Treatment of
  Animals, 1831–32, vol. 5
Select Committee on Constitution, Efficiency, Emoluments and Finances of Metro-
  politan Fire Brigade, 1877, vol. 14
Select Committee on Criminal and Destitute Juveniles, 1852, vol. 7
Select Committee on Performing Animals, 1921, vol. 7
Select Committee on Performing Animals, 1922, vol. 5
Select Committee on Regulation of Public Houses, Hotels, Beershops, Dancing Sa-
  loons, Coffee Houses, Theatres and Places of Public Entertainment, 1852–53, vol.
  37, and 1854, vol. 14
Select Committee on Temporary Dwellings Bill, 1887, vol. 13
Select Committee to inquire into Laws affecting Dramatic Literature, 1831–32, vol. 7
Select Committee to inquire into the Working of Acts for Licensing and Regulating of
  Theatres and Places of Public Entertainment, 1866, vol. 16

Royal Commission Reports

Royal Commission on Employment of Children, Young Persons and Women in Agriculture, 1868–69, vol. 13
Royal Commission for inquiring into Housing of the Working Classes, 1884–85, vol. 31
Royal Commission to inquire into working of Elementary Education Acts, 1887, vol.
  30

Accounts and Papers

Papers Relating to the Burning Down of the Brooklyn Theatre, 1877, vol. 68
Papers Relating to the Burning Down of the Brooklyn Theatre, 1878, vol. 61
Return of Licenses Granted under Act to amend Law relating to Cruelty to Animals,
  1877, vol. 68

BOOKS

A' Beckett, Arthur William. *Green Room Recollections.* Bristol: J. W. Arrowsmith,
  1896.
Adams, Charlotte. *The Stolen Child; or, Laura's Adventures with the Travelling Showman and His Family.* London: J. W. Parker, 1838.

A. G. S. *Jenny and the Showman; or, Mind What Mother Says.* London: Tiny Library, 1871.

Amherst, J. H. *The Battle of Waterloo.* London: Duncombe, 1874.

———. *Napoleon Bonaparte's Invasion of Russia; or, The Conflagration of Moscow.* London: Duncombe, 1854.

Astley, Philip. *Astley's System of Equestrian Education.* Dublin: Thomas Burnside, 1802.

———. *Description and Historical Account of the Places Now the Theatre of War in the Low Countries.* London, 1794.

———. *Modern Riding Master; or, A Key to the Knowledge of the Horse and Horsemanship.* London, 1775.

———. *Remarks on the Profession and Duties of a Soldier.* London, 1794.

Baker, Henry Barton. *The London Stage: Its History and Traditions from 1576–1888.* 1889. London: Routledge and Sons, 1904.

Ballantine, J. *The Life of David Roberts, R.A.* Edinburgh: Adam and Charles Black, 1866.

Banks, George Linnaeus, ed. *Blondin: His Life and Performance.* London: Routledge, Warne & Routledge, 1862.

Barlee, Ellen. *Pantomime Waifs: or, A Plea for Our City Children.* London: S. W. Partridge, 1884.

Barnum, P. T. *The Art of Money Getting.* London: Ward, Lock, 1883.

———. *Selected Letters of P. T. Barnum.* Ed. A. H. Saxon. New York: Columbia University Press, 1983.

———. *Struggles and Triumphs: or, Forty Years' Recollections of P. T. Barnum.* London: Sampson Low, 1869.

Blaikie, William. *Sound Bodies for Our Boys and Girls.* London: Sampson Low, 1884.

Blau, Henry. *Some Notes on the Stage and Its Influences on the Education of the Masses, Players, and Playgoers, Etc.* London: Society of Science Letters and Art of London, 1884.

Bostock, E. H. *Menageries, Circuses, and Theatres.* London: Chapman & Hall, 1927.

Browning, Robert. *Fifine at the Fair.* London: Smith, Elder, 1872.

Bulwer-Lytton, E. *The Lady of Lyons.* Paris: A and W. Galignani, 1838.

Bunce, John Thackray. *History of the Corporation of Birmingham.* Vol. 2. Birmingham: Cornish Brothers, 1885.

Burgin, George Brown. *Some More Memoirs.* London: Hutchinson, 1924.

Burke, Edmund. *A Philosophical Enquiry into the Origins of Our Ideas of the Sublime and the Beautiful.* 1757. Ed. Alan Philips. Oxford: Oxford University Press, 1990.

Cabinet of Curiosities; or, Wonder of the World Displayed. Forming a Repository of Whatever Is Remarkable in the Regions of Nature and Art, Extraordinary Events, Eccentric Biography, Etc. Etc. London: J. Limbard, 1831.

Carlyle, Thomas. *On Heroes, Hero Worship, and the Heroic in History.* 1841. Reprint, London: Cassell, 1908.

———. *Past and Present.* 1843. Reprint, London: J. M. Dent, 1902.

Catalogue of the Napoleon Museum . . . Now Exhibiting at the Egyptian Hall, Piccadilly from Ten till Dusk. . . . London, 1843.

Clive, Kitty. *Nada, the Circus Girl.* London: Sunday School Union, 1906.

Cody, William. *The Life of Buffalo Bill.* 1879. London: Senate, 1994.

———. *Story of the Wild West and Campfire Chats.* Philadelphia: Historical Publishing, 1888.

Collins, Wilkie. *Hide and Seek.* 1854. Reprint, Oxford: Oxford University Press, 1993.

Confessions of a Dancing Girl. London: Heath, Cranton & Ouseley, 1913.

Conklin, George. *The Ways of the Circus.* New York: Harper Bros., 1921.

Cook, Edward Dutton. *A Book of the Play.* 2 vols. London: Sampson Low, Marston, Searle & Rivington, 1876.

———. *On the Stage: Studies of Theatrical History and the Actor's Art.* 2 vols. London: Sampson Low, 1883.

Cooper, Anthony Ashley [7th Earl of Shaftesbury]. *Speeches and Addresses: Meeting at St. James's Hall.* London: National Education Union, 1872.

———. *Speeches and Addresses on Religious Services in Theatres.* London: B. Seeley, 1860.

———. *Speeches and Addresses on the Second Reading of the Factory Bill.* London: Chapman & Hall, 1874.

———. *Speeches and Addresses upon Subjects Having Relation . . . to the Labouring Class.* London, 1868.

Cooper, Frederick Renad. *Nothing Extenuate: The Life of Frederick Fox Cooper.* London: Barrie & Rockliff, 1964.

Darcy [Helen J. Eastwood]. *Darcy, the Young Acrobat.* London: Religious Tract Society, 1884.

Decastro, J. *The Memoirs of J. Decastro.* Ed. R. Humphrey. London: Sherwood, Jones, 1824.

de Goncourt, Edmond, *The Zemganno Brothers.* London: John and Robert Maxwell, 1879.

Denier, Tony. *How to Join the Circus and Gymnasium.* New York: A Happy Hours Co., 1877.

Dickens, Charles. *Hard Times.* 1854. Ed. George Ford and Sylvère Monod. New York: W. W. Norton, 1966.

———. *Hard Times.* 1854. Ed. Paul Schlicke. London: Oxford University Press, 1989.

———. *Nicholas Nickleby.* 1838–39. Ed. Michael Slater. Harmondsworth: Penguin Books, 1978.

———. *The Old Curiosity Shop.* 1840–41. Ed. Elizabeth M. Brennan. London: Oxford University Press, 1997.

———. *Sketches by Boz and Other Early Papers.* 1833–36. Ed. Michael Slater. London: J. M. Dent, 1993.

———. *The Uncommercial Traveller.* 1860. Ed. Edwin P. Whipple. New York: Hurd & Houghton, 1877.

Dickens, Charles [Boz, pseud.]. *Memoirs of Joseph Grimaldi.* Philadelphia: Lea & Blanchard, 1838.

Dibdin, Charles, the Younger. *Memoirs of Charles Dibden the Younger.* Ed. George Speaight. London: Society for Theatre Research, 1956.

Dolby, George. *Charles Dickens as I Knew Him.* London: T. Fisher Unwin, 1885.

Doss, Nundo Lall. *Reminiscences, English and Australasian: Being an Account of a Visit to England, Australia, New Zealand, Tasmania, Ceylon, &c.* Calcutta: M. C. Bhowmick, 1893.

Elliston, Robert William. *Copy of a Memorial Presented to the Lord Chamberlain by the Committee of Management of the Theatre Royal.* London: John Miller, 1818.

Esquiros, Alphonse. *The English at Home.* Trans. Lascelles Wraxall. 2 vols. London: Chapman & Hall, 1861.

Ferguson, Adam. *An Essay on the History of Civil Society.* 1767. Ed. Fania Oz-Salzberger. Cambridge: Cambridge University Press, 1995.

Frost, Thomas. *Circus Life and Circus Celebrities.* London: Tinsley Brothers, 1875.

——. *The Old Showmen and the Old London Fairs.* London: Tinsley Brothers, 1874.

——. *Reminiscences of a Country Journalist.* London: Ward & Downey, 1886.

Furber, Professor. *The Lady's Equestrian Companion; or, Golden Key to Equitation.* London: Saunders & Otley, 1847.

Ginisty, Paul. *Mémoirs d'une danseuse de Corde Mme. Saqui, 1786–1866.* Paris: Librairie Chapentier et Fasquelle, 1907.

Graf, Ferdinand. *Hints to Gymnasts: Being Sound Advice and Hints to Leaders and Teachers in Gymnasiums and Schools.* London: Dunn Collins, 1898.

Graham, Maria. *Journal of a Residence in India.* Edinburgh, 1812.

Grant, James. *The Great Metropolis.* 1836. 2 vols. Reprint, London: Saunders & Otley, 1838.

Gravelet, Jean Francois [Blondin]. *Dean's Moveable Book of Blondin's Astounding Exploits at the Crystal Palace.* London: Dean & Sons, 1862.

Greig, James. *The Farrington Diary.* 8 vols. London: Hutchinson, 1922–28.

Gresswell, Fred. *Bright Boots.* London: Robert Hale, 1956.

Hall, William Clarke. *The Law Relating to Children.* London: Stevens & Sons, 1894.

Hamilton, A. H. *The Summer Guide to the Amusements of London; and Provincial Excursionist for 1848.* London: Kent & Richards, 1848.

Harvey, Frederick James. *Physical Exercises and Gymnastics for Girls and Women.* London: Longmans, 1896.

Haweis, Rev. H. R. *Music and Morals.* London: Strahan, 1871.

Hibbert, Henry George. *Fifty Years of a Londoner's Life.* London: Grant Richards, 1916.

Hill, Benson Earle. *Playing About; or, Theatrical Anecdotes and Adventures.* 2 vols. London: printed for the author and sold by W. Sams, Bookseller to the Queen, 1840.

History of the Royal Circus. N.p., n.d.

Hodder, Edwin. *George Smith (of Coalville): The Story of an Enthusiast.* London: James Nisbet, 1896.

——. *Life and Work of the Seventh Earl of Shaftesbury.* London: Cassell, 1886.

Hood, Tom. *Harlequin Little Red Riding-Hood; or The Wicked Wolf and the Wirtuous Woodcutter.* In *Drawing Room Plays and Parlour Pantomimes,* ed. Clement Scott. London: Stanley Rivers, 1870.

Horne, Rev. Thomas. *Digest of Already Existing By-Laws in the United Kingdom, Affecting the Business of Open-Air Amusement Caterers.* Oldham: privately printed, 1899.

———. *The Showmen's Guild of Great Britain: The Story of Its Rise and Progress.* Oldham: privately printed, 1951.

Howison, John. *Foreign Scenes and Travelling Recreations.* 2 vols. Edinburgh: Oliver & Boyd, 1825.

Hunt, T. J. *The Life Story of T. J. Hunt: An Autobiography.* London, 1936.

Jones, Jack. *Unfinished Journey.* London: Hamish Hamilton, 1937.

Kant, Immanuel. *Observations on the Feeling of the Beautiful and the Sublime.* 1763. Trans. John T. Goldthwait. Berkeley: University of California Press, 1960.

Keith, Charlie. *Circus Life and Amusements.* Derby: Bewley & Roe, 1879.

Kilmer, A. J. *The Circus and Other Essays.* New York: Laurence J. Cromme, 1916.

Leotard [Gymnast]. *Dean's New Moveable Book of Leotard, Blondin as Ape, Blondin, Etc.* London: Dean & Sons, 1862.

———. *Mémoires de Léotard.* Paris: Simon, Bacon, 1860.

Le Roux, H., and Jules Garnier. *Acrobats and Mountebanks.* 1889. Trans. A. P. Morton. London: Chapman & Hall, 1890.

Liberty and Property Defence League. London: The League, 1889, 1893, 1894.

The Little Acrobat and His Mother. London: Religious Tract Society, 1872.

Lloyd, James. *My Circus Life.* London: Noel Douglas, 1925.

Mackie, Charles. *Norfolk Annals: A Chronological Record of Remarkable Events in the Nineteenth Century.* 2 vols. Norwich: Norfolk Chronicle Office, 1901.

Mayhew, Augustus. *Paved with Gold; or, The Romance and Reality of the London Streets, an Unfashionable Novel.* London: Ward, Lock, 1857.

Mayhew, Henry. *The Great World of London.* London: David Bogue, 1856.

———. *London Labour and the London Poor.* Vol. 3. London: Griffin, Bohn, 1861.

Meerza, Najaf Koolee. *Journal of a Residence in England, and a Journey from Syria . . . &c.* Trans. Assad Y. Kayat. 2 vols. London: privately printed, 1839.

Miller, D. P. *The Life of a Showman, to Which Is Added Managerial Struggles.* London: Lacy, 1849.

Montague, Charles W. *Recollections of an Equestrian Manager.* London: W. and R. Chambers, 1881.

Morley, Henry. *The Journal of a London Playgoer.* 1866. Reprint, Leicester: Leicester University Press, 1974.

———. *Memoirs of Bartholomew Fair.* Glasgow: George Routledge & Sons, 1892.

The Mountebank's Children. London: Society for Promoting Christian Knowledge, 1866.

Mukharji, T. N. *A Visit to Europe.* Calcutta: W. Newman, 1889.

Mulock, Dinah [Mrs. Craik, pseud.]. *The Unkind Word and Other Stories.* London: Hurst & Blackett, 1870.

Mundella, A. J. *Secular and Religious Education.* London: Sunday School Union, 1884.

Nadkarni, Rao B. G. N. *Journal of a Visit to Europe in 1896.* Bombay: D. B. Taraporevala & Sons, 1903.

Norris, S. *Phil, the Showman; or, Life in the Sawdust Ring.* London: Shurmer Sibthorp, 1902.

Nowrojee, Jehangeer, and Hirjeeboy Merwanjee. *Journal of a Residence of Two and a Half Years in Great Britain.* London: W. H. Allen, 1841.

Paterson, Peter [James Glass Bertram]. *Behind the Scenes: Being the Confessions of a Strolling Player.* Edinburgh: D. Mathers, 1859.

———. *Glimpses of Real Life as Seen in the Theatrical World and in Bohemia: Being the Confessions of Peter Paterson, a Strolling Comedian.* Edinburgh: William P. Nimmo, 1864.

A Peep at Bartholomew Fair Containing an Interesting Account of the Amusements and Divisions of That Famous Metropolitan Carnival, etc. London: Macdonald, 1837.

Pepys, Samuel. *The Diary of Samuel Pepys.* Vol. 9. *1668–69.* Ed. Robert Latham and William Matthews. 1971. Reprint, London: HarperCollins, 2000.

Planché, James Robinson. *The Recollections and Reflections of J. R. Planché.* 2 vols. London: Tinsley Brothers, 1872.

Pyne, W. H., and William Combe. *The Microcosm of London; or, London in Miniature.* 3 vols. London: R. Ackermann, 1808–11.

Ram, Jhinda. *My Trip to Europe.* Lahore: Mufid-I-Am Press, 1893.

Reade, Amye. *Ruby: A Novel Founded on the Life of a Circus Girl.* London: Author's Co-operative, 1889. Reprinted as *Ruby: or, How Girls Are Trained for Circus Life. Founded on Fact.* London: Trischler, 1890.

———. *Slaves of the Sawdust.* London: F. V. White, 1892.

Rede, Leman Thomas. *The Road to the Stage; or, The Performer's Preceptor.* London: Joseph Smith, 1827.

Report of the Proceedings of the Actors' Benevolent Fund, 1898–1909. London, 1898.

Robinson, Henry Crabb. *The London Theatre, 1811–1866: Selections from the Diary of Henry Crabb Robinson.* Ed. Eluned Brown. London: Society for Theatre Research, 1966.

Sala, George Augustus. *Twice Round the Clock; or, The Hours of the Day and Night in London.* London: Houlston & Wright, 1859.

Salter, Joseph. *The East in the West; or, Work among the Asiatics and Africans in London.* London: S. W. Partridge, 1896.

Sanger, George. *Seventy Years a Showman.* 1908. Intro. Colin MacInnes. London: MacGibbon & Kee, 1966.

Smith, Albert, ed. *Gavarni in London: Sketches of London Life and Character.* 1849. London: Dean & Son, 1859.

———. *Natural History of the Ballet Girl.* London: D. Bogue, 1847.

Smith, Elmer Boyd. *The Circus and All about It.* New York: Frederick A. Stokes, 1909.

Smith, George. *George Smith of Coalville: A Chapter in Philanthropy.* London: Haughton, 1881.

———. *George Smith of Coalville and His Work for Children: A Letter Signed by G. Smith.* Rugby, 1893.

———. *Gipsy Life: Being an Account of Gipsies and Their Children.* London: Haughton, 1880.

———. *I've Been a Gipsying; or, Rambles among Our Gipsies and Their Children, Etc.* London: T. Fischer Unwin, 1883.

———. *A Lecture by George Smith Delivered before the Association of Public Sanitary Inspectors.* London, 1888.

Smith, Thomas. *Recollections of the British Institution for Promoting the Fine Arts in the United Kingdom.* London, 1860.

Spencer, Charles. *Modern Gymnastics.* London: Frederick Ware, 1866.

S.R. *The Life of Zaeo: "Diva dell' Aria" and the Story of the Vigilance Persecution.* London: Universal Press Agency, 1891.

Stratton, Frances. *Nan, the Circus Girl.* London: John F. Shaw, 1898.

Strehly, G. *L'Acrobatie et les acrobates: Texte et dessins.* Paris: Librairie Ch. Delagrave, 1904.

Stretton, Hesba [Sara Smith]. *An Acrobat's Girlhood.* London: Society for Promoting Christian Knowledge, 1889.

Stutt, Joseph. *Sports and Pastimes of the People of England.* London: J. White, 1801.

The Thespian Preceptor; or, A Full Display of the Scenic Art. London: J. Roach at the Theatrical Library, 1811.

Third Annual Report of the Executive Committee of the National Vigilance Association. London, 1887.

Timbs, John. *Curiosities of London: Exhibiting the Most Rare and Remarkable Objects of Interest in the Metropolis.* 1855. Reprint, London: Longmans, Green, Reader & Dyer, 1868.

Van Hare, G. *Fifty Years of a Showman's Life; or, The Life and Travels of Van Hare.* London: W. H. Allen, 1888.

Vasey, George. *The Philosophy of Laughter and Smiling.* London: J. Burns, 1875.

Walker, John, and W. Dimond. *Napoleon, the Hunter of the Alps.* London, 1828.

Wallett, W. F. *The Public Life of W. F. Wallett, the Queen's Jester: An Autobiography.* Ed. John Luntley. London: Benrose & Sons, 1870.

Walton, O. F. *A Peep behind the Scenes.* London: Religious Tract Society, 1877.

Watkins, H. L. *Four Years in Europe: The Barnum and Bailey Greatest Show on Earth in the Old World, 1897–1901.* Paris [?]: privately printed, 1901.

Waugh, B. *Benjamin Waugh: Founder of the NSPCC and Framer of the Children's Charter.* London: C. W. Daniel, 1939.

Wild, Samuel. *The Original, Complete, and Only Authentic Story of Old Wild's.* Ed. Trim [William Broadley Megson]. London: G. Vickers, 1888.

William, Rev. John. *Notes and Narratives of Thirty Years' Missionary and Ministerial Labours in England and Wales.* London: Machynelleth, 1885.

Wonderful! Wonderful! Wonderful!!! The Life and Extraordinary Career of Blondin, the Ascentionist. London: C. Elliott, [ca. 1860?].

Wright, Thomas. *Some Habits and Customs of the Working Classes.* London: Tinsley Brothers, 1867.

Secondary Sources

Reference Works

Adams, W. Davenport. *Dictionary of the Drama.* Vol. 1. London: Chatto & Windus, 1904.

Banham, Martin. *The Cambridge Guide to the Theatre.* Cambridge: Cambridge University Press, 1992.

Boase, Frederick. *Modern English Biography.* London: Frank Cass, 1965.

Burnett, John, David Vincent, and David Mayall, eds. *The Autobiography of the Working Class: An Annotated and Critical Biography.* Vols. 1 and 3. Brighton, UK: Harvester, 1984–89.

Burnim, Kalman A., Philip H. Highfill Jr., and Edward A. Langhans. *A Biographical Dictionary of Actors.* 16 vols. Edwardsville: Southern Illinois Press, 1973–93.

Cheshire, D. F., U. Schneider, and L. Senelick. *British Music Hall, 1840–1923: A Bibliography and Guide to Sources.* Hamden, CT: Archon Books, 1981.

Delon, Michael, ed. *Encyclopedia of the Enlightenment.* 2 vols. London: Fitzroy Dearborn, 2001.

Enciclopedia dello spettacolo. Rome: Casa Editice Le Maschere, 1957.

Howard, Diana. *London Theatres and Music Halls, 1850–1950.* London: Library Association, 1970.

Mitchell, B. R., and Phyllis Deane. *Abstract of British Historical Statistics.* Cambridge: Cambridge University Press, 1962.

Pickering, David. *Encyclopedia of Pantomime.* Andover, Hants.: Gale Research International, 1993.

Scholes, Percy A. *Oxford Companion to Music.* 1938. Reprint, Oxford: Oxford University Press, 1991.

Stenton, Michael, and Stephen Lees, eds. *Dod's Parliamentary Companion.* 2 vols. Hassocks, UK: Harvester, 1976.

Thespian Dictionary. London: Ivy Lane, 1805.

Toole Stott, Raymond. *Circus and Allied Arts: A World Bibliography.* 4 vols. Derby: Derby & Sons, 1958–71

———. *Circus and Allied Arts, 1500–1982.* Vol. 5. Foreword by John Fisher. Formby: Circus Friends Association, 1992.

Turner, John. *Victorian Arena, the Performers: A Dictionary of British Circus Biography.* Vols. 1 and 2. Formby, UK: Lingdales, 1995–2000.

Wrigley, E. A., and R. Schofield. *The Population History of England, 1541–1871*. Cambridge: Cambridge University Press, 1981.

Books and Articles

Abrams, Anne Uhry. *The Valiant Hero: Benjamin West and Grand-Style History Painting*. Washington, DC: Smithsonian Institution Press, 1985.

Ackroyd, Peter. *Dressing Up: Transvestism and Drag, the History of an Obsession*. London: Jarrod & Sons, 1979.

Allen, Rick. "Munby Reappraised: The Diary of an English Flaneur." *Journal of Victorian Culture* 5, no. 2 (2000): 260–86.

Allen, Robert C. *Horrible Prettiness: Burlesque and American Culture*. Chapel Hill: University of North Carolina Press, 1991.

Altick, Richard. *Shows of London*. Cambridge: Harvard University Press, 1978.

Anderson, Benedict. *Imagined Communities: Reflections on the Origins and Spread of Nationalism*. London: Verso, 1983.

Ariès, Philippe. *Centuries of Childhood: A Social History of Family Life*. Trans. Robert Baldick. Harmondsworth: Penguin Books, 1973.

Ashfield, Andrew, and Peter de Bolla, eds. *The Sublime: A Reader in British Eighteenth-Century Aesthetic Theory*. Cambridge: Cambridge University Press, 1996.

Assael, Brenda. "Music in the Air: Noise, Performers, and the Contest over the Streets of the Mid-19th Century Metropolis." In *The Streets of London, 1660–1870*, ed. Tim Hitchcock and Heather Shore. London: Rivers Oram, 2002.

Aston Hall: A General Guide. Birmingham: Studio Press, 1987.

Avery, Gillian. *Childhood's Pattern: A Study of the Heroes and Heroines of Children's Fiction, 1770–1950*. London: Hodder & Stroughton, 1975.

Babcock, Barbara, ed. *The Reversible World: Symbolic Inversion in Art and Society*. Ithaca, NY: Cornell University Press, 1978.

Baer, Marc. *Theatre and Disorder in Late Georgian London*. Oxford: Clarendon, 1992.

Bailey, Peter. "Ally Sloper's Half Holiday: Comic Art in the 1880s." *History Workshop Journal* 16 (Autumn 1983): 4–31.

———. "Conspiracies of Meaning: Music Hall and the Knowingness of Popular Culture." *Past and Present*, no. 144 (1994): 138–70.

———. *Leisure and Class in Victorian England: Rational Recreation and the Contest for Control, 1830–1885*. 1978. London: Methuen, 1987.

———. "Leisure, Culture, and the Historian: Reviewing the First Generation of Leisure Historiography in Britain." *Leisure Studies* 8 (1989): 107–27.

———. "'A Mingled Mass of Perfectly Legitimate Pleasures': The Victorian Middle Class and the Problem of Leisure." *Victorian Studies* 21, no. 1 (1977): 7–28.

———. "'Naughty but Nice': Musical Comedy and the Rhetoric of the Girl, 1892–1914." In *The Edwardian Theatre: Essays on Performance and the Stage*, ed. Michael Booth and Joel H. Kaplan. Cambridge: Cambridge University Press, 1996.

———. "Parasexuality and Glamour: The Victorian Barmaid as Cultural Prototype." *Gender and History* 2, no. 2 (1990): 148–72.

———. "The Politics and Poetics of Modern British Leisure." *Rethinking History* 3, no. 2 (1999): 131–75.

———. *Popular Culture and Performance in the Victorian City.* Cambridge: Cambridge University Press, 1998.

———. "Theatres of Entertainment/Spaces of Modernity: Rethinking the British Popular Stage, 1890–1914." *Nineteenth Century Theatre* 26, no. 1 (1998). 5–24.

———. "'Will the Real Bill Banks Please Stand Up?' Towards a Role Analysis of Mid-Victorian Working Class Respectability." *Journal of Social History* 12.3 (1979): 336–53.

———, ed. *Music Hall: The Business of Pleasure.* Milton Keynes: Open University Press, 1986.

Bainbridge, Simon. *Napoleon and English Romanticism.* Cambridge: Cambridge University Press, 1995.

Baker, Michael. *The Rise of the Victorian Actor.* London: Croom Helm, 1978.

Bakhtin, Mikhail. *Rabelais and His World.* Trans. Hélène Iswolsky. 1968. Reprint, Bloomington: Indiana University Press, 1984.

Bann, Stephen. *The Clothing of Clio: A Study in the Representation of History in 19th Century Britain and France.* Cambridge: Cambridge University Press, 1984.

———. *Romanticism and the Rise of History.* New York: Macmillan, 1995.

Behlmer, George K. *Child Abuse and Moral Reform in England, 1870–1908.* Stanford: Stanford University Press, 1982.

———. "The Gypsy Problem in Victorian England." *Victorian Studies* 28, no. 2 (1995): 231–53.

Behrendt, Stephen C., ed. *History and Myth: Essays on English Romantic Literature.* Detroit: Wayne State University Press, 1990.

Belchem, John, and James Epstein. "The Nineteenth Century Gentleman Revisited." *Social History* 22, no. 2 (1997): 174–93.

Bennett, Susan. *Theatre Audiences: A Theory of Production and Reception.* London: Routledge, 1990.

Benson, John. *The Penny Capitalists: A Study of Nineteenth-Century Working Class Entrepreneurs.* Dublin: Gill & Macmillan, 1983.

———, ed. *The Working Class in England, 1875–1914.* London: Croom Helm, 1985.

Bergson, Henri. *Laughter: An Essay on the Meaning of the Comic.* London: Macmillan, 1911.

Best, Geoffrey. Review of *The Making of the English Working Class,* by E. P. Thompson. *Historical Journal* 8, no. 2 (1965): 271–81.

———. *Mid-Victorian Britain, 1851–70.* London: Fontana, 1979.

———. *War and Society in Revolutionary Europe, 1770–1870.* Leicester: University of Leicester Press, 1982.

Bettelheim, Bruno. *The Uses of Enchantment: The Meaning and Importance of Fairy Tales.* London: Thames & Hudson, 1976.

Billington, Sandra. *A Social History of the Fool*. New York: Harvester, 1984.

Bindman, D. *Hogarth*. London: Thames & Hudson, 1981.

Bland, Lucy. "'Purifying' the Public World: Feminist Vigilantes in Late Victorian England." *Women's History Review* 1, no. 2 (1992): 397–412.

Bogdan, Richard. *Freak Show: Presenting Human Oddities for Amusement and Profit*. Chicago: University of Chicago Press, 1988.

Bolt, Christine. *Victorian Attitudes towards Race*. London: Routledge, 1971.

Booth, Michael R. *English Melodrama*. London: Jenkins, 1965.

———. *Theatre in the Victorian Age*. Cambridge: Cambridge University Press, 1991.

———. *Victorian Spectacular Theatre*. London: Routledge & Kegan Paul, 1981.

Bouissac, P. *Circus and Culture: A Semiotic Approach*. Bloomington: Indiana University Press, 1976.

Bradby, D., L. James, and B. Sharralt, eds. *Performance and Politics in Popular Drama: Aspects of Popular Entertainment in Theatre, Film, and Television, 1800–1976*. Cambridge: Cambridge University Press, 1980.

Brantlinger, Patrick. *Rule of Darkness: British Literature and Imperialism, 1830–1914*. Ithaca, NY: Cornell University Press, 1988.

Bratton, J. S. "British Audiences and Black-Faced Acts." *Yearbook of English Studies* 11 (1981): 127–42.

———. "Hesba Stretton's Journalism." *Victorian Periodicals Review* 12, no. 2 (1979): 60–70.

———. *The Impact of Victorian Children's Fiction*. London: Croom Helm, 1981.

———, ed. *Music Hall: Performance and Style*. Milton Keynes: Open University Press, 1986.

Bratton, J. S., R. Cave, and M. Pickering, eds. *Acts of Supremacy: The British Empire and Stage, 1790–1930*. Manchester: Manchester University Press, 1991.

Bremmer, J., and Hermann Roodenberg, eds. *A Cultural History of Humour from Antiquity to the Present Day*. Cambridge: Polity, 1997.

Brereton, J. M. *The British Soldier: A Social History*. London: Bodley Head, 1986.

Briggs, Asa. *The Age of Improvement, 1783–1867*. 1959. London: Longman Group, 1979.

———. *Victorian Cities*. 1963. Harmondsworth: Penguin Books, 1968.

Bristow, Edward J. *Vice and Vigilance: Purity Movements in Britain since 1700*. Dublin: Gill & Macmillan, 1977.

Brooks, Peter. *The Melodramatic Imagination: Balzac, Henry James, Melodrama, and the Mode of Excess*. New Haven: Yale University Press, 1976.

Budd, Michael Anton. *The Sculpture Machine: Physical Culture and Body Politics in the Age of Empire*. Houndsmill: Macmillan, 1997.

Burn, W. L. *An Age of Equipoise: A Study of the Mid-Victorian Generation*. London: Unwin Books, 1964.

Burton, Antoinette. *At the Heart of the Empire: Indians and the Colonial Encounter in Late Victorian Britain*. Berkeley and Los Angeles: University of California Press, 1998.

——. "Making a Spectacle of Empire: Indian Travellers in *Fin de Siècle* London." *History Workshop Journal* 42 (Fall 1996): 127–46.

——, ed. *Gender, Sexuality and Colonial Modernities.* London: Routledge, 1995.

Canetti, Elias. *Crowds and Power.* Trans. Carol Stewart. London: Victor Gollancz, 1962.

Cannadine, David. "The Context, Performance, and Meaning of Ritual: The British Monarchy and the 'Invention of Tradition,' c. 1820–1977." In *The Invention of Tradition,* ed. Eric Hobsbawm and Terence Ranger. Cambridge: Cambridge University Press, 1983.

——. *Ornamentalism: How the British Saw Their Empire.* London: Allen Lane, 2001.

Chesney, Kellow. *The Victorian Underworld.* 1970. Reprint, Harmondsworth: Penguin Books, 1972.

Cohen, Morton N. *Lewis Carroll: A Biography.* London: Macmillan, 1995.

Cohen, Stanley. *Folk Devils and Moral Panics: The Creation of Mods and Rockers.* London: MacGibbon & Kee, 1972.

Colley, Linda. "Britishness and Otherness: An Argument." *Journal of British Studies* 31 (October 1992): 309–29.

——. *Britons: Forging The Nation, 1707–1837.* 1992. Reprint, London: Vintage, 1996.

——. *Captives: Britain, Empire and the World, 1600–1850.* London: Jonathan Cape, 2002.

——. "Whose Nation? Class and National Consciousness in Britain, 1750–1830." *Past and Present,* no. 113 (1986): 97–117.

Collins, Philip. "Dickens and Popular Amusements." *Dickensian* 61 (1965): 7–19.

——. "Queen Mab's Chariot among the Steam Engines: Dickens and 'Fancy.'" *English Studies* 42, no. 1 (1961): 78–90.

Columbus, Claudette K. "*Fifine at the Fair:* A Masque of Sexuality and Death Seeking Figures of Expression." *Studies in Browning and His Circle* 2, no. 1 (1874): 21–38.

Conolly, L. W. *The Censorship of English Drama, 1737–1824.* San Marino, CA: Huntington Library, 1976.

Cook, James W. *The Arts of Deception: Playing with Fraud in the Age of Barnum.* Cambridge: Harvard University Press, 2001.

Cordery, Simon. "Friendly Societies and the Discourse of Respectability in Britain, 1825–1875." *Journal of British Studies* 34 (January 1995): 35–58.

Coveney, Peter. *The Image of Childhood: The Individual and Society: A Study of the Theme in English Literature.* Harmondsworth: Penguin Books, 1967.

Coxe, A. H. "Historical Research and the Circus." *Theatre Notebook* 21, no. 1 (1966): 40–42.

——. "Lesser-Known Circuses of London." *Theatre Notebook* 13, no. 3 (1959): 89–100.

——. *A Seat at the Circus.* London: Evans Bros., 1951.

Crossick, Geoffrey. *An Artisan Elite in Victorian Society: Kentish London, 1840–1880.* London: Croom Helm, 1978.

——. "The Labour Aristocracy and Its Values: A Study of Mid-Victorian Kentish London." *Victorian Studies* 19, no. 3 (1976): 301–28.

Cunningham, Hugh. *Children and Childhood in Western Society since 1500.* London: Longman Group, 1995.

———. *Children of the Poor: Representations of Childhood since the Seventeenth Century.* Oxford: Blackwell, 1991.

———. "Employment and Unemployment of Children in England, 1680–1857." *Past and Present,* no. 126 (1990): 115–50.

———. "Jingoism in 1877–78." *Victorian Studies* 14, no. 4 (1971): 429–53.

———. "Language of Patriotism, 1750–1914." *History Workshop Journal* 12 (Autumn 1981): 8–33.

———. "Leisure and Culture." In *Cambridge Social History of Britain,* vol. 2, ed. F. M. L. Thompson. Cambridge: Cambridge University Press, 1990.

———. *Leisure in the Industrial Revolution, 1780–1880.* London: Croom Helm, 1980.

Cutt, Margaret Nancy. *Ministering Angels: A Study of Nineteenth Century Evangelical Writing for Children.* Wormley, Herts.: Five Owls, 1979.

———. *Mrs. Sherwood and Her Books for Children: A Study.* London: Oxford University Press, 1974.

da Costa Nunes, J. M. "O. G. Rejlander's Photographs of Ragged Children: Reflections on the Idea of Urban Poverty in Mid-Victorian Society." *Nineteenth Century Studies* 4 (1990): 105–36.

Daston, Lorainne. "Marvelous Facts and Miraculous Evidence in Early Modern Europe." In *Wonder, Marvels, and Monsters in Early Modern Culture,* ed. Peter G. Platt. Newark: University of Delaware Press, 1999.

Daston, Lorainne, and Katherine Park. "Unnatural Conceptions: The Study of Monsters in 16th and 17th Century France and England." *Past and Present,* no. 92 (1981): 20–54.

———. *Wonders and the Order of Nature, 1150–1750.* New York: Zone Books, 1998.

Daunton, M. J. "Poor Relief and Charity." In *Progress and Poverty: An Economic and Social History of Britain, 1700–1850,* ed. Daunton. Oxford: Oxford University Press, 1995.

Davidoff, Leonore. "Gender and Class in Victorian England: The Diaries of Arthur J. Munby and Hannah Cullwick." *Feminist Studies* 5 (Spring 1979): 87–141.

Davin, Anna. *Growing Up Poor: Home, School, and Street in London, 1870–1914.* London: Rivers Oram, 1996.

———. "Waif Stories in Late Nineteenth Century England." *History Workshop Journal* 52 (Autumn 2001): 67–98.

Davis, Jim. "British Bravery, or Tars Triumphant: Images of the British Navy in Nautical Melodrama." *New Theatre Quarterly* 4, no. 14 (1988): 122–43.

Davis, Jim, and Victor Emeljanow. *Reflecting the Audience: London Theatregoing, 1840–1880.* Hatfield, Herts.: University of Hertfordshire Press, 2001.

Davis, Natalie Zemon. *Society and Culture in Early Modern France.* 1975. Stanford: Stanford University Press, 1987.

Davis, Tracy C. *Actresses as Working Women: Their Social Identity in Victorian Culture.* London: Routledge & Kegan Paul, 1991.

———. "Does the Theatre Make for Good? Actresses' Purity and Temptation in the Victorian Era." *Queen's Quarterly* 93, no. 1 (1986): 33–49.

———. *Economics of the British Stage, 1800–1914.* Cambridge: Cambridge University Press, 2000.

———. "The Employment of Children in the Victorian Theatre: Training, Exploitation, and the Movement for Reform." *New Theatre Quarterly* 2, no. 6 (1986): 117–35.

———. "Labourers of the Nineteenth Century Theatre: The Economies of Gender and Industrial Organization." *Journal of British Studies* 33 (January 1994): 32–53.

———. "Private Women and the Public Realm." *Theatre Survey* 35 (May 1994): 65–72.

———. "Sex in Public Places: The Zaeo Aquarium Scandal and the Victorian Moral Majority." *Theatre History Studies* 10 (1990): 1–14.

———. "The Spectacle of Absent Costume: Nudity on the Victorian Stage." *New Theatre Quarterly* 20, no. 5 (1989): 321–33.

———. "Victorian Charity and Self-Help for Women Performers." *Theatre Notebook* 41, no. 3 (1987): 114–28.

Davis, Tracy C., and Ellen Donkin, eds. *Women and Playwriting in the Nineteenth Century.* Cambridge: Cambridge University Press, 1999.

Dawson, Graham. *Soldier Heroes: British Adventure, Empire, and the Imagining of Masculinities.* New York: Routledge, 1994.

Debord, Guy. *Society of Spectacle.* Detroit: Black and Red, 1977.

Dechamps, Jules. "Les défenseurs de Napoléon en Grand-Bretagne de 1815 à 1830." *Bulletin de la Classe des Lettres et des Sciences Morales et Politiques,* 5th ser., 44 (1958): 19–33.

de Mause, Lloyd. *History of Childhood.* London: Souvenir, 1976.

Disher, M. Willson. *The Greatest Show on Earth.* London: G. Bell & Sons, 1937.

Donajgrodzki, A. P., ed. *Social Control in Nineteenth Century Britain.* London: Croom Helm, 1977.

Donohue, Joseph. "Burletta and the Early Nineteenth Century English Theatre." *Nineteenth Century Theatre Research* 1, no. 1 (1973): 29–51.

———. "The Empire Theatre of Varieties Licensing Controversy of 1894." *Nineteenth Century Theatre Research* 15, no. 1 (1987): 50–60.

Douglas, Mary. "Jokes." In *Rethinking Popular Culture: Contemporary Perspectives in Cultural Studies,* ed. Chandra Mukerji and Michael Schudson. Berkeley and Los Angeles: University of California Press, 1991.

———. *Purity and Danger: An Analysis of the Concept of Pollution and Taboo.* 1966. Reprint, London: Routledge, 2002.

Drehr, Nan H. "The Virtuous and the Verminous: Turn of the Century Moral Panics in London's Public Parks." *Albion* 29, no. 2 (1997): 246–67.

Dyos, H. J., and M. Wolff, eds. *The Victorian City.* 2 vols. London: Routledge & Kegan Paul, 1973.

Elias, Norbert. *The Civilizing Process: The History of Manners.* 1939. Trans. Edmund Jephcott. Vol. 1. Oxford: Blackwell, 1983.

Elias, Norbert, and Eric Dunning. *The Quest for Excitement: Sport and Leisure in the Civilizing Process.* Oxford: Blackwell, 1986.

Epstein Nord, Deborah. "The City as Theatre: From Georgian to Early Victorian London." *Victorian Studies* 31, no. 2 (1988): 159–83.

Fairclough, Oliver. *The Grand Old Mansion: The Holtes and Their Successors at Aston Hall, 1618–1864.* Birmingham, UK: Birmingham Museum and Art Gallery, 1984.

Featherstone, Simon. "The Blackface Atlantic: Interpreting British Minstrelsy." *Journal of Victorian Culture* 3, no. 2 (1998): 234–51.

Feldman, David, and Gareth Stedman Jones, eds. *Metropolis London: Histories and Representations since 1800.* London: Routledge, 1989.

Fensham, Rachel. "'Making-Real' the Body: A Subordinate Reading of the Female Performer in the Nineteenth Century Australian Circus." *Australian Drama Studies* 30 (April 1997): 3–16.

Flaherty, Peter. "Reading Carnival: Towards a Semiotics of History." *Clio* 15, no. 4 (1986): 411–28.

Fletcher, Sheila. "The Making and Breaking of a Female Tradition: Women's Physical Education in England, 1880–1980." *British Journal of Sports History* 2 (1985): 29–39.

"For an America That Loved Freaks." *New York Times,* 20 August 1995, 38–43.

Forman, Ross G. "Peking Plots: Fictionalising the Boxer Rebellion of 1900." *Victorian Literature and Culture* 27, no. 1 (1999): 19–48.

Foucault, Michel. *Discipline and Punish: The Birth of the Prison.* Trans. Alan Sheridan. 1977. Harmondsworth: Penguin Books, 1991.

———. *The Order of Things: An Archaeology of the Human Sciences.* 1970. London: Routledge, 2001.

Foulkes, Richard, ed. *Scenes from Provincial Stages.* London: Society for Theatre Research, 1994.

French, Richard D. *Anti-Vivisection and Medical Science in Victorian Society.* Princeton: Princeton University Press, 1975.

Freud, Sigmund. *Wit and Its Relation to the Unconscious.* London, 1905.

Frost, Linda. "'Living Curiosities' and 'The Wonder of America.'" *Journal X: A Biannual Journal of Culture and Criticism* 1, no. 1 (1996): 85–111.

Frye, Northrop. "Myth, Fiction, and Displacement." *Fables of Identity: Studies in Poetic Mythology.* New York: Burlingame, 1963.

Gallagher, John, and Ronald Robinson. "The Imperialism of Free Trade." *Economic History Review* 6 (1953): 1–15.

Gamman, L., and M. Marshment, eds. *The Female Gaze: Women as Viewers of Popular Culture.* London: Women's Press, 1988.

Ganzel, Dewey. "Patent Wrongs and Patent Theatres: Drama and the Law in the Early Nineteenth Century." *PMLA* 76. no. 4 (1961): 384–96.

Gardner, Vivien, and Susan Rutherford, eds. *The New Woman and Her Sisters: Feminization and the Theatre, 1850–1914.* London: Harvester, 1992.

Gash, Norman. "After Waterloo: British Society and the Legacy of the Napoleonic Wars." *Transactions of the Royal Historical Society* 28 (1978): 145–57.

Gay, Peter. *The Cultivation of Hatred: The Bourgeois Experience from Victoria to Freud.* Vol. 3. London: HarperCollins, 1994.

Geertz, Clifford. *The Interpretation of Cultures.* 1973. London: Fontana, 1993.

———. *Local Knowledge: Further Essays in Interpretative Anthropology.* New York: Basic Books, 1983.

———. *Negara: The Theatre State in Nineteenth Century Bali.* Princeton: Princeton University Press, 1980.

Gillis, John. *Youth and History: Tradition and Change in European Age Relations.* New York: Academic Press, 1981.

Gilman, Sander L. "Black Bodies, White Bodies: Towards an Iconography of Female Sexuality in Late-19th Century Art, Medicine, and Literature." In *"Race," Writing, and Difference,* ed. Henry Louis Gates Jr. Chicago: Chicago University Press, 1986.

Girouard, Mark. *The Return to Camelot: Chivalry and the English Gentleman.* New Haven: Yale University Press, 1981.

Glennie, Paul, and Nigel Thrift. "Consumers, Identities, and Consumption Spaces in Early Modern England." Paper presented at the Historical Geography Seminar, Institute of Historical Research, London, 14 January 1995.

Goffman, Ernest. *The Presentation of Self in Everyday Life.* University of Edinburgh Monograph No. 2. Edinburgh: University of Edinburgh Social Science Research Centre, 1956.

Golby, J. M., and A. W. Purdue. *The Civilisation of the Crowd: Popular Culture in England, 1750–1900.* London: Batsford Academic and Educational, 1984.

Goodall, Jane R. *Performance and Evolution in the Age of Darwin.* London: Routledge, 2002.

Gordon, Linda, and Ellen DuBois. "Seeking Ecstasy on the Battlefield: Danger and Pleasure in 19th Century Feminist Thought." *Feminist Studies* 9 (Spring 1983): 7–25.

Gorham, Deborah. "The 'Maiden Tribute of Modern Babylon' Re-examined: Child Prostitution and the Idea of Childhood in Late Victorian England." *Victorian Studies* 21, no. 3 (1978): 353–79.

Gray, Donald J. "The Uses of Victorian Laughter." *Victorian Studies* 10, no. 2 (1966): 145–76.

Gray, Robert Q. *The Aristocracy of Labour in Nineteenth-Century Britain, c. 1850–1900.* London: Macmillan, 1981.

———. "The Labour Aristocracy in the Victorian Class Structure." In *Social Analysis of Class Structure,* ed. Frank Parkin. London: Tavistock, 1974.

Gregory, J. C. *The Nature of Laughter.* London: Kegan Paul, 1924.

Griffin, Emma. "Popular Culture in Industrializing England." *Historical Journal* 45, no. 3 (2002): 619–35.

———. "Sports and Celebrations in English Market Towns, 1660–1750." *Historical Research* 75 (May 2002): 187–208.

Haley, Bruce. *The Healthy Body and Victorian Culture.* Cambridge: Harvard University Press, 1978.

Hall, Catherine. *Civilising Subjects: Metropole and Colony in the English Imagination, 1830–1867.* Cambridge: Polity, 2002.

———, ed. *Cultures of Empire, A Reader: Colonizers in Britain and the Empire in the Nineteenth and Twentieth Centuries.* Manchester: Manchester University Press, 2000.

Hall, Donald, ed. *Muscular Christianity: Embodying the Victorian Age.* Cambridge: Cambridge University Press, 1994.

Hall, Stuart. "Cultural History and the Centre: Some Problematics and Problems." In *Culture, Media, Language: Working Papers in Cultural Studies, 1972–1979,* ed. Stuart Hall, D. Hobson, A. Lowe, and P. Willis. London: Hutchinson/Centre for Contemporary Cultural Studies, 1980.

———. "Spectacle of the 'Other.'" In *Representation: Cultural Representation and Signifying Practices,* ed. Hall. London: Sage, 1997.

Halttunen, Karen. "Humanitarianism and the Pornography of Pain in Anglo-American Culture." *American Historical Review* 100, no. 2 (1995): 303–34.

Hamilton Buckley, Jerome. *The Victorian Temper: A Study in Literary Culture.* London: George Allen & Unwin, 1952.

Harrington, Peter. *British Artists and the War: The Face of Battle in Paintings and Prints, 1700–1914.* London: Greenhill Books, 1993.

Harris, Jose. *Private Lives, Public Spirit: Britain, 1870–1914.* Oxford: Oxford University Press, 1993.

Harrison, Brian. "Animals and the State in Nineteenth-Century England." *English Historical Review* 88, no. 349 (October 1973): 786–820.

———. *Peaceable Kingdom: Stability and Change in Modern Britain.* Oxford: Clarendon, 1982.

———. "Philanthropy and the Victorians." *Victorian Studies* 9, no. 4 (1966): 353–74.

Harrop, J. *Victorian Portable Theatres.* London: Society for Theatre Research, 1989.

Hewitt, Martin, ed. *An Age of Equipoise? Reassessing Mid-Victorian Britain.* Aldershot: Ashgate, 2000.

Hichberger, J. W. M. *Images of the Army: The Military in British Art, 1815–1914.* Manchester: Manchester University Press, 1988.

Hiley, Michael. *Victorian Working Women: Portraits from Life.* London: Gordon Fraser, 1979.

Himmelfarb, Gertrude. *Victorian Minds.* London: Weidenfeld & Nicolson, 1968.

Hobsbawm, Eric. *Nations and Nationalism since 1780: Programme, Myth, and Reality.* Cambridge: Cambridge University Press, 1990.

Hoffenberg, Peter H. *An Empire on Display: English, Indian, and Australian Exhibitions from the Crystal Palace to the Great War.* Berkeley and Los Angeles: University of California Press, 2001.

Hoggart, Richard. *The Uses of Literacy.* London: Chatto & Windus, 1957.

Holt, Richard. *Sport and the British: A Modern History.* Oxford: Clarendon, 1989.

Hoppen, Theodore K. *The Mid-Victorian Generation.* Oxford: Clarendon, 1998.

Houghton, Walter E. *The Victorian Frame of Mind, 1830–1870.* New Haven: Yale University Press, 1957.

Howkins, A. "Whitsun in Nineteenth Century Oxfordshire." *History Workshop Pamphlets* 8 (1972).

Hudson, Derek. *Munby, Man of Two Worlds: The Life and Diaries of Arthur J. Munby, 1828–1910.* London: William Clowes & Sons, 1972.

Humpherys, Anne. *Travels into the Poor Man's Country: The Work of Henry Mayhew.* Athens: University of Georgia Press, 1977.

Hunt, Lynn, ed. *The New Cultural History.* Berkeley and Los Angeles: University of California Press, 1989.

Impey, Oliver, and Arthur MacGregor. *The Origins of Museums: The Cabinet of Curiosities in Sixteenth- and Seventeenth-Century Europe.* 1985. Reprint, London: House of Stratus, 2001.

James, Louis. *Fiction for the Working Man, 1830–1850.* Oxford: Oxford University Press, 1963.

Jan, Isabelle. *On Children's Literature.* Trans. Catherine Storr. London: Allen Lane, 1973.

Johnston, John. *The Lord Chamberlain's Blue Pencil.* London: Hodder & Stroughton, 1990.

Jones, Gareth Stedman. "Class Expression versus Social Control? A Critique of Recent Trends in the Social History of 'Leisure.'" *History Workshop Journal* 4 (Autumn 1977): 162–70.

———. "The Labours of Henry Mayhew: Metropolitan Correspondent." *London Journal* 10 (1984): 80–85.

———. *Languages of Class: Studies in English Working Class History, 1832–1982.* 1983. Reprint, Cambridge: Cambridge University Press, 1993.

———. *Outcast London: A Study in the Relationship between Classes in Victorian Society.* Harmondsworth: Penguin Books, 1976.

Jones, Robert W. "'The Sight of Creatures Strange to Our Clime': The London Zoo and the Consumption of the Exotic." *Journal of Victorian Culture* 2, no. 1 (1997): 1–26.

Jordan, Gerald, and Nicholas Rogers. "Admirals as Heroes: Patriotism and Liberty in Hanoverian England." *Journal of British Studies* 28 (July 1989): 201–24.

Joyce, Patrick. *Democratic Subjects: The Self and the Social in Nineteenth Century England.* Cambridge: Cambridge University Press, 1994.

———. *Visions of the People: Industrial England and the Question of Class, 1848–1914.* Cambridge: Cambridge University Press, 1991.

Judd, Denis. *Empire: The British Imperial Experience from 1765 to the Present.* London: HarperCollins, 1996.

Keating, Peter. *Into Unknown England, 1866–1913: Selections from the Social Explorers.* Glasgow: William Collins and Sons, 1976.

Kenny, Neil. *Curiosity in Early Modern Europe World Histories.* Wiesbaden: Harrassowitz Verlag, 1998.

Kitson Clark, G. *The Making of Victorian England.* London: Methuen, 1962.

Knoepflmacher, U. C. "The Balancing of Child and Adult: An Approach to Victorian Fantasies for Children." *Nineteenth-Century Fiction* 37, no. 4 (1983): 497–530.

Kwint, Marius. "The Legitimization of the Circus in Late Georgian England." *Past and Present,* no. 174 (2002): 72–115.

Laffan, William. *The Sublime and the Beautiful in Irish Art, 1700–1830.* London: Pyms Gallery, 2001.

Lang, Marjory. "Children's Champions: Mid-Victorian Children's Periodicals and the Critics." *Victorian Periodicals Review* 23, nos. 1–2 (1980): 17–31.

Lansbury, Coral. *Old Brown Dog: Women, Workers, and Vivisection in Edwardian England.* Madison: University of Wisconsin Press, 1985.

Leavis, F. R. *The Great Tradition.* 1948. Harmondsworth: Penguin, 1966.

Levine, Lawrence. *High Brow/Low Brow: The Emergence of Cultural Hierarchy in America.* Cambridge: Harvard University Press, 1988.

Lewis, Michael J. "American Sublime." *New Criterion* 21 (September 2002): 27.

Liesenfeld, Vincent J. *The Licensing Act of 1737.* Madison: University of Wisconsin Press, 1984.

Loeb, Lori Anne. *Consuming Angels: Advertising and Victorian Women.* New York: Oxford University Press, 1994.

Lynch, James J. *Box, Pit, and Gallery: Stage and Society in Johnson's London.* Berkeley: University of California Press, 1953.

MacKenzie, John M, ed. *Imperialism and Popular Culture.* Manchester: Manchester University Press, 1986.

———. *Popular Imperialism and the Military, 1850–1950.* Manchester: Manchester University Press, 1992.

———. *Propaganda and Empire: The Manipulation of British Public Opinion, 1880–1960.* Manchester: Manchester University Press, 1984.

Malamud, Margaret. "The Greatest Show on Earth: Roman Entertainments in Turn of the Century New York City." *Journal of Popular Culture* 35, no. 3 (2001): 43–58.

Malcolmson, R. W. *Popular Recreations in English Society, 1700–1850.* Cambridge: Cambridge University Press, 1973.

Mandler, Peter. "The Problem with Cultural History." *Cultural and Social History* 1, no. 1 (2004): 94–117.

Manning-Sanders, Ruth. *The English Circus.* London: Werner Laurie, 1952.

Marcus, Steven. *The Other Victorians: A Study of Sexuality and Pornography in Mid-Nineteenth Century England.* London: Weidenfeld & Nicolson, 1966.

Marshall, P. J., ed. *The Cambridge Illustrated History of the British Empire.* Cambridge: Cambridge University Press, 1996.

Martin, Jonathan D. "The Grandest and Most Cosmopolitan Object Teacher: *Buffalo Bill's Wild West* and the Politics of American Identity, 1883–1899." *Radical History Review* 66 (Fall 1996): 92–123.

Mason, Michael. *The Making of Victorian Sexual Attitudes.* Oxford: Oxford University Press, 1994.

------. *The Making of Victorian Sexuality.* Oxford: Oxford University Press, 1994.

Mathur, Saloni. "Living Ethnological Exhibits: The Case of 1866." *Cultural Anthropology* 15, no. 4 (2000): 492–524.

Matlaw, Myron, ed. *American Popular Entertainment: Papers and Proceedings of the Conference on the History of American Popular Entertainment.* Westport, CT: Greenwood, 1977.

Mayall, David. *Gypsy Travellers in Nineteenth Century Society.* Cambridge: Cambridge University Press, 1988.

Mayer, David. *Harlequin in His Element.* Cambridge: Harvard University Press, 1969.

McClintock, Anne. *Imperial Leather: Race, Gender, and Sexuality in the Colonial Contest.* London: Routledge, 1995.

McCullough, Jack W. *Living Pictures on the New York Stage.* Ann Arbor: UMI Research, 1983.

McGavran, James Holt, Jr., ed. *Romanticism and Children's Literature in Nineteenth-Century England.* Athens: University of Georgia Press, 1991.

McLaughlin, Joseph. *Writing the Urban Jungle.* Charlottesville: University Press of Virginia, 2000.

McWilliam, Rohan. "Melodrama and the Historians." *Radical History Review* 78 (Fall 2000): 57–84.

Meisel, Martin. *Realizations: Narrative, Pictorial, and Theatrical Arts in Nineteenth Century England.* Princeton: Princeton University Press, 1983.

Meller, H. E. *Leisure and the Changing City, 1870–1914.* London: Routledge, 1976.

Michie, Helena. *The Flesh Made Word: Female Figures and Women's Bodies.* Oxford: Oxford University Press, 1987.

Minois, Georges. *Histoire du rire et de la dérision.* Paris: Fayard, 2000.

Mitchell, Sally. *The Dictionary of British Equestrian Artists.* Suffolk: Antique Collectors' Club, 1985.

Monk, Samuel H. *The Sublime: A Study of Critical Theories in Eighteenth Century England.* Ann Arbor: University of Michigan Press, 1960.

Monro, D. H. *Argument of Laughter.* Carlton, Austral.: Melbourne University Press, 1951.

Moody, Jane. *Illegitimate Theatre in London, 1770–1840.* Cambridge: Cambridge University Press, 2000.

Morris, R. J. "Samuel Smiles and the Genesis of Self-Help: The Retreat to a Petit Bourgeois Utopia." *Historical Journal* 24, no. 1 (1981): 89–109.

Moss, Arthur W. *Valiant Crusade: A History of the R.S.P.C.A.* London: Cassell, 1961.

Mulvey, Laura. *Visual and Other Pleasures.* London: Macmillan, 1989.

------. "Visual Pleasures and Narrative Cinema." *Screen* 16, no. 3 (1975): 6–18.

Murphy, Thomas. *A History of the Showman's Guild, 1889–1948.* Oldham: privately printed, 1949.

Myerly, Scott Hughes. *British Military Spectacle: From the Napoleonic Wars through the Crimea.* Cambridge: Harvard University Press 1996.

Nardinelli, C. *Child Labor and the Industrial Revolution*. Bloomington: Indiana University Press, 1990.

Nead, Lynda. *The Female Nude: Art, Obscenity and Sexuality*. London: Routledge, 1992.

———. *Victorian Babylon: People, Streets and Images in 19th Century London*. New Haven: Yale University Press, 2000.

Nicholson, Watson. *The Struggle for a Free Stage in London*. 1906. Reprint, New York: Benjamin Blom, 1966.

Nicoll, Allardyce. *A History of English Drama, 1660–1900*. 6 vols. Cambridge: Cambridge University Press, 1952–59.

Paget, Guy. "Abraham Cooper, R.A., 1787–1868." *Apollo* 50, no. 295 (September 1949): 78–80.

Paley, Morton D. *The Apocalyptic Sublime*. New Haven: Yale University Press, 1986.

Paris, Michael. *Warrior Nation: Images of War in British Popular Culture, 1850–2000*. London: Reaktion, 2000.

Parry, Jonathan. *Rise and Fall of Liberal Government in England*. New Haven: Yale University Press, 1993.

Parssinen, Terry M. "Mesmeric Performers." *Victorian Studies* 21, no. 1 (1977): 87–104.

Pattison, Robert. *The Child Figure in Literature*. Athens: University of Georgia Press, 1978.

Paxton, Nancy L. "Mobilizing Chivalry: Rape in British Novels about the Indian Uprising of 1857." *Victorian Studies* 36, no. 1 (1992): 5–30.

Pears, Iain. "The Gentleman and the Hero: Wellington and Napoleon in the Nineteenth Century." In *Myths of the English*, ed. Roy Porter. Cambridge: Polity, 1992.

Pickering, Michael. "John Bull in Blackface." *Popular Music* 16, no. 2 (May 1997): 181–201.

Pilbeam, Pamela. *Madame Tussaud and the History of Waxworks*. London: Hambeldon, 2003.

Pinchbeck, Ivy, and Margaret Hewitt. *Children in English Society*. Vol. 2. London: Routledge & Kegan Paul, 1973.

Plumb, J. H., Neil McKendrick, and John Brewer, eds. *The Birth of a Consumer Society: The Commercialization of Eighteenth-Century England*. London: Europa, 1982.

Pollock, Linda A. *Forgotten Children: Parent-Child Relations from 1500–1900*. Cambridge: Cambridge University Press, 1983.

Pomian, Krysztof. *Collectors and Curiosities: Paris and Venice, 1500–1800*. Cambridge: Polity, 1990.

Porter, Andrew. *The Oxford History of the British Empire*. Vol. 3. Oxford: Oxford University Press, 1999.

Porter, Bernard. *The Lion's Share: A Short History of British Imperialism, 1850–1983*. 1975. Reprint, London: Longman, 1984.

Porter, Roy. "History of the Body." In *New Perspectives on Historical Writing*, ed. Peter Burke. Cambridge: Polity, 1991.

————. *London: A Social History.* Cambridge: Harvard University Press, 1994.

Pratt, Mary Louise. *Imperial Eyes: Travel Writing and Transculturation.* London: Routledge, 1992.

Prochaska, Frank K. "Philanthropy." In *Cambridge Social History of Britain*, vol. 3, ed. F. M. L. Thompson. Cambridge: Cambridge University Press, 1990.

Prothero, Iowerth. *Artisans and Politics in Nineteenth Century London.* London: Methuen, 1981.

Quennell, Peter. *Victorian Panorama: A Survey of Life and Fashion from Contemporary Photographs.* London: B. T. Batsford, 1937.

Radway, Janice. "Reception Study: Ethnography and the Problems of Dispersed Audiences and Nomadic Subjects." *Cultural Studies* 2, no. 3 (1988): 359–67.

Rees, Terence, and David Wilmore. *British Theatrical Patents, 1801–1900.* London: Society for Theatre Research, 1996.

Rehin, George F. "Blackface Street Minstrels in Victorian London and Its Resort: Popular Culture and Its Racial Connotations as Revealed in Polite Opinion." *Journal of Popular Culture* 15, no. 1 (1981): 19–38.

————. "Harlequin Jim Crow: Continuity and Convergence in Blackface Clowning." *Journal of Popular Culture* 9, no. 3 (1975): 682–701.

Reiss, Benjamin. *The Showman and the Slave: Race, Death, and Memory in Barnum's America.* Cambridge: Harvard University Press, 2001.

Richards, Thomas. *The Commodity of Culture in Victorian England: Advertising and Spectacle, 1851–1914.* Stanford: Stanford University Press, 1990.

Ritvo, Harriet. *The Animal Estate: The English and Other Creatures in the Victorian Age.* 1987. Harmondsworth: Penguin Books, 1990.

————. *The Platypus and the Mermaid and Other Figments of the Classifying Imagination.* Cambridge: Harvard University Press, 1997.

Robbins, Louise E. *Elephant Slaves and Pampered Parrots: Exotic Animals in Eighteenth-Century Paris.* Baltimore: Johns Hopkins University Press, 2002.

Roberts, Andrew. *Napoleon and Wellington.* 2001. Reprint, London: Phoenix, 2002.

Rose, Jonathan. *The Intellectual Life of the Working Classes.* New Haven: Yale University Press, 2001.

Rose, Lionel. *The Erosion of Childhood: Child Oppression in Britain, 1860–1918.* London: Routledge & Kegan Paul, 1991.

Rowell, George. *The Victorian Theatre, 1792–1914: A Survey.* 1956. Cambridge: Cambridge University Press, 1978.

Russell, Gillian. *The Theatres of War: Performance, Politics, and Society, 1793–1815.* Oxford: Clarendon, 1995.

Said, Edward W. *Orientalism.* 1978. London: Penguin Books, 1991.

Samuel, Raphael, ed. *Patriotism: The Making and Unmaking of British National Identity.* 3 vols. London: Routledge & Kegan Paul, 1989.

Saxon, A. H. *Enter Foot and Horse.* New Haven: Yale University Press, 1968.

————. *The Life and Art of Andrew Ducrow and the Romantic Age of the English Circus.* Hamden, CT: Archon Books, 1978.

———. *P. T. Barnum: The Legend and the Man.* New York: Columbia University Press, 1989.

———. "Shakespeare and Circuses." *Theatre Survey* 7 (November 1966): 59–79.

———. "The Tyranny of Charity: Andrew Ducrow in the Provinces." *Nineteenth Century Theatre Research* 1, no. 2 (1973): 95–105.

Scarry, Elaine. *The Body in Pain: The Making and Unmaking of the World.* New York: Oxford University Press, 1985.

Schama, Simon. "The Unruly Realm: Appetite and Restraint in 17th Century Holland." *Daedalus* 108, no. 3 (1979): 103–23.

Schlicke, Paul. "Circus." In *Oxford Reader's Companion to Dickens,* ed. Schlicke. Oxford: Oxford University Press, 1999.

———. *Dickens and Popular Entertainment.* London: Allen & Unwin, 1985.

———. "Dickens in the Circus." *Theatre Notebook* 67, no. 1 (1993): 2–19.

Schwartz, Vanessa. *Spectacular Realities: Early Mass Culture in Fin de Siècle Paris.* Berkeley and Los Angeles: University of California Press, 1998.

Semmel, Stuart. "Reading the Tangible Past: British Tourism, Collection, and Memory after Waterloo." *Representations* 69 (Winter 2000): 9–37.

Senelick, Lawrence. "Politics as Entertainment: Victorian Music Hall Songs." *Victorian Studies* 19, no. 2 (1975): 149–80.

Sharpe, Jenny. *Allegories of Empire: The Figure of the Woman in the Colonial Text.* Minneapolis: University of Minnesota Press, 1993.

Shelton, Anthony Alan. "Cabinets of Transgression: Renaissance Collections and the Incorporation of the New World." In *The Cultures of Collecting,* ed. John Elsner and Roger Cardinal. London: Reaktion, 1994.

Silver, Carole G. *Strange and Secret Peoples: Fairies and Victorian Consciousness.* New York: Oxford University Press, 1999.

Simmel, Georg. *On Individuality and Social Forms: Selected Writings.* Ed. Donald N. Levine. Chicago: University of Chicago Press, 1971.

Simpson, Margaret. "*Hard Times* and Circus Times." *Dickens Quarterly* 10, no. 3 (1993): 131–46.

Skelley, Alan R. *The Victorian Army at Home.* London: Croom Helm, 1977.

Snitow, Anne, Christine Stansell, and Sharon Thompson, eds. *Power of Desire: The Politics of Sexuality.* New York: New York Monthly Press, 1983.

Sommerville, C. John. *The Rise and Fall of Childhood.* London: Sage, 1982.

Speaight, George. *A History of the Circus.* London: Tantivy, 1980.

Spiers, Edward M. *The Army and Society, 1815–1914.* London: Longman, 1980.

Springhall, John. *Coming of Age: Adolescence in Britain, 1860–1890.* Dublin: Gill & MacMillian, 1986.

———. *Youth, Empire, and Society: British Youth Movements, 1883–1940.* London: Croom Helm, 1977.

Stacey, J. *Star Gazing: Hollywood and Female Spectatorship.* London: Routledge, 1994.

Stallybrass, Peter, and Allon White. "Bourgeois Hysteria and the Carnivalesque." In *The Cultural Studies Reader,* ed. Simon During. London: Routledge, 1993.

———. *The Politics and Poetics of Transgression.* Ithaca, NY: Cornell University Press, 1986.

Starsmore, Ian. *English Fairs.* London: Thames and Hudson, 1975.

Steedman, Carolyn. *Strange Dislocations: Childhood and the Idea of Human Interiority, 1780–1930.* London: Virago, 1995.

Stephens, John Russell. *The Censorship of English Drama, 1824–1901.* Cambridge: Cambridge University Press, 1980.

———. *The Profession of the Playwright, British Theatre, 1800–1900.* Cambridge: Cambridge University Press, 1992.

Storch, Robert, ed. *Popular Culture and Custom in Nineteenth Century England.* London: Croom Helm, 1982.

Storey, John, ed. *Cultural Theory and Popular Culture: A Reader.* 1994. Hemel Hempstead, Herts.: Prentice Hall, 1998.

Tait, Hugh. *Catalogue of the Waddesdon Bequest in the British Museum III: The "Curiosities."* London: British Museum Press, 1991.

Thomas, Keith. *Man and the Natural World: Changing Attitudes in England, 1500–1800.* 1983. Reprint, Harmondsworth: Penguin Books, 1984.

———. "The Place of Laughter in Tudor and Stuart England." *Times Literary Supplement,* January 1977, 77–81.

———. "Work and Leisure in Pre-Industrial Society." *Past and Present,* no. 29 (1964): 50–66.

Thompson, E. P. *Customs in Common.* 1991. Harmondsworth: Penguin Books, 1993.

———. *The Making of the English Working Class.* 1963. Reprint, London: Victor Gollancz, 1980.

———. "Patrician Society, Plebeian Culture." *Journal of Social History* 7, no. 4 (1974): 382–405.

Thompson, E. P., and E. Yeo. *The Unknown Mayhew.* 1971. Reprint, Harmondsworth: Penguin Books, 1984.

Thompson, F. M. L., ed. *Cambridge Social History of Britain.* 3 vols. Cambridge: Cambridge University Press, 1990.

———. "Nineteenth-Century Horse Sense." *Economic History Review* 29 (1976): 60–79.

———. *The Rise of Respectable Society: A Social History of Victorian Britain, 1830–1900.* London: Fontana, 1988.

———. "Social Control in Victorian Britain." *Economic History Review* 34, no. 2 (May 1981): 189–208.

Thomson, Rosemary Garland, ed. *Freakery: Cultural Spectacles of the Extraordinary Body.* New York: New York University Press, 1996.

——— "Narratives of Deviance and Delight: Staring at Julia Pastrana, the Extraordinary Lady." In *Beyond the Binary: Reconstructing Cultural Identity in a Multicultural Context,* ed. Timothy B. Powell. New Brunswick, NJ: Rutgers University Press, 1999.

Toll, C. *Blackening Up: Minstrel Shows in Nineteenth-Century America.* New York: Oxford University Press, 1974.

Troubridge, T. St. Vincent. *The Benefit System in the British Theatre.* London: Society for Theatre Research, 1967.

Tucker, Herbert, ed. *A Companion to Victorian Literature and Culture.* Oxford: Blackwell, 1999.

Turner, Victor. *The Forest of Symbols: Aspects of Ndembu Ritual.* 1967. Reprint, Ithaca, NY: Cornell University Press, 1970.

———. *From Ritual to Theatre: The Human Seriousness of Play.* New York: Performing Arts Journal, 1982.

Twitchell, James B. *Romantic Horizons: Aspects of the Sublime in English Poetry and Painting, 1770–1850.* Columbia: University of Missouri Press, 1983.

Tyrwhitt-Drake, Garrard. *The English Circus and Fairground.* London: Methuen, 1946.

Vance, Norman. *The Sinews of the Spirit: The Ideal of Christian Manliness in Victorian Literature and Religious Thought.* Cambridge: Cambridge University Press, 1985.

Vincent, David. *Bread, Knowledge, and Freedom: A Study in Nineteenth Century Working Class Autobiography.* London: Methuen 1983.

———. *Literacy and Popular Culture in England, 1750–1914.* Cambridge: Cambridge University Press, 1989.

Voskuil, Lynn M. "Feeling Public: Sensation, Theatre, Commodity Culture, and the Victorian Public Sphere." *Victorian Studies* 44, no. 2 (2002): 245–74.

Wagner-Lawlor, Jennifer A., ed. *The Victorian Comic Spirit: New Perspectives.* Aldershot: Ashgate, 2000.

Walkowitz, Judith R. *City of Dreadful Delight: Narratives of Sexual Danger in Late-Victorian London.* Chicago: University of Chicago Press, 1992.

———. *Prostitution and Victorian Society.* Cambridge: Cambridge University Press, 1980.

———. "The 'Vision of Salome': Cosmopolitanism and Erotic Dancing in Central London, 1908–1918." *American Historical Review* 108, no. 2 (2003): 337–76.

Waller, P. J. "Laughter in the House." *Twentieth Century British History* 5.1 (1994): 4–37.

Walters, Margaret. *The Nude Male: A New Perspective.* New York: Paddington, 1978.

Walton, John K. "The Demand for Working-Class Seaside Holidays in Victorian England." *Economic History Review* 34 (1981): 249–65.

Walton, John K., and James Walvin, eds. *Leisure in Britain, 1780–1939.* Manchester: Manchester University Press, 1983.

Walvin, James. *Beside the Seaside: A Social History of the Popular Seaside Holiday.* London: Allen Lane, 1978.

———. *Leisure and Society, 1830–1950.* London: Longman, 1978.

Walvin, James, and J. A. Mangan. *Manliness and Morality: Middle Class Masculinity in Britain and America, 1800–1940.* Manchester: Manchester University Press, 1997.

Waters, Hazel. "'That Astonishing Clever Child': Performers and Prodigies in the Early and Mid-Victorian Theatre." *Theatre Notebook* 50, no. 2 (1996): 78–94.

Waters, Karen Volland. *The Perfect Gentleman: Masculine Culture in Victorian Men's Fiction, 1870–1901.* New York: Peter Lang, 1997.

Weber, Eugen. "Gymnastics and Sports in Fin-de-Siècle France: Opium of the Classes?" *American Historical Review* 76, no. 3 (1971): 70–98.

Welsford, Enid. *The Fool: His Social and Literary History.* London: Faber & Faber, 1935.

Whitaker, Katie. "The Culture of Curiosity." In *Cultures of Natural History,* ed. N. Jardine, J. A. Secord, and E. C. Spary. Cambridge: Cambridge University Press, 1996.

Williams, Raymond. *Culture and Society, 1780–1950.* 1958. Harmondsworth: Penguin, 1961.

Wilton, Andrew. *Turner and the Sublime.* London: British Museum, 1980.

Winter, James. *London's Teeming Streets, 1830–1914.* London: Routledge, 1993.

Yarrington, Alison. *The Commemoration of the Hero, 1800–1864: Monuments to the British Victors of the Napoleonic Wars.* London: Garland, 1988.

Yeo, S., and E. Yeo. *Popular Culture and Class Conflict, 1590–1914.* Brighton: Harvester Press, 1981.

Dissertations and Theses

Assael, Brenda. "The Circus and Respectable Society in Victorian Britain." Ph.D. diss., University of Toronto, 1997.

Bold, Christine. "Selling the Wild West: Popular Western Fiction, 1860–1960." Ph.D. diss., University College, London, 1983.

Crowhurst, Andrew. "The Music Hall, 1885–1922: The Emergence of a National Entertainment Industry in Britain." Ph.D. diss., Cambridge University, 1992.

Crozier, B. A. M. "Notions of Childhood in London Theatres, 1800–1905." Ph.D. diss., Cambridge University, 1981.

Daum, Paul Alexander. "The Royal Circus, 1782–1809: An Analysis of Equestrian Entertainments." Ph.D. diss., Ohio State University, 1973.

Girard, C. A. "The Equestrian Drama in the Nineteenth Century." Ph.D. diss., Louisiana State University, 1939.

Kwint, Marius. "Astley's Amphitheatre and the Early Circus in England, 1768–1830." Ph.D. diss., Oxford University, 1995.

Lin, Patricia. "Extending Her Arms: Military Families and the Transformation of the British State, 1793–1815." Ph.D. diss, University of California, Berkeley, 1997.

Mayall, David. "Itinerant Minorities in England and Wales in the Nineteenth and Twentieth Centuries: A Study of Gypsies, Tinkers, Hawkers, and Other Travellers." Ph.D. diss., University of Sheffield, 1981.

Monsanto, Anthony, Jr. "The Living Proof: The Barnum and Bailey Circus and the Reification of Racial Categories, 1884–1896." M.A. thesis., Princeton University, 1992.

Moody, Jane. "Aspects of Cultural Politics in the London Minor Theatres of the Early Nineteenth Century." Ph.D. diss., Oxford University, 1993.

Myrone, David Martin. "Body Building: British Historical Artists in London and Rome and the Remaking of the Heroic Ideal, 1760–1800." Ph.D. diss., Courtauld Institute, University of London, 1998.

Sexton, R. D. "Travelling People in the U.K. in the First Half of the Twentieth Century." Ph.D. diss., University of Southampton, 1989.

Tuttle, George P. "A History of the Royal Circus, Equestrian and Philharmonic Academy, 1782–1816." Ph.D. diss, Tufts University, 1972.

Index

Recent Books in the Victorian Literature and Culture Series

Linda Dowling   *The Vulgarization of Art: The Victorians and Aesthetic Democracy*

Tricia Lootens   *Lost Saints: Silence, Gender, and Victorian Literary Canonization*

Matthew Arnold   *The Letters of Matthew Arnold*, vols. 1–6
Edited by Cecil Y. Lang

Edward FitzGerald   *Edward FitzGerald*, Rubáiyát of Omar Khayyám: *A Critical Edition*
Edited by Christopher Decker

Christina Rossetti   *The Letters of Christina Rossetti*, vols. 1–3
Edited by Antony H. Harrison

Barbara Leah Harman   *The Feminine Political Novel in Victorian England*

John Ruskin   *The Genius of John Ruskin: Selections from His Writings*
Edited by John D. Rosenberg

Antony H. Harrison   *Victorian Poets and the Politics of Culture: Discourse and Ideology*

Judith Stoddart   *Ruskin's Culture Wars:* Fors Clavigera *and the Crisis of Victorian Liberalism*

Linda K. Hughes and Michael Lund   *Victorian Publishing and Mrs. Gaskell's Work*

Linda H. Peterson   *Traditions of Victorian Women's Autobiography: The Poetics and Politics of Life Writing*

Gail Turley Houston   *Royalties: The Queen and Victorian Writers*

Laura C. Berry   *The Child, the State, and the Victorian Novel*

Barbara J. Black   *On Exhibit: Victorians and Their Museums*

Annette R. Federico   *Idol of Suburbia: Marie Corelli and Late-Victorian Literary Culture*

Talia Schaffer   *The Forgotten Female Aesthetes: Literary Culture in Late-Victorian England*

Julia F. Saville   *A Queer Chivalry: The Homoerotic Asceticism of Gerard Manley Hopkins*

Victor Shea and William Whitla, Editors   *Essays and Reviews: The 1860 Text and Its Reading*

Marlene Tromp   *The Private Rod: Marital Violence, Sensation, and the Law in Victorian Britain*

Dorice Williams Elliott   *The Angel out of the House: Philanthropy and Gender in Nineteenth-Century England*

Richard Maxwell, Editor   *The Victorian Illustrated Book*

Vineta Colby   *Vernon Lee: A Literary Biography*

E. Warwick Slinn   *Victorian Poetry as Cultural Critique: The Politics of Performative Language*

Simon Joyce   *Capital Offenses: Geographies of Class and Crime in Victorian London*

Caroline Levine   *The Serious Pleasures of Suspense: Victorian Realism and Narrative Doubts*

Emily Davies   *Emily Davies: Collected Letters, 1861–1875*
Edited by Ann B. Murphy and Deirdre Raftery

Joseph Bizup   *Manufacturing Culture: Vindications of Early Victorian Industry*

Lynn M. Voskuil   *Acting Naturally: Victorian Theatricality and Authenticity*

Sally Mitchell   *Frances Power Cobbe: Victorian Feminist, Journalist, Reformer*

Constance W. Hassett   *Christina Rossetti: The Patience of Style*

Brenda Assael   *The Circus and Victorian Society*